Practice-Sensitive
Social Work Education:
An Empirical Analysis of Social Work
Practice and Practitioners

by

Robert J. Teare

and

Bradford W. Sheafor

Council on Social Work Education
Alexandria, Virginia

Library of Congress Cataloging-in-Publication Data

Practice-sensitive social work education: an empirical analysis of social work
    practice and practitioners / by Robert J. Teare and Bradford W. Sheafor.
        p.   cm.
    Includes bibliographic references.
    ISBN 0-87293-046-7
    1. Social work education—United States—Curricula..   2. Social
workers—Job descriptions—United States.. I. Sheafor, Bradford W. II. Title.
HV11.T414   1995
361.3'2'071073—dc20   95-31474
                                                                          CIP

Manufactured in the United States of America.

Table of Contents

Preface

Professional education requires that schools prepare their graduates for two purposes: to perform the practice activities currently expected of that discipline, and to be at the cutting edge of practice innovation. Aside from the somewhat general guidelines evident in the Council on Social Work Education's (CSWE) latest Curriculum Policy Statement (CSWE, 1992), the social work profession has provided its schools with limited guidance for selecting curriculum content to achieve either goal. The National Social Work Task Analysis Studies provide a unique empirical database for assisting the social work profession to understand the nature of its practice and to use that data in curriculum development. Hence our use of the term "practice-sensitive" social work education.

It is our contention that the information contained within provides perhaps the most accurate understanding of the characteristics of social work practitioners and their practice activities to date. In Chapter 1, we demonstrate that this study represents a new generation in social work's long-standing effort to describe its diverse set of practice activities. The strength of the research lies in the fact that the data are derived from a substantial representative sample of social workers ($N=7,000$) and are underpinned by a nonpartisan methodology. Unlike many prior efforts to depict social work, this approach has avoided imposing any particular practice model on the data. It is our belief that this comprehensive database of information on social work practice and practitioners can serve to inform policies that will guide social work education and assist schools in selecting curriculum content.

In this monograph, we present selected data from the task analysis studies in a format that we anticipate will be useful in both formulating educational policy and making curriculum decisions at the baccalaureate and master's levels. The first chapter is designed to provide background about social work's attempts over the years to develop practice depictions; the next three chapters present the data. Chapter 2, "Baccalaureate-Level Social Workers: Who Are They and What Do They Do?", summarizes the responses from 1,449 baccalaureate social work practitioners. In Chapter 3, parallel data from 5,272 master's degree in social workers are presented. Each is organized to be of particular use to the colleges and universities offering professional social work education programs at those levels. In Chapter 4, "Comparisons between BSW and MSW Social Workers," data about practitioners and practice activities at the two levels are compared. Similarities and differences in the demographic characteristics of workers are highlighted and, in particular, the activities of social workers who occupy direct service, supervisory, and administrative/management positions are compared. This information, we anticipate, will assist committees and commissions from both CSWE and the National Association of Social Workers (NASW) in the formulation of policies that affect practice at the two entry levels. We also expect them to be helpful in facilitating the work of the schools as they design foundation curricula and examine concentrations for the various levels.

In the hope of minimizing the influence of our own biases in presenting these findings (although some of our own viewpoints are no doubt present), we have selected a group of knowledgeable and respected social work educators to react to the data and identify the implications for general educational policy and for curriculum development at the school or program level. These commentaries can be found in Chapter 5, "Implications for Social Work Education and Planning," and in several of the appendices.

Three technical appendices are included to assist the reader who is interested in an in-depth understanding of the methodology and data. Appendix A, "Personal History Variables and Task Cluster Descriptions," lists all of the variables included in the first section of the Job Analysis Questionnaire (JAQ) that were subsequently used to describe the practitioners and to provide contextual information for interpreting practice findings. This appendix also contains the task statements grouped into various clusters.

Appendix B, "Data Collection and Data Analysis Procedures," details the methodology used in this research. Although we anticipate publishing other reports of these data elsewhere in the social work literature, this appendix will serve as the primary reference point regarding the study methodology. To help the reader assess the strengths and limitations of the methodology used, an independent commentary on this methodology has been provided by Walter Hudson, a highly respected research methodologist and social work educator.

Appendix C, "A Technique for Establishing the Job Relatedness of Social Work Curricula," describes an approach developed to assist schools in analyzing their curricula in a format that is parallel to the clusters of practice activity identified in this study. The format, originally developed for NASW's Curriculum Validation Project (Teare,

Higgs, Gauthier, & Feild, 1984), has been modified in subsequent applications of that model (Sheafor, Teare, Hancock, & Gauthier, 1985; Teare, 1987). This appendix includes guidelines for developing time and content budgets and a method for scoring the curriculum emphasis on each of the clusters of practice activity. A commentary on this approach is provided by two social work educators, Barbara Shank and Angeline Barretta-Herman, who have experienced its use in curriculum evaluation.

As a final note, we offer several cautions in the use of these data. First of all, although the baccalaureate-level data were gathered in 1989-90, the data on master's degree social workers were collected in the mid-1980s. There is, however, no evidence of systematic changes in the nature of practice during the ensuing time period. In fact, recent findings from updated NASW membership records show consistent task/responsibility patterns in the employment settings and practice areas reported by social workers over the past decade (Gibelman & Schervish, 1993)—patterns that are very similar to the ones in our composite 7,000 sample. Changes in some social programs and new problem areas, e.g., AIDS and homelessness, may have affected the activities of subsets of social workers and there is no way to adjust these data for those changes. Readers are therefore urged to adapt their interpretations to account for any changes about which they are aware.

Second, when using these data as a basis for curriculum development or educational policy revision, the reader is reminded that these data reflect what social workers were *actually* doing in their practice, not what they ought to have been doing or how well they did it. As such, these data provide the important element of reality but do not necessarily reflect the vision for the profession's future that should be a part of curriculum and educational policy decisions. The reader, school, or professional organization making use of these data must add that vision.

We want to thank several people who played a special role in making this work possible. In particular, we thank our wives, Marge and Nadine. Thanks are also due to Thom Gauthier, Myles Johnson, Leila Whiting, the late Vern Lyons, and other NASW staff members who facilitated the development of this material; to NASW and the University of Alabama for providing funds that supported the collection of data; Barbara Shank and students at the University of St. Thomas and College of St. Catherine who made it possible to collect the data on baccalaureate-level practitioners; our colleagues at the University of Alabama and Colorado State University who covered for us when we received sabbatical leaves to work on this project; Thomas Stem of the University of Alabama Institute for Social Science Research, and Catherine Teare-Ketter of the University of Georgia, who provided valuable assistance in data processing and analysis; a number of social workers in the Tuscaloosa, Alabama area who worked with us to define and label the clusters of task in terms that would be meaningful to the social work profession; and finally, numerous of our colleagues who have offered suggestions, critique, and encouragement at many stages of the development of this project—especially those who prepared commentaries for this book: Joseph Anderson, Diane Bernard, Charles Guzzetta, Angeline Barretta-Herman, Walter Hudson, Leslie Leighninger, Donald Pilcher, William Reid, and Barbara Shank. We thank you all.

Robert J. Teare
Bradford W. Sheafor

References

Council on Social Work Education, "Curriculum Policy Statement," Alexandria, VA, 1992.

Margaret Gibelman and Philip Schervish, *Who We Are: The Social Work Labor Force As Reflected in the NASW Membership*. Washington, DC: National Association of Social Workers, 1993.

Bradford W. Sheafor, Robert J. Teare, Mervyn J. Hancock, and Thomas P. Gauthier, "Curriculum Development through Content Analysis: A New Zealand Experience," *Journal of Social Work Education*, 21 (Fall 1985): pp. 113-124.

Robert J. Teare, Catherine Higgs, Thomas P. Gauthier, and Hubert S. Feild, *Classification Validation Processes for Human Service Positions*, 7 vols., Silver Spring, MD: National Association of Social Workers, 1984.

Robert J. Teare, *Validating Social Work Credentials for Human Service Jobs*, Silver Spring, MD: National Association of Social Workers, 1987.

Foreword

If social work were a city, you might be hard put to find it. The directions you would get would be contradictory. "Just keep going straight ahead, you can't miss it," some would say. Ask others, and you would be told, "You're heading in the wrong direction! Go back the way you came and continue until the mountains become misty. It's somewhere back there." When you think you have arrived, you ask, "Is this really social work?" The response you hear might be, "Well, it could be, but nobody knows for sure."

The reason our search for the nature of social work has been more a matter of groping than grasping is that we have always lacked a clear picture of what social workers actually do. Our descriptions of the profession have been invariably partial and fuzzy, based as they have been on insular perspectives, fragmentary data, and personal agendas.

The research reported here by Bob Teare and Brad Sheafor goes a long way toward giving us this clear picture. It presents the most thorough, empirical description we have ever had of the many-faceted activities of professional social workers. It is a description based on the painstaking aggregation and analysis of data on the tasks actually performed by a representative sample of over 7,000 social workers. Through the use of cluster and factor analyses, information on 131 discrete tasks was organized into broader descriptive categories. These categories are used to spell out the broad sweep of social work as it is actually practiced. One can see its major foci and variations across different levels of professional preparation. Moreover, these analyses have produced an important breakthrough in conceptualizing social work: the social work practice framework provides a way of explicating and organizing the key components of professional social work activity.

Some empirically based knowledge of social work practice has been accumulated over the years through a number of "process" studies based on analyses of case records, tape recordings, and the like. Although such studies have been useful, they have also been limited by small and often atypical samples, by their focus on clinical activities, and by their restriction to master's-level practitioners. In Teare and Sheafor's work, we have a complete view of professional social work in all its many aspects. It is a major step forward in the profession's research endeavors, extending over the past half-century, to ground the complexities of social work practice in empirical data.

Over the years a good deal of writing, speculation, and debate has taken place on the allocation of tasks and responsibilities between baccalaureate- and master's-level social workers. The data provided by Teare and Sheafor show quite clearly the similarities and differences in the activities of BSW and MSW practitioners. Especially illuminating are findings that suggest that MSWs have access to a much wider range of job functions than BSWs, and findings that indicate that when MSWs and BSWs occupy similar positions, they tend to perform similar functions. Although such findings will not resolve the many issues in education and practice concerning different levels of training, they will enable us to tackle these issues in a more rational manner. Here, as elsewhere, reliable information about current realities is helpful in planning those realities we hope to achieve.

Over the years, we have also tried to resolve the question of social work's unique role. What special contribution distinguishes social work from the other helping professions? This book provides some interesting data on this point. The time-honored notion that a special province of social work is to help people obtain resources and effect changes in their immediate environments receives support. One of the major factors identified as characterizing social work practice turns out to be the "client situation change" factor. However, the historic self-proclaimed mission of social work to bring about changes in peoples' larger environments seems more wishful thinking than reality, if one can judge from these data analyses. As a rule, social workers' efforts to bring about change seem to be largely concentrated on clients and their situations. This finding poses a particular challenge to social work education. Should we abandon the apparently unrealized ideal that social workers be actively involved, as professionals, in changing larger systems? Or should we renew our efforts to attain this ideal? As the authors cogently ask at the end of their narrative: "To what degree should the schools lead or follow practice?"

But another kind of perspective on the special nature of social work might be gleaned from this volume. As I reflected on the authors' descriptions and conceptualizations of social work practice, I began to realize that the uniqueness of social work may not lie so much in any particular task, but rather in how these tasks are clustered in relation to the range of client problems and agency settings that characterize most social work practice. In other words, the essence of social work may not lie in bits of practice but in the picture of practice that is formed when these bits are organized into larger gestalts.

I have just illustrated what readers are likely to find plenty of in this book—food for thought. Read and enjoy!

William J. Reid
Albany, New York

1

Documenting
Social Work Practice

T he profession of social work has a long history of asserting its
claim to certain practice activities because it has experienced repeated challenges to its domain from other human service disciplines—
both in colleges and universities where practitioners are educated and
in organizations where they practice. To strengthen its claim on uniqueness among the helping professions, social work has sought to clearly
identify and define the practice activities of social workers. The formulation of such practice descriptions, however, has proven difficult.

This book represents a new chapter in the effort to capture the
nature of social work: It presents a comprehensive description of practice activities based on *actual* data from the work place. As such, it
has the potential to clarify the realities of the profession and to influence a variety of policy and curriculum decisions that affect social
work education. A review of two developments—the evolution of conceptual descriptions of social work practice and the application of job
analysis techniques to social work practice—provide the backdrop
against which this empirical framework was created and form an important foundation for understanding and interpreting these data.

Characterizing Social Work Practice: A Brief History

At various times in its history, the social work profession has attempted to define its objectives and related professional activities. These
efforts have met with some success, but have been complicated by the
breadth of activities encompassed by social work practice and their
susceptibility to changing social conditions and policies. Three factors
have limited the usefulness of previous attempts at accurate practice
description. First, most have been assertions about the nature of practice based on the observations of individual authors or panels of experts. As such, many of these assertions were unduly influenced by

the particular experiences and orientations of their proponents. Second, many were limited to a single employment setting, practice modality, educational level, or region of the country. Thus, they failed to represent the whole of social work practice or to provide a basis for comparison between subsets of practitioners or practice applications. Finally, although many of these descriptions were conceptually sound, they were not empirically based and thus offered no assurance that they reflected the realities of social work practice. The identification of a few mileposts in the evolution of these practice formulations helps to identify the place of this study in social work's continuing effort to firm up its perception of the work of social workers.

Evolution of Practice Formulations

Although the assignment of historical beginnings is always somewhat arbitrary, most social work historians would identify Mary Richmond's book *Social Diagnosis* as the initial attempt to describe the essential elements of social work (Richmond, 1917). No doubt earlier efforts were made to describe the provision of human services, but it is clear that by around 1910 a philosophical shift had begun to separate social work from other helping efforts. Where before the "character" of the client was viewed as the source of the problem in social functioning, it was at this time that the environment was beginning to be seen as having an important influence. Richmond's writing reflected this dual focus on person and environment that has characterized social work ever since. But there was still little clarity about the essential nature of social work practice. This fact was brought home clearly by Abraham Flexner (1916) in a speech to the National Conference on Charities and Correction entitled "Is Social Work a Profession?" Flexner concluded that social work lacked specificity in aim (i.e., definition) and a sense of identification with other social workers (i.e., a professional organization).

In her 1922 book, *What is Social Case Work?*, Richmond attempted to deal with the first deficit. She defined social case work at a very high level of abstraction, concluding that it encompassed "those processes which develop personality through adjustments consciously effected, individual by individual, between men and their social environment" (Richmond, 1922, pp. 98-99). This definition was abstract enough to bridge the differences in various settings where social work practice occurred, but still did not identify the specific activities in which social workers should be engaged. With regard to the second deficit identified by Flexner, the 1910s and 1920s saw the formation of several professional social work associations that focused on specific settings in which practice took place, as well as the formation of the more generic American Association of Social Workers (AASW). This mix of generic and specialized organizations did little to provide clarity about the essence of social work.

In an attempt to identify the factors that were common to all of social work practice, 17 key social workers met in Milford, Pennsylvania in 1923 under the auspices of the AASW. Although the Milford Conference met regularly over the next five years, the participants were able to agree only on the principle that "generic social case work" was much more substantial than any of the emphases in the various fields and settings. The final committee report stated that many of the questions addressed by the group could not "be satisfactorily discussed" without assembling research data "which are not now available" (AASW, 1929, p. 10). As will be seen, the absence of hard data would continue to plague those who sought clarification.

Throughout the 1930s, social work practitioners continued to emphasize the provision of tangible resources for the solution of daily living problems, but also began to give more attention to the interdependence of personality and the environment in shaping one's social condition. Along with a return to an emphasis on the individual's personality as a primary contributor to social problems came a decision that many social workers believed would strengthen the profession's status—the requirement that all accredited social work education should be conducted in universities at the master's level. With the coming of the Great Depression, the New Deal, and the Social Security Act, social work became a central part of the effort in this country to meet the needs of vulnerable citizens. The dramatic change in the human services created by the federal government's expanded role in social programs led to substantial changes in social work practice and, subsequently, in education. In this context, it was impracticable (if not impossible) to advance efforts to define the nature of social work practice.

By the early 1940s, the range of activities carried out by practitioners had become more apparent and practice descriptions had become more complex. In her 1942 book *Social Work: An Analysis of a Social Institution*, Helen Witmer concluded that social work had become an institutionalized part of U.S. society and thus required more accurate public interpretation. She identified administration, community organization, social action, and research as elements of social work that should be considered in any description of the profession, which further complicated the task of defining practice activities.

The post-World War II era was dominated by a spirit of unity and cooperation within the profession. In 1955, after six years of negotiation, the six specialized practice organizations and the AASW were consolidated to form the National Association of Social Workers (NASW). One of NASW's first efforts to identify the factors that unified social workers was the creation of a Commission on Practice. The *Working Definition of Social Work Practice*, published in 1958, was the Commission's most important product. The political intent of the document was to "define social work practice in a way acceptable to the seven organizations that were subsumed" in the newly organized NASW (Delahanty, 1988, p. vi). Cast in fairly general terms, the *Working Definition* finessed many of the issues that polarized the profession and asserted that social work was best recognized by its unique "constellation of values, purpose, knowledge and method" (Bartlett, 1958, p. 5).

This same period saw the formation, in 1952, of the Council on Social Work Education (CSWE) out of organizations representing two competing factions in social work education. The dominant group was the AASW, which argued for social work education only at the graduate level. Competing with that perspective was the renegade National Association of Schools of Social Administration, which embraced both undergraduate and graduate preparation for professional practice. Shortly after its founding, CSWE began a comprehensive curriculum study to identify the appropriate educational base for practice at both levels. The project's chairperson, Werner Boehm, pointed again to the absence of empirical data on which to formulate curriculum policies: "No single, widely recognized, or generally accepted statement exists on the aims and purposes of the practice of social work. The core activities of social work, as distinct from the activities of other helping professions, have not yet been authoritatively stated and differentiated" (Boehm, 1959, p. 40). Clearly, practice-sensitive curriculum development continued to be problematic for the schools.

The 1960s ushered in yet another period of profound change in America's human services. Heightened public awareness of long-standing social problems and injustice was coupled with the belief that these social problems could be dealt with through the release of sufficient resources and the delivery of appropriate services. As perhaps never before (or since), the federal government was viewed as the most viable resource for financing and orchestrating attacks on social problems. At the same time, there was a perception that traditional social agencies and organizations had not been sufficiently responsive to the needs of the poor and, to correct that, major changes had to be made in the channels through which funding came and the manner in which personnel were utilized. Although, historically, social services had been diverse in nature, there was a call for an even wider array of services, an increased emphasis on social action, and drastic changes in entitlement programs. Professionally trained social workers were required to deliver many of these programs, but the supply was insufficient for the increased demand.

In the mid-1960s, a task force was appointed by Wilbur Cohen, Secretary of the U.S. Department of Health, Education, and Welfare (HEW), to examine the extent of this labor force problem and explore the need for people prepared at different levels to deliver the increasingly diverse human service programs. The task force concluded that, through careful job differentiation, an appropriately prepared work force could quickly be put into place (U.S. Department of HEW, 1965). That conclusion was consistent with the emerging belief that indigenous personnel (i.e., former clients and recipients) could draw on their personal experiences and, by so doing, be effective providers of some services (Pearl & Riessman, 1965; Reiff & Riessman, 1964). By 1970, the labor force in the human services—that is, social welfare, health, education, mental health, vocational rehabilitation, and corrections— was being energized by more than one hundred separate grant-in-aid, programs administered by eight federal departments and agencies (Teare, 1978). The result of all this diversification of services and differentiation in personnel was a human service system and a social work profession that were even harder to characterize than before. Furthermore, little information was available on which to base such characterizations.

Emergence of Differential Practice Frameworks

The disjointed infusion of large amounts of money and many different kinds of workers into the human service systems in the 1960s resulted in a delivery system that was driven by contradictory motives, fragmented in nature, and perceived by many as inefficient and ineffective. Large numbers of service providers had been employed without traditional credentials, and those with professional credentials were often viewed with suspicion. As time went on, it became evident that a clear rationale was needed for organizing human service programs and for using the skills of the different types of workers who were providing these services.

To maintain its prominent place in the human services, the social work profession had to define the qualifications and competencies required for various levels of practice. NASW responded by forming a Committee on the Study of Competence, which released its first document, *Guidelines for the Assessment of Professional Practice in Social Work*, in 1968. The report defined four levels of social work practice: (1) premaster's degree practice, (2) professional practice at the beginning level (i.e., the new MSW graduate), (3) self-regulated practice, and (4) senior-level practice (NASW, 1968, pp. 3-4). Because the report described the basic competencies required at each practice level, it served as an important basis for curriculum development in social work education.

Subsequent work on utilization frameworks reflected the emergence of undergraduate social work education as an important contributor to a sufficient supply of social workers. In 1968, the Social and Rehabilitation Service of HEW awarded a grant to the Southern Regional Education Board (SREB) to develop guidelines for the use of workers with BSW and BA degrees in the delivery of human services. Although SREB concentrated on the baccalaureate-level social worker, it developed a framework that encompassed a wide range of worker preparation—from those with a few weeks of in-service training to those with terminal degrees. To provide a rationale for this worker differentiation scheme, a task force of practice experts assisted SREB in developing a framework that incorporated 12 practice "roles" linked to 9 major objectives of social welfare interventions (Teare & McPheeters, 1970).

In 1969, the NASW membership approved a referendum that granted professional status to graduates of CSWE-recognized baccalaureate social work programs. CSWE began developing the accreditation standards that would determine which educational programs would be recognized, while NASW revisited and updated its labor force classification system *Standards for Social Service Manpower* (NASW, 1973).

The increased differentiation in social work again turned the attention of the profession to a search for a conceptual framework that would help to identify the similarities, as well as the differences, in the several formulations of social work practice. This search was led by the NASW Publications Committee, which identified as a top priority for the latter half of the 1970s a response to prevailing concerns among practitioners as to the purpose of social work and social workers, and as to whether any consensus existed in social work that cut across "the profession's various specialties and interests" (Minahan & Briar, 1977, p. 339). To this end, the Committee commissioned papers from several experts and held a conference to discuss the issues raised. In comparison to the 1923 conference in Milford, PA, this conference was intended to address the *whole* of social work, not just social casework. The results, however, were comparable to those of the Milford effort—a call to "articulate what is common within the evident diversity" in social work practice (Briar, 1977, p. 415).

At this point, the accepted definitions, conceptualizations, and classification systems had all been based on the deliberations of task forces and, at best, represented the consensus of subject matter experts. A recognized limitation in these descriptions of social work was that they were not based on a *systematically collected body of data* about the nature of social work practice activities. External forces, largely outside the control of the social work profession, would soon make this type of database a necessity.

Development of Practice Task Banks

In the 1970s various funding sources and policy makers became concerned about perceived overlaps in effort among programs staffed by different disciplines. As a result, they demanded more efficient operations and the elimination of program duplication. In part to realize efficiency, agencies pushed to make workers in the various disciplines interchangeable. Thus, while social work was struggling to define its uniqueness, employing agencies were searching for commonality among the helping disciplines. This pressure was most strongly felt at the state level, where both public and private agencies competed for limited funds and drew from a small and increasingly undifferentiated labor pool. For better or worse, the age of "human services integration" had arrived.

Because little attention had been given to the classification of service personnel within most of the newly integrated agencies, no clear rationale existed for the division of labor among the disciplines. Further, no provision was made for horizontal or vertical career mobility for these workers. The need for clarity and definition, previously felt by disciplines like social work, was now felt just as strongly by the organizations that employed social workers and other human service providers. The information most frequently sought related to details of the work activities of different kinds of workers and the relevance of these activities to their job credentials (i.e., degree and experience prerequisites and/or examination cut scores). This, however, was precisely the type of information that was not available.

To remedy this information deficit, several states turned their attention to the systematic collection of job information within these integrated agencies. In 1972, the state of Florida began a three-year labor force planning project, funded by the Division of Social and Rehabilitation Services of HEW. The focus of the project was to design a personnel classification system for the large state human service agency (15,000 employees) that included several diverse service divisions. Self-report work diaries obtained from a representative sample of employees were used to identify a number of specific tasks that employees performed as a part of their jobs. These task statements were then edited and refined into a bank of 358 standardized human service activities (Austin, Smith, & Skelding, 1975; Pecora & Austin, 1987).

At approximately the same time, a similar need for information was felt by Alabama's freestanding public welfare department. Because of the proliferation of programs and changes brought about by federal participation in funding, the job functions of many social workers in the department had been altered. It became necessary to generate a new system of job classification and worker utilization. Because the forces that argued for the interchangeability of professionals were likely to challenge the association of specific credentials with positions in the new job classification system, it was especially important that the system be defensible. The job descriptions, therefore, had to be based on accurate data. Drawing on the SREB material and the Florida task bank, a task analysis survey was developed[1] and self-reported job data were collected from a representative sample of 661 social workers. These job data were analyzed in such a way that social workers with similar job content, regardless of their job titles, could be grouped together. The results of this survey became the basis of a new classification for social work positions in Alabama (Teare, 1981).

These and similar efforts in other states represented the beginnings of a process that would result in the gradual accumulation of specific content about the activities of social workers and others who provided the vast array of social and human services. Although these efforts provided much needed information, the usefulness of the data for the description of social work practice was limited by the fact that a substantial number of social service workers, especially in the public sector, did not possess social work credentials. Because of this, the data could neither address the question of the proper content of social work

---

[1] This became the prototype of the Job Analysis Questionnaire (JAQ), subsequent versions of which were used to generate the database described here. The task statements contained in the JAQ, and a subsequent version entitled the Social Work Activity Inventory (SWAI), have been copyrighted (1984, 1989, 1995) by Robert J. Teare. They may not be reproduced in any fashion without the written permission of the author.

education nor shed light on the activities performed by social workers who were prepared at different educational levels.

Comment generated by the September 1977 special issue of *Social Work*, which addressed the status of social work's conceptual frameworks, stimulated the NASW Publications Committee to convene another group (in 1979) to again consider the nature of social work. The process this time was to have experts in various specialties offer judgments concerning social work's relevance for their practice areas. The goal was to determine if consensus could be achieved among the different practice specialties. This process resulted in a second special issue of *Social Work*, about which Brieland (1981) noted: "This second special issue on frameworks has produced new insights and new issues for a profession in transition. An analysis of the articles makes it evident that specializations have apparently increased the difficulties in arriving at a satisfactory consensus for a framework for the profession" (p. 83).

Given the absence of an accepted conceptual framework or a suitable database from which to work, NASW continued to use the opinions of experts in rationalizing the use of different levels of social workers for various job classifications. In 1981, the NASW Board of Directors accepted a second report from the Task Force on Labor Force Classification entitled *Standards for the Classification of Social Work Practice*. This revision of the 1973 standards was designed to guide strategies for (1) identifying appropriate personnel for service provision in private practice, voluntary agencies, and the public sector, (2) obtaining legal regulation for social work practice, and (3) addressing the problem of "declassification" in social work.[2] The report has also served as a basis for distinguishing between the "basic social worker" (BSW level) and the "specialized social worker" (MSW level) in the formulation of professional education curricula.

Need for a Standardized Approach to Practice Description

As the 1970s drew to an end, the need for detailed occupational data became even more acute. A survey of 47 state merit systems carried out by NASW between 1979 and 1981 indicated that there was

---

[2]The terms "declassification" and "reclassification" have been used to refer to the removal or alteration of social work training and experience from social work positions that have typically required them. At the height of the agency integration movement, it was one of the strategies used to liberalize hiring practices or to avoid credential challenges.

little uniformity in the way training and education requirements were established for social work positions in the public sector (Teare, Higgs, Gauthier, & Feild, 1984), and there was evidence that the situation was essentially the same in the private sector. The link between minimum job requirements, that is, educational or licensing credentials and experience, and the job duties performed by social workers was increasingly under challenge. Thus, while the profession struggled with definitions and consensus, its hold on its traditional occupational turf was slipping.

Other pressures conspired to further loosen the profession's grip. Title VII of the Civil Rights Act, several rulings of the U.S. Supreme Court in the early and mid-1970s, and federal guidelines issued by the Equal Employment Opportunity Commission in 1978 and 1979 had all focused on job requirements. These rulings and guidelines stated that evidence of the "job relatedness" of employment requirements needed to be demonstrated if their use had an adverse impact on minorities. Because minorities of gender and color constituted a large segment of the social work labor force, it was particularly important that any such possibilities be minimized for jobs in human services. Rather than run the risk of discriminating, many agencies elected to reclassify positions by eliminating all but the most rudimentary job requirements.

If social work was to lay claim to a particular sector of the job market, it had to establish the validity of any discipline-specific job requirements related to positions in that sector. Donald Brieland (1977), who issued a call for continuing research aimed at differentiating the levels of social work practice, clearly described the situation:

> Unless the profession validates the skills necessary to perform duties in public agencies, the trend toward declassification will continue. If the differences in levels of work cannot be established, specifications will be based on the assumptions that high school graduates, BSWs, and MSWs do the same thing—and are interchangeable. (p. 339)

NASW Job Analysis Projects

In 1982, NASW decided to undertake validation of its Academy of Certified Social Workers (ACSW) examination, which was, in some instances, used as a qualification for employment and was being marketed to state regulatory boards as a qualifying examination for MSW-

or doctoral-level licensing. The essential ingredient in the validation of any procedure used to set minimum job requirements involves establishing the job-relatedness of the assessment procedure. Several validation strategies are commonly used; NASW elected to use the content validation approach.[3] Simply put, content validation provides evidence that any mechanism or instrument used to screen job applicants contains a representative sample of the content of the job. This, of course, requires considerable information about the job in question.

To be able to demonstrate the job-relatedness of the ACSW examination (and, subsequently, of the Academy of Certified Baccalaureate Social Workers [ACBSW] exam), it was necessary to collect detailed information about the job activities of social workers. As a result, NASW commissioned a series of national job analyses that produced the data presented in this book. These studies took place, intermittently, from 1983 through 1990. Although these studies were not originally conceived of as connected, they all used the same methodological approach and were conducted by a core group of NASW staff members and technical consultants. This continuity made it possible to compile an unusually large base of compatible information about the work of social workers. In all, three studies were conducted.

The ACSW Study

The Job Analysis Questionnaire (JAQ) was the primary data collection instrument used in the 1983 ACSW study. The task statements in this instrument were derived from earlier work with the task banks, but were expanded and updated during a series of workshops attended by social work practitioners and subject matter experts. In formulating revisions, emphasis was placed on the comprehensiveness of content, clarity of the statements, and avoidance of technical jargon. The revised version of the JAQ contained 135 task statements that required respondents to rate, using a five-point scale, "how often" they performed each task and "how important" it was to their job. A personal history section was included to provide demographic data on each respondent. The format of the personal history items was identical to that used in the NASW Data Bank Questionnaire (a membership database), allowing direct comparisons to be made to member characteristics. (See Appendix A for a list of the personal history variables in the JAQ.)

---

[3] For more details about the validation of social service jobs and the NASW validation project background, the reader is urged to read the technical reports produced by NASW (Teare et al., 1984).

Using the NASW membership database as a sample population, investigators selected a stratified random sample of 7,255 NASW members. These individuals received the JAQ in the mail. Of the 5,936 (79%) returned questionnaires, 5,397 were usable. (For a full description of this study, see Teare, 1987a.)

The Occupational Social Work Study

In 1985, NASW's Commission on Employment and Economic Support undertook a national study of people who identified themselves as occupational social workers. Most were MSWs, but the study also included some BSWs and some without any type of social work credential at all. As with the ACSW study, the survey instrument of choice was the JAQ, which was revised by subject matter experts who added, deleted, and revised tasks to make the survey contents and language more compatible with occupational social work practice. To maximize content overlap with the ACSW study, 128 of the task statements were maintained in identical form or with very similar content to those used in the ACSW version. The personal history section also was changed as little as possible.

The sampling frame was a composite of NASW local chapter Occupational Social Work Committee rosters and practitioner lists of various kinds. The lists were merged and purged, yielding 2,220 unduplicated names. These individuals received the JAQ in early spring of 1985. In all, 1,068 (49%) surveys were returned. After these were screened to ensure that respondents possessed social work credentials and met the definition of occupational social work set down for the study, 499 surveys were deemed usable. (For a full description of this study, see Teare, 1987b.)

The BSW Practitioner Study

The most recent data resulted from a 1987 NASW decision to develop a process for certifying baccalaureate social workers. Since the process was to resemble the ACSW procedure, a job content study from a national sample of BSW practitioners was required. As with the graduate level exam, the results of the job analysis would be used to derive content for the ACBSW examination. As before, workshops were held to revise the instrument so that it would be appropriate for BSW workers, but minimal changes were made to content and language. The BSW version contained 132 task statements; of these, 129 were identical or directly comparable to those in the ACSW version.

In the BSW study, however, identification of potential respondents was much more difficult than with the previous studies. Because few BSW graduates were NASW members, existing membership lists were far from representative of the population. In the absence of a single comprehensive list to use as a sampling frame, lists of graduates were requested from all 349 CSWE-accredited undergraduate programs. A representative sample of 149 schools replied and, when added to the persons on the NASW roster, a list of 22,075 unduplicated names was compiled. An elaborate screening process was used to locate graduates (many addresses were outdated) and to eliminate those who were not currently employed as social workers or who had gone on for further graduate training. In all, 5,244 BSW graduates were located; of these, 2,488 met the criteria for inclusion in the study—full-time employment as a social worker for at least six months with the BSW degree being the sole job credential. By the cutoff date in early 1990, 1,480 of the 2,488 potential respondents (59.5%) had returned completed surveys. Of these, 1,363 were confirmed as meeting the eligibility criteria. (For a more complete report of this study, see Teare, Shank, and Sheafor, 1990.)

Combining the Project Samples

By the time the third study was completed, data had been collected from a total of 7,259 social work practitioners, comprising a data set that was truly unique in size and scope. Taken as an aggregate, the analysis of such a database would permit, for the first time, the construction of an empirically based depiction of the framework of social work practice, an analysis of the content of task activities, a clearer understanding of how the division of labor is influenced by education and work setting, and a comprehensive description of social work practitioners. The potential in these data to inform both practice and education was evident.

The first step was to combine the three data sets. Tasks were retained if they had been used in the ACSW and at least one other survey; 131 tasks met this criterion. After careful editing and data transformation, a composite sample of 7,000 surveys was selected for analysis. All had only minor omissions in demographic and task data. All respondents in this group had at least one social work degree from an accredited program and all had been employed as full-time social workers for at least six months.

Demographic Characteristics

The data in Table 1.1 show that the sample is quite diverse. Respondents worked in all parts of the country and were found in virtually all of the employment settings where social workers hold positions. The primary job responsibility for most respondents (57.9%) was the provision of direct services to clients. Most of the remainder were employed to manage organizations, supervise workers, or teach. As indicated by age, experience, and job tenure, the typical respondent was a seasoned, mature practitioner. In short, the composite sample can be considered a representative, comprehensive, cross-section of contemporary social work practitioners. (See Appendix B for more information on the representativeness of the sample.)

Table 1.1. **Composite Study Sample: Demographic Data**

(*N* = 7,000)

Location			Ethnicity			Gender		
Northeast	2,264	32.2%[a]	Asian	96	1.4%	Female	4,606	65.8%
Northcentral	2,136	30.5%	Afr. Amer.	502	7.2%	Male	2,366	30.8%
South	1,505	21.5%	Am. Indian	45	0.6%			
West	1,060	15.1%	White	6,178	88.0%			
			Chicano/					
			Mex. Am.	47	0.7%			
Age			Puerto Rican	27	0.4%			
41.8 years (Mean)			Other Hispanic	40	0.6%			
39.0 years (Median)								

Education Level			Employment Setting			Employment Function		
(Highest Degree)			Social services	2,170	30.1%	Direct service	4,053	57.9%
BSW	1,449	20.7%[b]	Private practice	472	6.8%	Supervision	640	9.1%
MSW	5,272	75.3%	Membership org.	76	1.3%	Mgt./admin.	1,639	23.4%
DSW or			Hospital	1,354	19.3%	Policy/		
PhD	279	3.9%	Institution	266	3.8%	planning	83	1.2%
			Outpat. facility	1,171	16.7%	Consultation	128	1.8%
Social Work Experience			Group home	178	2.5%	Educ/training	420	6.0%
12.2 years (Mean)			Nursing home	220	3.0%			
9.0 years (Median)			Court/crim.			**Time In Current Position**		
			justice	118	2.6%	6.1 years (Mean)		
			College/			4.0 Years (Median)		
			university	390	5.6%			
			Elem/sec.					
			school	418	6.0%			

[a]Percentages may not total 100% because of missing values on some variables.
[b]Degrees in social work do not always have the same designation. To be included in this study, a respondent must have completed a bachelor's or master's degree from a social work program accredited by the Council on Social Work Education, or a doctoral degree in social work.

Developing the Practice Framework

Cluster Analysis

Individual ratings of 131 tasks by 7,000 respondents generated a mass of data. It was obvious that some form of data reduction and organization was in order. At the same time, it was strongly felt that the organizational framework should be based on relationships inherent in the data rather than imposed by the researchers. In keeping with this rationale, the 131 tasks were grouped, on an ex posteriori basis, by using a hierarchical cluster analysis procedure developed by Ward (1963). (See Appendix B for a detailed description of data reduction.) Researchers made comparisons among all the tasks and combined those that were most similar, using a statistically derived index of similarity, into a more limited number of clusters. Conceptually, the process began by treating the 131 tasks as independent "clusters" and iteratively decreasing their number until all tasks were combined into a single cluster. The ideal number of groups is assumed to be somewhere between the two extremes—at the point where the differences *between* clusters is maximized and the differences *within* clusters is minimized. Previous empirical studies of portions of the JAQ data suggested that a cluster analysis of the entire data set should result in somewhere between 15 and 25 clusters of work activity.

Following the guidance of recognized methodologists in this area (Aldenderfer & Blashfield, 1984; Everitt, 1979), investigators used a blend of statistical and judgmental criteria to select the ideal number of clusters and their identifying labels. Three criteria—stability, meaningfulness, and homogeneity—were applied to the cluster solution.

Stability

A good cluster scheme is stable—that is, one would get the same results with repeated analyses of independent samples. To assess the stability of the clusters, the 7,000 records in the data were randomized. Four independent data subsets of 1,500 records each and a fifth containing the remaining 1,000 records were created. By carrying out a separate cluster analysis on all five subsamples, each served as both a derivative and a confirmatory sample for the others.[4] Only clusters that were repeated in at least three of the five subsamples were considered stable enough to be included in the final classification; 18 clusters met this criterion.

---

[4]Looking for replicated patterns of relationships in exploratory multivariate analyses of different samples represents a type of convergent construct validity. See Carmines and Zeller (1979) and Camasso and Geismar (1992).

Meaningfulness

A good classification system should also "make sense" within the context of the population from which it was derived. With these data it meant that a cluster should only contain tasks that, from a practice point of view, can be connected logically to one another. If the tasks can be, it becomes a relatively straightforward matter to assign labels and define the clusters in a manner that will communicate the meaning of the clustered tasks. The meaningfulness of the labels is particularly important since they become the shorthand for communication about the set of activities represented in each cluster.

The authors took great care in assigning cluster labels and descriptions. Once the 18 clusters were identified, the tasks in each cluster were examined for their commonalities, a capsule summary (definition) was created for each cluster, and a label was assigned. To increase the likelihood that the labels and definitions used would communicate accurately to other social workers, the investigators made them consistent with those contained in *The Social Work Dictionary* (Barker, 1987) and the *Encyclopedia of Social Work* (Minahan, 1987) whenever possible. When clustered tasks did not clearly fit generally accepted terminology, an effort was made to introduce entirely new descriptions that would not be confused with existing ones. To validate these definitions and labels, a group of social workers from varied settings were assembled to critique the appropriateness of the definitions for the related tasks and the accuracy of the labels as representations of the clusters.

Homogeneity

In a classification system, the elements contained within each cluster should be as similar as possible. This homogeneity can be estimated statistically by computing a measure of internal consistency reliability called Cronbach's alpha (Cronbach, 1951). In each cluster description that follows, this coefficient is reported. (See Appendix B for a more complete description of Cronbach's alpha.) All of the alpha coefficients in this study were statistically significant and, with the exception of only one cluster (Dispute Resolution), they were quite high.

Description of the Clusters

Using the process described above, the following 18 clusters were identified, defined, and labeled. The reader is encouraged to study these clusters carefully as they will be used repeatedly in depicting social work practice throughout this book. The notations for each cluster identify the assigned label, Cronbach's alpha (ranging from .54 to .95), the number of tasks that fell into each cluster, and the mean score for the frequency of performance of the tasks in the cluster for the composite sample (mean scores can range from 1.00 to 5.00). For each cluster a one-sentence definition is given (in italics) along with elaboration to enhance understanding of the cluster. (See Appendix A for a listing of the tasks contained in each cluster.)

1. Interpersonal Helping
($\alpha = .81$) (4 tasks) (mean = 3.98)

Use basic helping skills (e.g., interviewing, questioning, counseling) to assist individuals and/or families in understanding the problems they experience in social functioning and helping them to examine possible options for resolving those problems. In carrying out these activities, the worker actively involves individuals and families in discussions designed to explore options for solving problems. The worker encourages people to express their points of view and share their feelings. Throughout this process the worker attempts to communicate an understanding of other people's points of view and establish a relationship of trust with clients.

2. Group Work
($\alpha = .68$) (4 tasks) (mean = 2.43)

Use small groups as an environment for teaching clients skills for effective performance of daily living tasks, communicating information to enhance social functioning, or for facilitating problem resolution or therapeutic change. In these tasks, the worker consciously uses the group process in order to teach individuals how groups work and how to act as a member of the group. These tasks involve the worker in therapeutic groups as well as task-oriented work groups in organizations and in communities.

3. Individual/Family Treatment
($\alpha = .84$) (3 tasks) (mean = 3.24)

Select and use clearly defined formal treatment modes or models to help individuals and/or families improve their social functioning or resolve social problems. Activities include the use of any of a wide array of interventive techniques and strategies ranging from non-directive to confrontational approaches.

4. Risk Assessment/Transition
(α = .79) (8 tasks) (mean = 2.79)

Assess case situation to determine its difficulty (i.e., risk, urgency, or need) and engage clients either in making use of services or preparing them for transition or termination. Tasks include the observation of individuals and the gathering of information in order to decide whether special services or routine services are required. In certain circumstances, the worker will be expected to deal with hostile or uncooperative clients. A number of the tasks focus on the preparation of clients for movement, transition, or service termination.

5. Protective Services
(α = .79) (4 tasks) (mean = 2.03)

Collect and analyze data to be used in assessing at-risk clients and presenting information to appropriate authorities if clients are judged to be in danger of physical or emotional maltreatment or having their basic rights violated. This includes the observation and assessment of children and/or adults to determine whether they have been abused or neglected. As part of this process, the worker may be expected to start legal proceedings and testify or participate in court hearings involving custody, competence, outplacement, or institutionalization.

6. Case Planning/Maintenance
(α = .90) (11 tasks) (mean = 3.46)

Perform ongoing case planning, coordinate any additional services the client requires, monitor and evaluate case progress, obtain case consultation when appropriate, and complete required paperwork for case records. Tasks include preparing and reviewing case materials to assess progress, coordinating service planning with internal staff and providers from other agencies, and carrying out appropriate procedures, e.g., obtaining consent, explaining rights, maintaining security, to ensure that client's rights are protected.

7. Service Connection
(α = .75) (6 tasks) (mean = 2.30)

Employ techniques that help clients to connect with established services, take action to eliminate barriers that prevent clients from receiving those services, and evaluate the success of services clients have received. Activities in this cluster center on the linkage function, although some advocacy on the part of the worker may be required. Tasks include arranging for transportation, following up people by phone, and carrying out intake procedures.

8. Tangible Service Provision
($\alpha = .75$) (12 tasks) (mean = 1.60)

Deliver a variety of "hard," tangible services designed to assist people in coping with problems or activities associated with daily living. In contrast to the more therapeutically oriented services, these activities focus on meeting the needs of clients as they cope with everyday life. Tasks include teaching budgeting, money management, food preparation, and homemaking skills, helping clients find jobs and housing, and putting them in touch with people of similar backgrounds and experience. Workers may visit clients to assess the suitability of living arrangements and take part in leisure activities to help reduce loneliness.

9. Professional Development
($\alpha = .65$) (7 tasks) (mean = 3.64)

Engage in activities that strengthen one's own practice effectiveness and expand one's professional competence. Some of the tasks involve self-assessment, i.e., periodically taking stock of one's performance by evaluating actions and decisions made within the context of practice. Other tasks involve attendance at workshops, seminars, or professional meetings as well as reading professional journals, magazines, and newspapers in order to keep abreast of new developments. The focus of the cluster is the perception that professional development is an ongoing process.

10. Staff Deployment
($\alpha = .88$) (6 tasks) (mean = 2.08)

Recruit and select staff (e.g., professional and clerical employees, volunteers, and students), arrange staffing patterns and workload assignments, monitor staff productivity, and oversee compliance with organizational policies. Tasks in this cluster concentrate on the assurance of staff coverage and equitable workload distribution within an organizational setting. They include scheduling and coordinating working hours, leave, and vacation, reviewing personnel actions, recruiting and screening applicants, and monitoring service demands in order to establish staffing requirements.

11. Staff Supervision
($\alpha = .94$) (9 tasks) (mean = 2.62)

Guide the day-to-day work of staff members (e.g., professional and clerical employees, volunteers, and/or students) by orienting them to the organization and its requirements, assigning work and teaching them to perform their jobs, as well as monitoring and assessing their performance. The tasks in this cluster encompass the array of tasks typically associated with supervision. They include the provision of job orientation and job training by means of regular case review and critique, clarification of job duties and work expectations with individuals and groups, and the evaluation, interpretation, and feedback of job performance evaluations.

12. Dispute Resolution
(α = .54) (4 tasks) (mean = 2.30)

Use advocacy, negotiation, and mediation to resolve interpersonal problems among staff members or between client/staff and the organization. These tasks involve interactions in a "charged" organizational climate. The worker is expected to listen to dissatisfied parties and mediate disputes at various levels in the organization.

13. Staff Information Exchange
(α = .66) (4 tasks) (mean = 2.94)

Organize and/or participate in meetings or use other means of communication to exchange information with staff members, resolve job-related problems, and/or make decisions that affect agency functioning. The essence of the tasks in this cluster is the presentation and receiving of information, with individuals and in group meetings, in order to accomplish task-centered objectives.

14. Organizational Maintenance
(α = .91) (16 tasks) (mean = 1.82)

Manage the ongoing operation of a program or administrative unit to assure its efficient and effective functioning by securing, allocating, and overseeing the utilization of its resources (e.g., staff, funds, office supplies, space) and marketing its services. This cluster includes a wide array of tasks concerned with the operation of an existing program or unit. Some of the tasks center on financial operations, e.g., estimating budgets, documenting and reviewing expenditures, and compiling billings, cost reimbursement, and cost control documents. Others deal with the maintenance of a physical plant and the control of inventory. Some of the tasks involve working with staff and vendors in order to ensure smooth program operations.

15. Delivery System Knowledge Development
(α = .74) (7 tasks) (mean = 3.09)

Learn about the community's service delivery system and develop an understanding of various regulations, policies, and procedures that affect social programs. The focus of this cluster is on the gathering of information about the network of services and service resources within the geographic area in which the worker is located. Activities include visiting agencies, attending meetings, and making contacts in order to become acquainted with or keep up to date with changes in the services provided, developing cooperative service arrangements among agencies, and keeping up to date on regulations, organizational policies, and agency guidelines.

16. Program Development
(α = .93) (15 tasks) (mean = 2.27)

Document and interpret the need for additional human service programs, develop working relationships with relevant resources for program support (e.g., boards, funding sources, legislative bodies, referral sources), oversee implementation of new programs, and evaluate program success. This cluster differs from Organizational Maintenance (Cluster 14) in that the emphasis of most tasks in this cluster is on the development of *new* programs or units or the *alteration* of existing ones. Workers convert program goals and concepts into specific plans, develop budgets and staffing plans, "sell" the program(s) to funding sources and other decision makers, and compile data for evaluation purposes. In this cluster, workers meet with resource people, explain needs, and encourage volunteer or other resource contributions. Workers may also make public appearances and disseminate information in order to garner public support for programs.

17. Research/Policy Development
(α = .75) (7 tasks) (mean = 1.72)

Collect, analyze, and publish data, present technical information to the general public, legislators, or other decision makers responsible for changes in human service programs or community conditions, and/or interact with community groups. While the tasks in this cluster involve a wide assortment of research, public relations, and community outreach activities, most of them are concerned with influencing public opinion, public policy, or legislation. The worker may collect and compile information, conduct surveys, present or publish finding from studies, testify as an expert witness, or organize and take part in campaigns and demonstrations.

18. Instruction

($\alpha = .81$) (4 tasks) (mean = 2.20)

Plan, arrange, conduct, and evaluate programs that enhance the knowledge or increase the skills of staff members, students, agency volunteers, or participants in community groups. This cluster deals with formal instruction rather than the kind of informal teaching associated with orientation or on-the-job training. Activities involve course planning, syllabus design, test construction, group instruction, and course evaluation.

The cluster analysis reduced the 131 task statements to 18 clusters of work activity. A more convenient way to characterize practice is to calculate the mean score for each of the clusters and use this pattern of means as a depiction. This has been done for the total sample ($N = 7,000$) and is displayed below in Figure 1.1. In interpreting these cluster

Figure 1.1. Mean Cluster Scores: All Respondents

($N = 7,000$)

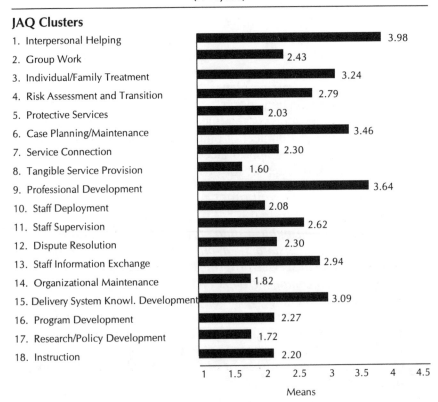

JAQ Clusters

1. Interpersonal Helping — 3.98
2. Group Work — 2.43
3. Individual/Family Treatment — 3.24
4. Risk Assessment and Transition — 2.79
5. Protective Services — 2.03
6. Case Planning/Maintenance — 3.46
7. Service Connection — 2.30
8. Tangible Service Provision — 1.60
9. Professional Development — 3.64
10. Staff Deployment — 2.08
11. Staff Supervision — 2.62
12. Dispute Resolution — 2.30
13. Staff Information Exchange — 2.94
14. Organizational Maintenance — 1.82
15. Delivery System Knowl. Development — 3.09
16. Program Development — 2.27
17. Research/Policy Development — 1.72
18. Instruction — 2.20

Means

means, it is useful to note that a score of 1.50 to 2.49 represents a group of tasks that, as a cluster, were "seldom" performed, 2.50 to 3.49 represents tasks "occasionally" performed, and 3.50 to 4.49 represents tasks "frequently" performed.

The definitions of the tasks and clusters makes clear the range of rather discrete activities carried out by social workers. Figure 1.1 indicates that, when one looks at social workers as an intact group, some task clusters were seldom performed (e.g., Protective Services, Tangible Services, Organizational Maintenance, Research and Policy Development), while others had such high mean frequency scores in the composite sample that they seemed virtually universal in social work practice (e.g., Interpersonal Helping, Professional Development). As will be seen, many more differences in cluster patterns will become apparent when the data are broken down by other variables (e.g., education level, job function, setting). Even at this cursory level, however, the data have practice and curricular implications.

Factor Analysis of the Clusters

As part of the initial data analysis, a matrix of the intercorrelations among the clusters was calculated. Inspection of that matrix revealed a wide range of negative and positive correlations among the clusters and suggested that it might be useful to carry out a factor analysis using the cluster scores as variables. Unlike cluster analysis, which is designed to form groups or classes, factor analysis attempts to explain relationships (e.g., correlations) among variables in terms of fewer, more abstract constructs.

A principle components factor analysis was carried out using the 18 cluster scores for each of the 7,000 practitioners.[5] Based on accepted statistical criteria, a five-factor solution was deemed most appropriate. The factors were labeled by concentrating on those clusters that correlated with or "loaded" most strongly on each factor. (See Appendix B for a listing of the factor loadings for each cluster.) Each task statement in the JAQ contained an "in order to" clause identifying the purpose for which the task was performed. The higher order abstractions that seemed to best explain the pattern of factor loadings were the purposes for which the clusters of activity were intended. The factor labels were chosen to reflect these. Also, since some clusters of worker activity addressed more than one purpose, some clus-

---

[5]Cluster means, rather than total scores, were used in the factor analysis. Thus, regardless of the number of tasks, the score in each cluster ranged from 1.0 to 5.0.

ters loaded on more than one factor. For example, Risk Assessment and Transition Management activities loaded on both the "Client Change" and "Client Situation Change" factors. Following are descriptions of the five factors, and their mean factor scores, for the entire sample.[6]

The Factors

Factor 1: Client Change *(Mean = 13.11)*

The first factor is defined primarily by five clusters that have a common focus on the provision of direct services to clients, individually and in groups, by means of a combination of formal intervention strategies and more generalized techniques of problem solving and helping. The two most important clusters in the definition of this factor were "Interpersonal Helping" and "Individual/Family Treatment." The clusters dealing with "Group Work," "Risk Assessment/Transition Management," and "Case Planning/Maintenance" also loaded heavily on the factor. As one reads through the tasks contained in these clusters, the emphasis seems to be on bringing about changes in the clients themselves.

Factor 2: Client Situation Change *(Mean = 12.44)*

Like the first factor, the second is also client-oriented. Factor 2, however, is defined by clusters which focus more on situations that impinge on clients and on the resources that are brought to bear on dealing with their problems. Involving clusters such as "Protective Services," "Service Connection," and "Tangible Service Provision," this factor seems to be describing a domain of activities designed to reduce risks and marshal resources for individuals, families, and groups. In short, the factor is oriented toward client situation change, and has been so labeled. Since both Factors 1 and 2 dealt with the change process as it pertains to clients, it is not surprising that "Risk Assessment/Transition Management" and "Case Planning/Maintenance" have substantial loadings on the two factors.

Factor 3: Professional Competence Development *(Mean = 9.42)*

The third factor is defined almost entirely by the "Professional Development" cluster. It is the only factor that seems to focus on the practitioner-centered activities associated with growth, self-awareness,

---

[6]Unlike the cluster frequency mean scores, factor scores have no standardized range. The best explanation is: the higher the factor score, the greater the involvement of the worker in tasks designed to achieve that purpose.

and evaluation. Given this orientation, it is not surprising that it also derives its definition from the cluster called "Delivery System Knowledge Development."

Factor 4: Organization/Unit Operation (Mean = 14.39)

The fourth factor is generically different from the preceding three in that it is not directly related to the provision of services to clients. The clusters that define this factor deal primarily with the management of organizational units and the supervision of staff. Five clusters, "Staff Deployment," "Staff Supervision," "Organizational Maintenance," "Staff Information Exchange," and "Program Development" load most heavily on this factor. With the exception of the "Program Development" cluster, the emphasis appears to be on the organizational maintenance of ongoing or existing delivery system elements, that is, programs, units, and organizations.

Factor 5: Resource/Service Change (Mean = 6.78)

Factor 5 is similar to the previous factor in that it does not deal with the provision of direct services to clients. It has been defined primarily by those clusters that focus more on the community and the larger service delivery system. "Research/Policy Development" and "Instruction" load most heavily on this factor. It encompasses activities associated with needs analyses, social action, and the provision of expert technical assistance to various groups outside the organization. It also focuses on the development and evaluation of programs of formal instruction to a variety of individuals. Given the emphasis on both formal and informal group interaction, it is not surprising that the "Group Work" cluster also loads substantially on this factor.

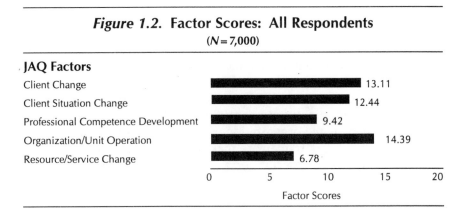

Figure 1.2. Factor Scores: All Respondents
(N = 7,000)

JAQ Factors	Factor Scores
Client Change	13.11
Client Situation Change	12.44
Professional Competence Development	9.42
Organization/Unit Operation	14.39
Resource/Service Change	6.78

The factor scores for the total sample again reveal differences in emphasis placed on the activities associated with various practice objectives. Figure 1.2 shows the pattern of the scores for each factor.

Couched in the most global terms, the work of the 7,000 practitioners encompasses five major practice objectives. Factor 1 (Client Change) and Factor 2 (Client Situation Change) reflect client-centered tasks and clusters, while Factor 3 (Professional Competence Development) is worker centered. Factor 4 (Organization and Unit Operation) and Factor 5 (Resource/Service Change) are system- and environment-centered. As Figure 1.2 shows, the client-centered activities, generally accepted as typifying social work, manifest as important objectives. However, the factor data also suggest some departures from the ways in which social work is typically portrayed. For example, it is clear from the data that a very important focus of social work activity on is the operation of service delivery units and organizations (Factor 4). In typical descriptions of social work practice, this component is normally not emphasized as much as the client-centered activities. Finally, social workers seem to be far less involved in tasks designed to bring about changes in resources and services (Factor 5); in fact, this factor had the lowest loading in the work activities of the total sample. This finding sharply contrasts with the image of the profession as a "social change agent." In short, even this cursory inspection of the results gives one pause to reflect on the educational and practice implications of the data.

Practice Framework

The analyses of the task data resulted in the formulation of a social work practice framework that can be conceptualized at four levels of abstraction. At the most specific level, the 131 task statements give detailed information about the content of social work practice. Next, the cluster analysis grouped these tasks into 18 mutually exclusive groups of related activity. Then the factor analysis revealed that these activities seem organized around 5 basic objectives. Finally, the authors suggest one more level: Social work objectives may be defined as client centered, practitioner centered, and delivery system centered. Figure 1.3 depicts the organization of these four levels into one practice framework. This framework makes it possible, depending on the need or objective, to describe social work practice in very specific or more general terms.

Agreement of the Practice Framework with Theoretical Formulations

Two properties were considered to be important in developing the JAQ instrument. First, it had to be sufficiently comprehensive to encompass the breadth of social work practice. Second, it had to be "model-fair," that is, not oriented toward any particular model(s) of

Figure 1.3. **The Social Work Practice Framework**

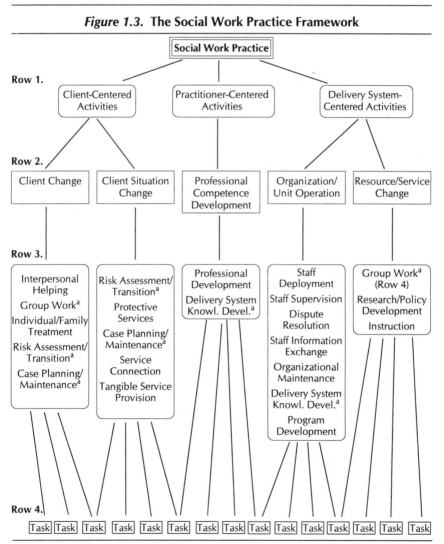

[a]Cluster loaded on more than one factor.

practice or any specific organization of practice domain. The intent was to include on the questionnaire a set of tasks that represented the activities of social workers, and then to allow the data to define the practice framework and the depiction of social work. From the outset, this rationale was followed. To what extent, then, is the practice framework that emerges from the data consistent with the theoretical formulations described in the beginning of this chapter?

It seems to be congruent with a number of the theoretical formulations regarding the nature of social work practice. At the most global level of the framework (see row 1 of Figure 1.3), for example, the client-centered practice content closely resembles the "direct work" domain identified by Witmer (1942) and referred to since as "direct services" or "direct practice" (see, for example, Briar, 1987; Brieland, 1987; Meyer, 1987). The delivery system-centered content, too, seems analogous to the "indirect service" component mentioned by a number of authors (see, for example, Briar, 1987; Meyer, 1987). Also, analysis of the data indicates a considerable difference in the work content of these two practice areas, which has been a persistent theme in the literature relating to supervision and management (Austin, 1981; Holloway & Brager, 1989; Kadushin, 1992; Patti, 1983).

The empirical model and the profession's theoretical formulations are congruent in another way: The five factors correspond rather closely to the objectives of social work outlined in the "Working Statement on the Purpose of Social Work" (Minahan, 1981, p. 6). Here, the stated objectives of social work are to "help people enlarge their competence and increase their problem-solving and coping abilities," which corresponds closely to the Client Change factor; "help people obtain resources (and) . . . facilitate interactions between individuals and others in their environment," which corresponds closely to the Client Situation Change factor; "make organizations responsive to people," which is encompassed in the activities reflected in the Organization/Unit Operation factor; and "influence social and environmental policy" and "interactions between organizations and institutions," which corresponds to the Resource/Service Change factor. Finally, the range of clientele served by the 7,000 respondents clearly supports the assertion that the clients of social workers "may be individuals, a family, a group, a community, or an organization." Note that the cluster concerned with the development and maintenance of the worker's professional competence, a central concern of social work education, was omitted from the "Working Statement."

Although the framework recognizes these theoretical bases, the data from the composite sample relating to both cluster and factor scores suggest that social work practice may be more often related to helping clients change themselves or their situations than to working to change the delivery system. This finding only partially supports the claim that a unique feature of social work practice is its "simultaneous dual focus" on person and environment. Social workers assist clients in addressing issues in their "near environment," but appear to do little in the way of community or delivery system change.

The 18 clusters of practice activity appear to parallel the many roles posited for social workers in the practice literature (Bisno, 1971; Connaway & Gentry, 1988; Sheafor, Horejsi, & Horejsi, 1994; Soby, 1977; Teare & McPheeters, 1970). In many ways, the framework generated by the data requires no startling departures from the conceptualization that has been used for years within the profession. The scope of social work practice described by the data illustrates why it has been so difficult for the profession to agree on the nature of social work practice and the educational content required to prepare graduates for that practice. As a matter of fact, the scope serves to underscore Meyer's concern about social work's "being all things to all people" and, therefore, being uniquely vulnerable to a wide range of alien and unfriendly forces (Meyer, 1981, p. 70).

Concluding Comments

Throughout its evolution as a profession, social work has been concerned with accurately identifying the core of activities that are performed by all (or most) social workers—the practice activities that bind practitioners to a common profession. In addition, it has been concerned with documenting the uniqueness in practice activities in various practice settings, job functions, and practice areas, and with different client groups. This definition and documentation has been viewed as important for establishing social work's professional domain and for identifying the "center of gravity" for its professional education.

Historically, social work has depended primarily on subjective assertions about the nature of practice. Increasingly there has been a demand for more explicit and well-documented evidence to support its claim for a unique role among the human service professions. This increased impetus to document the nature of practice, the existence of a standardized tool for data collection (the JAQ), and the availability of computer packages to analyze large data sets have made possible a new generation of practice-sensitive social work formulations. This book presents the results of research toward that end. That the results of this meta-analysis of practice data are largely congruent with the theoretical conceptions already in place strengthens the claims that social work has made. The data do, however, suggest very different practice emphases and orientations when one partitions them by education level. For this reason, selective analyses of the data organized by education level (BSW and MSW) will be the basis on which subsequent chapters are organized. Throughout the book, the implications of these data for social work education will be thoroughly explored.

References

Mark S. Aldenderfer and Roger K. Blashfield, *Cluster Analysis*, Sage University Paper Series on Quantitative Applications in the Social Sciences, 07-044. Beverly Hills: Sage, 1984.

American Association of Social Workers, *Social Casework: Generic and Specific, A Report of the Milford Conference*. New York: National Association of Social Workers, 1974. (Original work published in 1929.)

Michael J. Austin, Phillip L. Smith, and Alexis Skelding, *The Florida Human Services Task Bank*. Tallahassee: Office of Career Planning, State University System of Florida, 1975.

Michael J. Austin, *Supervisor Management for the Human Services*. Englewood Cliffs, NJ: Prentice-Hall, 1981.

Robert L. Barker, *The Social Work Dictionary*. Silver Spring, MD: National Association of Social Workers, 1987.

Harriett M. Bartlett, "Toward Clarification and Improvement of Social Work Practice," *Social Work*, 3 (April 1958): pp. 3-9.

Herbert Bisno, "A Theoretical Framework For Teaching Social Work Methods and Skills, With Particular Reference to Undergraduate Social Welfare Education," in Frank Loewenberg and Ralph Dolgoff (eds.), *Teaching of Practice Skills in Undergraduate Programs in Social Welfare and Other Helping Services*. New York: Council on Social Work Education, 1971: pp. 72-78, 84-85.

Werner W. Boehm, *Objectives of the Social Work Curriculum of the Future*, Vol. 1. New York: Council on Social Work Education, 1959.

Scott Briar, "Summing Up," *Social Work*, 22 (September 1977): pp. 415-416.

Scott Briar, "Direct Practice: Trends and Issues," in Anne Minahan (ed.), *Encyclopedia of Social Work*, Vol. 1. Silver Spring, MD: National Association of Social Workers, 1987, pp. 393-398.

Donald Brieland, "To Make Chicken Soup, Start With a Chicken...," *Social Work*, 22 (September 1977): pp. 338 and 444.

Donald Brieland, "Definition, Specialization, and Purpose of Social Work," *Social Work*, 26 (January 1981): p. 83.

Donald Brieland, "History and Evolution of Social Work Practice," in Anne Minahan (ed.), *Encyclopedia of Social Work*, Vol. 1. Silver Spring, MD: National Association of Social Workers, 1987, pp. 739-754.

Michael J. Camasso and Ludwig L. Geismar, "A Multivariate Approach to Construct Reliability and Validity Assessment: The Case of Family Functioning," *Social Work Research and Abstracts*, 28 (December 1992): pp. 16-26.

Edward G. Carmines and Richard A. Zeller, *Reliability Assessment*, Sage University Paper Series on Quantitative Applications in the Social Sciences, 07-017. Beverly Hills: Sage, 1979.

Ronda S. Connaway and Martha Gentry, *Social Work Practice*. Englewood Cliffs, NJ: Prentice-Hall, 1988.

Lee J. Cronbach, "Coefficient Alpha and the Internal Structure of Tests," *Psychometrika*, 16 (September 1951): pp. 297-334.

Delores S. Delahanty, "Foreword" to Harriett M. Bartlett, *Analyzing Social Work Practice by Fields*, revised ed. Silver Spring, MD: National Association of Social Work, 1988. (Original work published in 1961.)

B. S. Everitt. "Unresolved Problems in Cluster Analysis," *Biometrics*, 35 (March 1979): pp. 169-181.

Abraham Flexner, "Education for Social Work," in *Proceedings of the National Conference on Charities and Correction, 1915*. Chicago: National Conference on Charities and Correction, 1916.

Stephen Holloway and George Brager, *Supervising in the Human Services: The Politics of Practice*. New York: The Free Press, 1989.

Alfred Kadushin, *Supervision in Social Work*, 3rd ed. New York: Columbia University Press, 1992.

Carol H. Meyer, "Social Work Purpose: Status by Choice Or Coercion," *Social Work*, 26 (January, 1981): p. 70.

Carol H. Meyer, "Direct Practice in Social Work: Overview," in Anne Minahan (ed.), *Encyclopedia of Social Work*, Vol. 1. Silver Spring, MD: National Association of Social Workers, 1987: pp. 409-422.

Anne Minahan and Scott Briar, "Introduction to Special Issue," *Social Work*, 22 (September 1977): p. 339.

Anne Minahan, "Purposes and Objectives of Social Work Revisited," *Social Work*, 26 (January 1981): pp. 5-6.

Anne Minahan, ed., *Encyclopedia of Social Work*, 2 vols. Silver Spring, MD: National Association of Social Workers, 1987.

National Association of Social Workers, *Guidelines for the Assessment of Professional Practice in Social Work*. New York: Author, 1968.

National Association of Social Workers, *Standards for Social Service Manpower*. Washington, DC: Author, 1973.

National Association of Social Workers, *NASW Standards for the Classification of Social Work Practice*. Silver Spring, MD: Author, 1981.

Rino Patti, *Social Welfare Administration*. Englewood Cliffs, NJ: Prentice Hall, 1983.

Arthur Pearl and Frank Riessman, *New Careers for the Poor: The Nonprofessional in Human Service*. New York: The Free Press, 1965.

Peter J. Pecora and Michael J. Austin, *Managing Human Services Personnel*, 2nd ed. Newbury Park, CA: Sage, 1987.

Robert Reiff and Frank Riessman, *The Indigenous Nonprofessional: A Strategy of Change in Community Action and Community Mental Health Programs*. New York: National Institute of Labor Education, 1964.

Mary Richmond, *Social Diagnosis*. New York: Russell Sage Foundation, 1917.

Mary Richmond, *What Is Social Case Work?* New York: Russell Sage Foundation, 1922.

Bradford W. Sheafor, Charles R. Horejsi, and Gloria A. Horejsi, *Techniques and Guidelines for Social Work Practice*, 3rd ed. Boston: Allyn and Bacon, 1994.

Francine Soby, ed., *Changing Roles in Social Work Practice*. Philadelphia: Temple University Press, 1977.

Robert J. Teare and Harold McPheeters, *Manpower Utilization in Social Welfare*. Atlanta: Southern Regional Education Board, 1970.

Robert J. Teare, "Paraprofessional Utilization Issues," in Michael J. Austin (ed.), *Professionals and Paraprofessionals*. New York: Human Services Press, 1978.

Robert J. Teare, *Social Work Practice in a Public Welfare Setting*. New York: Praeger, 1981.

Robert J. Teare, Catherine Higgs, Thomas P. Gauthier, and Hubert S. Feild, *Classification Validation Processes for Social Service Positions-Volume I: Overview*. Silver Spring, MD: National Association of Social Workers, 1984.

Robert J. Teare, *Validating Social Work Credentials for Human Service Jobs*. Silver Spring, MD: National Association of Social Workers, 1987a.

Robert J. Teare, *National Survey of Occupational Social Workers*. Silver Spring, MD: National Association of Social Workers, 1987b.

Robert J. Teare, Barbara W. Shank, and Bradford W. Sheafor, "The National Survey of BSW Practitioners," in Kenneth J. Kazmerski (ed.), *New Horizons: Expanding Directions for Baccalaureate Education*. Orlando: University of Central Florida, 1990: pp. 97-102.

U.S. Department of Health, Education and Welfare, *Closing the Gap*, Report of the Departmental Task Force on Social Work Education and Manpower. Washington, DC: HEW, 1965.

Joe H. Ward, "Hierarchical Grouping to Optimize an Objective Function," *Journal of the American Statistical Association*, 58 (March 1963): pp. 236-244.

Helen Leland Witmer, *Social Work: An Analysis of a Social Institution*. New York: Farrar & Rinehart, 1942.

2

Baccalaureate-Level Social Workers: Who Are They and What Do They Do?

D etermining the appropriate preparation of students for baccalaureate social work (BSW) practice has been a challenge for social work educators since the approval/accreditation process for undergraduate programs was reestablished in 1970. The sanctioning of BSW practice by the profession legitimized existing BSW programs and created the impetus for new programs to be established. Educators were required to make judgements about the types of students who would be attracted to social work, the jobs that would become available, and the competencies required for those jobs. At the same time, various groups were initiating curriculum development projects designed to clarify the roles and functions of the baccalaureate social worker. The Southern Regional Education Board identified a set of practice roles (Teare & McPheeters, 1970), and later Baer and Federico (1978-79) identified a set of entry-level competencies and outlined the curriculum content needed to attain them. BSW graduates entered the job market believing they had the necessary knowledge and skills to practice as entry-level social workers.

Today, nearly a quarter century later, the occupational niche of the baccalaureate practitioner has been clearly established. With a substantial number of BSW graduates now occupying social work jobs, curriculum designers and educational policy makers can avail themselves of the knowledge of what these social workers actually do in the context of their employment. This study is one source of that knowledge. Using these data, it is possible for BSW programs to develop "practice-sensitive curricula."

This chapter was co-authored by Barbara W. Shank, University of St. Thomas and College of St. Catherine, Co-Investigator for the National Study of BSW Practitioners.

Table 2.1. **Personal Characteristics of Baccalaureate Practitioners**
(*N* = 1,449)

Location		Ethnicity		Gender	
Northeast	29.2%[a]	American Indian	1.4%	Male	8.9%
Northcentral	38.8%	Asian/Pacific Islander	0.6%	Female	90.8%
South	21.2%	African American	7.3%		
West	10.4%	Chicano/Mexican American	1.2%		
		Puerto Rican	0.5%		
		Other Hispanic	0.5%		
		White	87.4%		
Mean Age = 33.4		**Mean Yrs. in Present Position** = 3.2		**Mean Yrs. in Social Work** = 5.3	

[a]Percentages may not total 100% because of missing values on some variables.

Demographic Characteristics

As indicated in Chapter 1, the criteria for being included in the national undergraduate study were that a person must (a) have completed a social work degree from a program accredited by the Council on Social Work Education and, (b) at the time of the survey, have been employed as a full-time social worker for at least six months. The demographic data generated by the study shed much light on who the baccalaureate social workers are, where they are employed, and who they serve.[1]

Who They Are

A few characteristics of these baccalaureate social workers are summarized in Table 2.1. The typical baccalaureate-level practitioner was a relatively young (roughly 60% of those in practice were age 30 or younger), white female with a moderate amount of practice experience. Also, more than two-thirds of these BSW practitioners were concentrated in the Northeast and Northcentral regions of the United States (i.e., a region bounded by Kansas, Nebraska, and North and South Dakota at the western end, along a line from Kansas to the southern tip of New Jersey on its southern border, and from New Jersey north through Maine on the eastern seaboard). As compared to the composite sample (see Chapter 1), there was a particularly heavy

---

[1]The data obtained from the screening process (*n*=5,375) and from the job analysis (*n*=1,449) have already provided some clarity about career patterns of BSW graduates. See the authors' article entitled "Separating Reality From Fantasy: A Depiction of BSW Practice" (1992).

concentration of BSWs in the Northcentral states and a disproportionately small number in the West.

What They Do and Where They Work

If one is committed to the notion of practice-sensitive undergraduate education, it is particularly important to have a clear understanding of the jobs that BSW practitioners hold. Table 2.2 begins the description of these data. Using the language developed in Chapter 1, one would have to say that the BSW practitioner is overwhelmingly "client-centered." Almost 81% reported holding direct service jobs; few (14.8%) indicated that they were employed in management or supervisory positions. Further, virtually all of these BSW social workers began their practice in direct service positions (90.2%). Relatively few moved into other job functions without first returning to school for additional education. This has obvious implications for a continued emphasis on the development of direct service practice skills in undergraduate curricula.

The practitioners were asked about the size of the community in which they were employed. A considerable proportion (43.9%) reported working in relatively small communities having a population of 40,000 or less; only 30.8% said they worked in cities with 100,000 or

Table 2.2. **Employment Characteristics of Baccalaureate Practitioners**

(*N* = 1,449)

Primary Job Function		Size of Practice Community		Perceived Autonomy	
Direct service	80.9%[a]	Fewer than 10,000	16.7%	Almost complete	19.7%
Supervision	6.6%	10,001 to 40,000	27.2%	Considerable	42.4%
Management/adm.	8.2%	40,001 to 100,000	25.3%	Moderate	26.1%
Other	3.5%	100,001 to 500,000	19.1%	Little	9.1%
		More than 500,000	11.7%	Almost none	2.7%

Practice Setting		Primary Practice Area	
Social service agency	46.4%	Children and youth	18.8%
Hospital	13.7%	Services to the aged	16.5%
Nursing home/hospice	11.5%	Family services	13.7%
Outpatient facility	8.7%	Medical and health care	12.8%
Group home/residential care	6.3%	Mental health	9.9%
Psychiatric institution	4.4%	Dev. disabilities/mental retardation	9.6%
Courts/criminal justice	2.8%	Alcohol and substance abuse	3.2%
Elementary/secondary school	2.1%	Public assistance/welfare	3.1%
Non-social service agencies	1.2%	Corrections/criminal justice	2.7%
Private practice	0.9%	School social work	1.4%
Other	1.7%	Other	8.3%

[a]Percentages may not total 100% because of missing values on some variables.

more people. For BSW programs, particularly those located in rural areas, these data suggest that it may be important to address the uniqueness of service delivery in rural areas and small communities.

To gain some understanding of the autonomy they have to determine their practice activities, the BSW practitioners were asked to indicate the amount of control or choice they had in determining what their job tasks would be or how often they carried them out. Many (62.1%) felt they had "considerable" or "almost complete" job autonomy while another 26.1% reported having a "moderate" degree. When controlled for length of time on the job, no pattern of difference was found. The reported autonomy of BSW graduates in determining their day-to-day job activities differs significantly from that implied in the NASW Classification Standards (NASW, 1981). Undergraduate social work programs, then, might do well to prepare their graduates for the challenges and responsibilities of more autonomous practice.

The vast majority (91.0%) of all BSW social workers were concentrated in six employment settings: social service agencies, hospitals, nursing homes or hospice organizations, outpatient psychiatric clinics, group homes, and psychiatric institutions. The largest number, 46.4%, were employed in social service agencies, which included both public social service or public welfare agencies and small nonprofit human service agencies. Knowledge of the high concentration of baccalaureate social workers in these six settings may be particularly useful in the selection and development of field instruction sites since these seem to be the settings most likely to offer employment to the graduates.

The deployment of BSW practitioners across primary practice areas is a bit more uniform. As Table 2.2 shows, between 9% and 19% of the respondents reported that they were providing services in the following practice areas: children and youth, services to the aged, family services, medical and health care, mental health, and developmental disabilities or mental retardation. When planning human behavior, social policy, and practice course content, schools will want to be sure that their graduates have the necessary knowledge and skills to serve clients in these various practice areas.

What Their Clients Are Like

A basic premise of professional education is that its graduates will be prepared to meet the needs of individual clients or client groups. When time and resources are limited, deciding which content to include and which to leave out of a curriculum can be a difficult one.

Setting content priorities relating to human behavior, human diversity, and practice content can be made easier by knowing who BSW graduates are most likely to serve.

Practitioners were asked to indicate the gender make-up of the clients they served in their practice. Although overall they reported that 57.4% of their clients were female (see Table 2.3), the gender composition of caseloads varied considerably with the job setting and the primary practice area associated with that job. For example, respondents working in nursing homes reported a 72.3% female clientele, as opposed to respondents in psychiatric institutions who reported a female clientele of 43.3%. Similarly, when practice area was considered, working with the aged population or offering family services meant working with a predominantly female population, while serving clients who were mentally retarded or developmentally disabled meant that one was likely to be working with predominantly male clients.

The BSW practitioners were asked to identify as many as three racial or ethnic groups they regularly served in their practice. More than 91% of these BSW workers reported working with white clients and 46.2% reported having African-American clients as part of their caseloads. Understanding the cultural, demographic, and socioeconomic differences and similarities of these two groups would therefore seem to be essential for all BSW graduates. Furthermore, these con-

Table 2.3. **Client Characteristics and Problems—Baccalaureate Practitioners** (*N* = 1,449)

Client Gender		Client Ethnicity[a]		Client Age[a]	
Female (mean)	57.4%	American Indian	6.6%	Infants (0–5)	14.6%
Male (mean)	42.6%	Asian/Pacific Islander	2.9%	Children (6–12)	19.5%
		African American	46.2%	Youth (13–20)	29.5%
		Chicano/Mexican Am.	9.7%	Adults (21–60)	54.7%
		Puerto Rican	6.6%	Aged (over 60)	34.6%
		Other Hispanic	4.8%		
		White	91.1%		

Percentage of Time Each Client Problem Was Cited[a]

Family functioning difficulties	38.6%	Skill or knowledge development	10.5%
Health problems	26.8%	Shelter or housing needs	10.5%
Problems with aging	23.6%	School problems	8.4%
Behavior problems	23.5%	Job or work needs	8.1%
Mental illness or mental retardation	21.6%	Legal problems	6.4%
Alcohol or substance abuse	20.1%	Group interaction problems	3.9%
Interpersonal relationship problems	18.2%	Recreation needs	2.3%
Anxiety or depression	15.6%	Membership development	1.0%
Financial problems	14.9%	Civil rights or affirmative action	0.9%
Physical disabilities	11.8%		

[a]Percentages total to more than 100% because respondents could name more than one category.

cepts need to be linked to appropriate practice approaches. Only a small percentage of BSW practitioners reported working with clientele from any racial or ethnic group other than white or African American, and those clientele varied substantially from one region of the country to another. If one were going to conserve curricular resources, it would seem appropriate that only students most likely to come into contact with certain ethnic minority populations would need to acquire in-depth knowledge about their relevant characteristics and the appropriate practice approaches for working with them.

Each respondent was also asked to identify two age groups that most characterized their clients. These data indicate that about 15% of the BSW social workers worked with infants (birth through 5 years); nearly 20% provided services for children (6 through 12 years); almost 30% worked with youths (13 through 20 years); more than 50% worked with adults (21 through 60 years); and almost 35% provided services to the aged (over 60 years). This clear evidence that BSW graduates work with substantial numbers of clients from all age groups strongly suggests the need for undergraduate curriculum content in human development over the entire life cycle.

Finally, the BSW practitioners were asked to identify the three most prevalent needs or problems their clients experienced. These responses indicate that the BSW practitioners were involved with a great variety of client problem situations. Clearly the most dominant client need was related to family functioning: 38.6% of the respondents reported addressing problems in that area. In addition, more than 20% of the BSWs were dealing with clients who had either health problems, problems associated with aging, behavior problems, problems related to mental illness or mental retardation, or alcohol or substance abuse problems. Table 2.3 provides a more detailed distribution of the needs/problems of clients served by BSW practitioners.

Client needs and problems varied considerably from one setting to another.[2] The differing array of problems associated with each setting suggests specific curriculum content to which students should be exposed prior to beginning a field placement or employment in these settings. Table 2.4 identifies the four most prevalent client problems in the five settings in which BSWs were most frequently employed.

---

[2]Whenever differences are described in the narrative, they have been tested and found to be statistically significant ($p < .05$). Given the large size of the samples, however, it is possible to achieve statistical significance without differences of a practical significance being attained. Only those differences that are also large enough to have clear implications for curriculum design are highlighted in the discussion.

In the social service agencies, the focus was on the provision of services to clients and families faced with a variety of physical, social, psychological, and financial difficulties. In hospitals, the BSW workers helped individuals and families cope with disease and physical disabilities, both short-term and chronic. In nursing homes and hospices, the emphasis shifted to the elderly and problems associated with chronic care and impending death. In the outpatient facilities, group homes, and residential treatment centers, practitioners tended to handle problems associated with mental illness and mental retardation as their clients attempted to make the transition from institutional to community-based living.

Task Analysis of the Baccalaureate Practitioners

Cluster Scores

A more detailed understanding of the practice activities of the BSW social worker can be gained by examining the mean scores for each

Table 2.4. Client Problems Addressed in Primary BSW Settings

Type of Setting	Client Problems Addressed[a]

Social Service Agencies (n = 673)	Family functioning (54.1%)
	 Character or behavior problems (24.2%)
	    Alcohol or substance abuse (23.2%)
	    Interpersonal relations (22.4%)

Hospitals (n = 199)	Health problems (65.3%) Problems associated with aging (31.7%) Family functioning (25.6%) Anxiety or depression (22.1%)
Nursing Homes or Hospices (n = 167)	Problems associated with aging (86.2%) Health problems (61.7%) Anxiety or depression (37.1%) Family functioning (20.4%)
Outpatient Psychiatric Facilities (n = 126)	Mental illness or mental retardation (57.1%) Anxiety or depression (30.2%) Alcohol or substance abuse (26.2%) Family functioning (26.2%)
Group Homes or Residential Treatment Centers (n = 92)	Character or behavior disorders (45.7%) Mental illness or mental retardation (39.1%) Interpersonal relationships (25.0%) Developing living skills (23.9%)

[a]Percentages total to more than 100% because respondents identified up to three client needs most frequently addressed.

task cluster. Figure 2.1 shows the distribution of practice activities for the 1,449 BSW-level social workers. It is evident from examination of this chart that there is considerable variability in the frequency with which the various clusters of work activity were performed.[3]

The predominance of direct service activities in the top section of Figure 2.1 underscores the client-centered nature of baccalaureate practice (Clusters 1-8). Two clusters of activity dominated the work of these social workers: Interpersonal Helping (Cluster 1), and Case Planning/Maintenance (Cluster 6).[4] The typical BSW practitioner "frequently" performed the tasks associated with these clusters. The clusters of activity that were "occasionally" performed by these practitioners included Individual/Family Treatment (Cluster 3), Risk Assessment/Transition Services (Cluster 4), and Service Connection (Cluster 7). To deliver these direct services to clients, the practitioners had to engage in certain kinds of indirect service activities. They reported being "frequently" involved in tasks that fostered their own growth and professional development (Cluster 9). To use the service system, they had to become knowledgeable about it (Cluster 15) and coordinate their efforts with other staff members (Cluster 13). Helping students develop the competence needed to perform each of these clusters of activity would appear to be a minimal goal for BSW programs.

Factor Scores

The factor scores give an even clearer picture of the basic orientation of BSW practice. Because 80.9% of the BSW practitioners reported that they were employed in direct service positions, their practice activities tended to focus on clients' needs. This finding is consistent with CSWE's Curriculum Policy Statement, which states that BSW programs "prepare(s) students for direct services with client systems of various sizes and types" (CSWE, 1994, B5.2, p. 98). As Figure 2.2 illustrates, the factor scores for BSW practitioners indicate a strong and almost equal focus on client-centered objectives (Client Change and Client Situation Change). To a somewhat lesser but still signifi-

---

[3] To interpret the cluster means, the reader should relate the score in the chart to the rating made by the respondents when completing the JAQ. For example, "almost never" is represented by a score 1.0 to 1.49, "seldom" by 1.5 to 2.49, "occasionally" by 2.5 to 3.49, "frequently" by 3.5 to 4.49, and "almost always" by 4.5 to 5.0. The longer the bar in the graph, the more frequently (on the average) the tasks in a given cluster were performed on the job.

[4] Descriptions of all of these clusters can be found in Chapter 1. The tasks in each cluster are listed in Appendix A.

cant extent, they reported being involved in tasks that maintained and supported the operation of the organizations in which they worked (Organization/Unit Operation); they reported devoting little attention

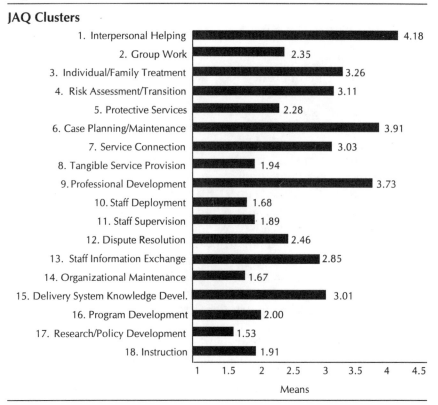

Figure 2.1. **Mean Cluster Scores: All BSW Respondents** (*N* = 1,449)

JAQ Clusters

Cluster	Mean
1. Interpersonal Helping	4.18
2. Group Work	2.35
3. Individual/Family Treatment	3.26
4. Risk Assessment/Transition	3.11
5. Protective Services	2.28
6. Case Planning/Maintenance	3.91
7. Service Connection	3.03
8. Tangible Service Provision	1.94
9. Professional Development	3.73
10. Staff Deployment	1.68
11. Staff Supervision	1.89
12. Dispute Resolution	2.46
13. Staff Information Exchange	2.85
14. Organizational Maintenance	1.67
15. Delivery System Knowledge Devel.	3.01
16. Program Development	2.00
17. Research/Policy Development	1.53
18. Instruction	1.91

Means

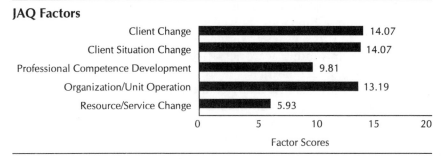

Figure 2.2. **Factor Scores: All BSW Respondents** (*N* = 1,449)

JAQ Factors

Factor	Score
Client Change	14.07
Client Situation Change	14.07
Professional Competence Development	9.81
Organization/Unit Operation	13.19
Resource/Service Change	5.93

Factor Scores

to activities that would enhance the resources or strengthen the services available in their communities (Resource/Service Change); and, as all other groups of social workers described in this study, they reported paying a moderate amount of attention to enhancing their own development and increasing their knowledge of the existing human service delivery system (Professional Competence Development).

Job Function and the BSW Social Worker

Worker Demography

When they filled out the JAQ, the BSW workers indicated their primary job function. Nearly 96% of them were employed in three job functions—direct services, supervision, and management or administration. (Because BSWs were rarely employed primarily as consultants, as educators, or in policy/research/planning jobs, these job functions are not analyzed further in this chapter.) Relatively little variation in worker demographics was found in these three primary job functions. Females made up 91.8% of the direct service providers, 88.4% of the supervisors, and 89.1% of those engaged in management/administration; and there was little intrafunction difference in worker ethnicity, age, and practice experience. The BSWs in supervisory jobs were only one year older (mean=34.2 years) than the direct service workers, and the managers and administrators averaged just one more year of age (mean=35.2 years) than the supervisors. Further, the managers and administrators had only about one more year of experience in social work practice (6.3 years) than the supervisors and direct service workers. In short, worker demography appeared to differ very little with job function among the BSW respondents. None of the rather minor variations would suggest that BSW programs should adapt their curricula to respond to them.

Client Characteristics and Needs

In each of the three primary job functions, the gender and ethnic backgrounds of clients were fairly similar. There were some differences in the three functions, however, with respect to the age of clients. Compared to the direct service workers, the BSWs who were managers/administrators were less likely to be dealing with clients under the age of 21 and much more likely to be working with the elderly. This suggests that many of the BSW practitioners who were supervisors or administrators were employed in nursing homes.

When compared to the supervisors and managers, the direct service BSW workers were somewhat more likely to deal with client needs related to family functioning, anxiety/depression, and alcohol or substance abuse. They were less likely to address matters related to job and work performance, knowledge and skill development, and the use of recreation or leisure services. BSW supervisors were more likely to deal with school problems, and less likely to work with health-related and financial problems than the other two groups. Managers/administrators were more likely to deal with organizational membership issues, and were much less likely to deal with persons experiencing severe emotional problems such as character or behavior disorders than their direct service counterparts. As will be seen later, administrative roles in agencies serving people with these problems appeared to be the responsibility of MSWs or other professionals.

Job Function and Work Content

One of the major determinants of BSW practitioners' on-the-job activities was the primary job function they reported on the JAQ. The activity patterns of the workers in direct services, supervision, and management/administration were significantly different, as the factor scores depicted in Figure 2.3 show clearly. First, it is evident that when one moves from a direct services to an administrative or supervisory job there is a reduction in client-centered activities and a marked increase in emphasis on organizational and service delivery system operation. Given the direct services orientation of most BSW pro-

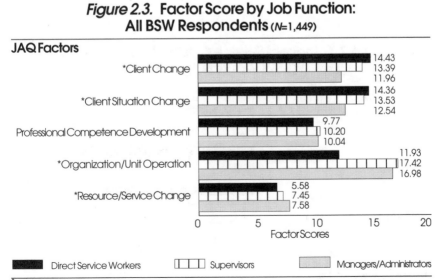

Figure 2.3. Factor Score by Job Function: All BSW Respondents (N=1,449)

JAQ Factors

Factor	Direct Service Workers	Supervisors	Managers/Administrators
*Client Change	14.43	13.39	11.96
*Client Situation Change	14.36	13.53	12.54
Professional Competence Development	9.77	10.20	10.04
*Organization/Unit Operation	11.93	17.42	16.98
*Resource/Service Change	5.58	7.45	7.58

Factor Scores

■ Direct Service Workers   ⊞ Supervisors   ▨ Managers/Administrators

*Indicates significant differences (*p*<.05) among the three primary job functions on that factor.

grams, some additional education or training (e.g., continuing education) might be required for BSW practitioners making this dramatic change in job function and work activity.

The cluster data shed even more light on this. As indicated in Figure 2.4, the workers who were in supervisory or management/administrative positions had a much greater involvement in activities associated with Staff Supervision (Cluster 11), Staff Deployment (Cluster 10), and Staff Information Exchange (Cluster 13) activity. It would be expected that educational programs preparing students for direct service work would impart many of the generic interpersonal skills needed for the performance of supervisory and administrative jobs at the baccalaureate level. Thus, the content of any supplemental, continuing education, or training programs for BSW practitioners moving into administration or supervision might do well to focus on technical topics such as administrative supervision, staffing, employee evaluation, and work-centered communications.

Because more than 90% of the BSW practitioners began employment as direct service workers, and only 10% subsequently gravitated into other job functions, it would seem that BSW programs should continue to place their emphasis on preparation for direct service practice. Baccalaureate social workers performing in other job functions appear to be exceptions and need not be a prime consideration in educational planning. The remaining sections of this chapter will focus on various aspects of direct service practice.

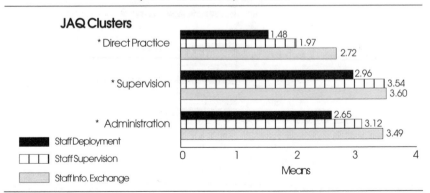

Figure 2.4. **Indirect Service Clusters by Job Function (BSW Workers)** (*N*=1,449)

JAQ Clusters

* Direct Practice — 1.48 / 1.97 / 2.72

* Supervision — 2.96 / 3.54 / 3.60

* Administration — 2.65 / 3.12 / 3.49

▪ Staff Deployment
▢ Staff Supervision
▨ Staff Info. Exchange

Means (0 1 2 3 4)

* Indicates significant differences (p<.05) among at least one pair of cluster means.

BSW Practitioner as a Generalist

The Generalist as a Practice Formulation

The factor and cluster data provide a partial answer to the difficult question: Does baccalaureate social work practice reflect generalist practice as required by the Curriculum Policy Statement? (CSWE, 1994, B6.9). The question can only be partially answered because the concept of generalist practice is defined in various ways (see Schatz, Jenkins, & Sheafor, 1990, pp. 218-220; Sheafor & Landon, 1987, pp. 664-665). A theme common to all generalist conceptions, however, is the expectation of "job breadth," which in terms of the practice framework in this study would be evidenced by BSW workers regularly engaging in a broad array of "client-centered" and "delivery system-centered" activities.

The factor scores for the direct service practitioners (see Figure 2.5) show a high concentration of activity in the "client-centered" aspects of the job. Clearly, the respondents provided services targeted to both the clients and the situations that caused those clients to seek services. In terms of social work's dual perspective on person and environment, it appears that the BSW practitioners were actively engaged with both person (client) and that person's "near" environment, helping their clients to cope with personal problems and to change troublesome conditions in their lives. These direct service practitioners were also engaged, to a lesser extent, in activities designed to help their organizations operate more effectively and to enhance their own professional development. Very striking, however, is the very low score for Resource/Service Change, which suggests that the BSW

Figure 2.5. Factor Scores: Direct Service BSW Respondents
(*n* = 1,172)

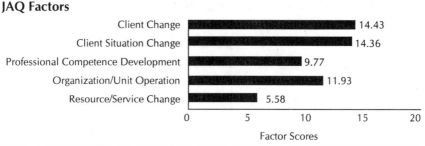

JAQ Factors	
Client Change	14.43
Client Situation Change	14.36
Professional Competence Development	9.77
Organization/Unit Operation	11.93
Resource/Service Change	5.58

Factor Scores

practitioners were relatively uninvolved in trying to bring about change in the macro or "distant" environment.

Figure 2.6 provides more detail about the clusters that make up the various factors. As with the factors, the level of involvement across the various task clusters varied considerably. Three of the eight "client-centered" clusters—Group Work, Protective Services, and Tangible Service Provision—were "seldom" performed. The other five were either "occasionally" or "frequently" performed. Of the nine delivery system-centered clusters, only two—Staff Information Exchange and Delivery System Knowledge Development—reached the "occasionally" performed level. It was primarily the activities associated with these two clusters that contributed to the moderate Organization/Unit Operation factor score. The other clusters associated with the delivery system-centered activities were all "seldom" performed.

Figure 2.6. **Mean Cluster Scores: Direct Service BSW Respondents**

(*n* = 1,172)

JAQ Clusters

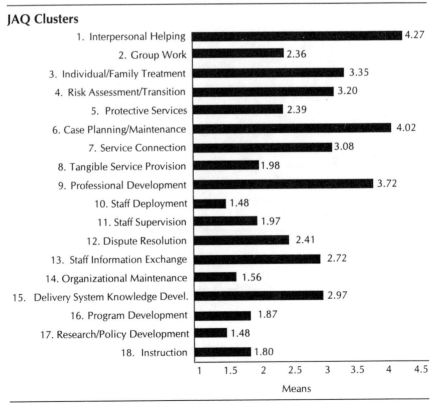

These data help define the job breadth of generalist social work practice. The BSW practitioners were heavily client-centered, using some formal treatment modalities with individuals and families, but primarily taking a less formal approach to helping clients (e.g., interviewing, counseling, advising) and maintaining case loads. Although they reported some activity associated with exchanging information about the agency and the human services delivery system, they engaged in relatively little practice that extended beyond specific cases. If one interprets the Curriculum Policy Statement's expectations for baccalaureate programs to mean that program curriculum should focus on both client change and client situation change, the actual work activity of BSW practitioners matches with these policies. However, if one interprets the CPS's expectations to include frequent involvement in organization and community change activities, the fit is not as close.

The Generalist as a Labor Force Strategy

When the generalist concept was formally introduced into social work and ascribed to baccalaureate social work education, it was intended primarily as a labor force penetration strategy. A combination of forces—the need for labor force differentiation, a demand for social work practitioners that exceeded the supply from master's programs, and NASW's recognition of the baccalaureate-level practitioner as "professional" in the late 1960s (see Chapter 1)—created the need to establish a focus that would distinguish the BSW practitioner from both the "new careerist" and the MSW social worker engaged in specialized practice (Teare & Sheafor, 1992, pp. 10-13). The goal was to carve out as broad a market share for the BSW social worker as possible.

Has this objective been achieved? If it has, BSW practitioners should now be found in a wide range of practice settings and in a variety of practice areas. The data presented in Table 2.2 suggest that the penetration effort has met with success: Baccalaureate practitioners were found in many settings and practice areas. Although there were differences in where MSW and BSW practitioners were concentrated, the deployment of BSWs was as diffuse, in terms of practice settings and areas, as that of the MSWs.[5]

---

[5]More comparisons between BSWs and MSWs are made in Chapters 3 and 4.

Employment Setting and Practice Activity

Another important consideration is discovering any differences that exist in practice content and clients served in various settings. This has important implications for baccalaureate education. If differences are not of practical importance, the "one curriculum fits all" approach can be considered viable. If they are, it seems more appropriate for BSW programs to develop unique educational experiences for students intending to seek employment in different settings and practice areas. In short, programs would need to move toward increased specialization.

To shed some light on this, the average factor and cluster scores in the six settings with the largest number of BSW practitioners (i.e., social service agencies, hospitals, nursing homes, outpatient clinics, group homes, and psychiatric institutions) were compared with one another.[6] As with the analyses described earlier, the large sample size produced statistical significance but, in general, these differences were not large enough to be of practical importance. The pattern of factor scores across the various settings tended to be basically the same as that seen in Figure 2.4. Regardless of setting, respondents tended to emphasize client change (Factor 1) and changes in the situations in which the clients found themselves (Factor 2), and to have little involvement in resource and service change (Factor 5).

Analyses of the cluster data provided a few more details, but essentially told the same story. Again, Figure 2.5 serves as a good summary. BSW practitioners "frequently" engaged in interpersonal helping (Cluster 1), regardless of the employment setting. Group Work (Cluster 2) was "seldom" carried out, except in group homes and nursing homes where workers "occasionally" carried out these activities. More formal helping techniques in Individual/Family Treatment (Cluster 3) were "occasionally" used, most often in group homes and least often in hospitals. Risk Assessment (Cluster 4) was "seldom" carried out by the respondents, but most often occurred in nursing homes. When Protective Services (Cluster 5) were delivered, they were delivered in social service agencies. The BSWs "frequently" carried out Case Planning/Maintenance tasks (Cluster 6), most often in hospitals and nursing homes. Although involvement in Service Connection (Cluster 7) was typically low, it was found, not surprisingly, more often in social service agencies, outpatient settings, and nursing homes and hospices.

---

[6]Single classification ANOVAs across the six settings for each of the five factors and 18 clusters were computed.

The delivery of Tangible Services (Cluster 8) was "seldom" done in any setting. All workers, regardless of setting, reported that they "frequently" were involved in activities associated with professional growth and development (Cluster 9). Of the nine remaining "delivery system-centered" clusters, all but two were "seldom" carried by direct service workers in any setting. The two exceptions were Staff Information Exchange (Cluster 13) and Delivery System Knowledge Development (Cluster 15), which were "occasionally" carried out by practitioners in a few settings.

Practice Area and Practice Activity

To determine whether BSWs carried out different tasks in different areas of practice, the same analyses of factor and cluster means were carried out using data from the six practice areas in which most of the BSW practitioners were found (i.e., children and youth, services to the aged, family services, medical and health care, mental health, and developmental disabilities and mental retardation). The results were essentially the same as those produced by the setting data—some statistically significant differences were found but few were large enough to have practical implications. Figure 2.5 still serves as a good summary of these data. As far as the factor scores were concerned, the predominance of activities were directed toward Client Change (Factor 1) and Client Situation Change (Factor 2), regardless of practice area. As before, the data indicate no practice area in which the BSW workers were highly involved in bringing about changes in resources or services (Factor 5).

The mean cluster scores of the BSW workers also showed fairly consistent patterns from one practice area to another. Figure 2.6 summarizes the data fairly well. When present, statistical differences served mainly to underscore, for certain practice areas, the practice orientations of the total group. The practitioners "frequently" engaged in interpersonal helping activities (Cluster 1) regardless of their primary practice area. Work with groups (Cluster 2) was "seldom" done by any of the practitioners except for those in the mental health practice area where workers "occasionally" used the group process as a means of providing services and improving functioning. The BSWs tended to use more formal intervention techniques (Cluster 3) in services to children, youths, and families, and were least likely to use formal intervention techniques in providing medical and health-related social work services. Assessment of risk and the preparation for movement or transition (Cluster 4), when provided, was more likely to be carried out in association with services to families and children. The same was true for Protective Services (Cluster 5). Case Planning/Maintenance (Cluster 6), prominent in the overall sample, was "frequently" carried out regardless of the practice area of the worker. Helping clients connect with established services (Cluster 7) and delivering hard, "tangible" services (Cluster 8) was "seldom" done by most of the BSW practitioners. Regardless of their practice area, the workers reported that they "frequently" engaged in tasks that contributed to their Professional Development (Cluster 9). The remaining clusters, all dealing with "indirect services" were rarely performed by these direct service BSW practitioners.

These data, then, do not suggest that substantial differences in practice activity occurred in different practice areas. The design of curricula for specific practice areas would appear to be unnecessary.

Differences among Client Groups

Client Demography

The clients served by the BSW practitioners varied considerably from one employment setting to another. These differences may be useful to keep in mind when developing content for undergraduate curricula. Of particular note was the relative absence of male and minority clients in nursing home/hospice settings, and the greater prevalence of male and minority clients in group homes and psychiatric institutions. The age of clients served also varied considerably from one setting to another. Workers in social service agencies reported dealing with the widest array of client age groups—from infants (birth through 5 years of age) to the elderly (over 60 years). These same workers also reported a significantly higher involvement with infants and children (birth to 12 years) than any other setting. In group homes and psychiatric institutions, BSW practitioners were most likely to be working with youths (13 to 20 years); in hospitals, they were most likely to be working with adults and the elderly (21 and older). With the exception of those working in hospitals and nursing homes, BSWs in all other settings reported working with a relatively high percentage of teen-aged clients (13 to 20 years). Workers in hospitals and nursing homes reported an exceptionally high percentage of elderly individuals in their case loads.

Client Needs

Noting these age differences and recognizing that different practice settings have different missions to perform, it is not surprising that workers in each of the six practice settings reported trying to meet various types of client needs. Although somewhat predictable, these differences were quite striking and, when coupled with the task data, presented a relatively clear picture of the nature of practice as it varied from one setting to another.

For example, practitioners in social service agencies were most likely to deal with problems of family functioning (54.1%); they also dealt with substance and alcohol abuse (23.2%), interpersonal relations (22.4%), and character or behavior disorders (24.2%).[7]

For BSWs working in hospitals, the central problem involved clients experiencing health problems (65.3%). These workers also dealt with related needs such as aging (31.7%), family functioning (25.6%), anxiety and depression (22.1%), mental illness (21.1%), and the need for financial assistance (20.6%).

In nursing homes, problems associated with aging (86.2%) and related health needs (61.7%) dominated the workers focus. BSW practitioners also helped people cope with anxiety and depression (37.1%) and family functioning (20.4%). These workers rarely dealt with problems of job and work performance, substance and alcohol abuse, mental illness, or legal problems.

Workers in outpatient settings most frequently reported dealing with problems of mental illness (57.1%) and anxiety and depression (30.2%). They were the largest single group dealing with substance and alcohol abuse (26.2%); as one would expect, they also provided services to families dealing with these problems (26.2%).

BSWs in group homes and residences dealt predominantly with individuals struggling with the problems associated with transitional living. Almost half (45.7%) of the workers dealt with character and behavioral problems, many of these (39.1%) associated with mental illness or mental retardation. Given this pattern, it is not surprising that the BSWs also focused on problems with interpersonal relations (25.0%), family functioning (21.7%), and clients experiencing anxiety and depression (17.3%).

---

[7]It should be remembered that respondents could report up to three client problems or issues they addressed in their practice. The numbers in parentheses represent the percentage of workers in a given setting who cited the problem (see Table 2.4).

BSW workers employed in psychiatric hospitals and institutions reported dealing with a predictable array of client problems: mental illness or mental retardation (46.9%) and character and behavior problems (42.2%). Family functioning was also mentioned frequently (31.0%). Unlike BSWs in community-based settings, these workers dealt with more health problems (23.4%) and alcohol and substance abuse (18.8%).

In contrast to the task data, which indicated little difference in the activities of BSWs from one practice area to another, data on client demography and client problems clearly revealed setting-specific differences. BSW programs that offer courses targeted to specific practice areas may want to include content related to the client demographics and high-emphasis client needs reported in those areas.

Table 2.5. **Core Tasks Carried Out by Direct Service BSW Workers**
(*n* = 1,172)

Cluster/Task	% of Direct Service BSWs
Interpersonal Helping	
Discuss options with individuals in order to help them resolve a problem. (Task 3)	90%
Express understanding of people's points of view in order to establish relationships. (Task 9)	89%
Talk with individuals about problems in order to provide support/reduce anxiety. (Task 5)	82%
Encourage and help people to discuss their points of view to increase their insight. (Task 8)	76%
Individual/Family Treatment	
Confront individuals about unacceptable behavior in order to promote adjustment. (Task 4)	59%
Use specific intervention techniques in order to improve functioning and adjustment. (Task 12)	55%
Risk Assessment/Transition Service	
Counsel individuals in order to prepare for the termination of services or financial help. (Task 6)	60%
Review service plans in order to ensure that clients' rights are protected. (Task 42)	54%
Work with hostile clients in order to gain their cooperation. (Task 66)	52%
Case Planning/Maintenance	
Carry out appropriate procedures in order to see that individuals' rights are protected. (Task 62)	86%
Tell people about services in order to promote their use. (Task 28)	84%
Record/dictate information in order to update records, document or terminate services. (Task 68)	86%

continued on next page . . .

The Practice "Core"

To develop a "job-related" curriculum, those involved should identify a core of activities common to the jobs for which the curriculum serves as preparation. This can be done for the 1,172 direct service BSWs in the sample, who represented over 80% of the BSW respondents. In Table 2.5, these "core" tasks are grouped in the clusters to which they belonged. A task was included only if at least 50 percent of the direct service workers reported that they carried it out "frequently" or "almost always." To the right of each task is the percentage of direct service BSWs who reported carrying out the task.

By the completion of a BSW program, graduates should be able to carry out these 25 tasks.

Table 2.5. Core Tasks Carried Out by Direct Service BSW Workers (con't)

Cluster/Task	% of Direct Service BSWs
Review files and records in order to become familiar with a case situation. (Task 57)	81%
Obtain information in order to carry out intake or admission procedures. (Task 39)	79%
Exchange case information with colleagues/supervisors in order to get guidance. (Task 59)	78%
Review case records in order to evaluate progress and alter service plans if needed. (Task 65)	76%
Analyze case background in order to arrive at a plan for services or financial help. (Task 64)	75%
Discuss proposed actions with individuals in order to provide full understanding. (Task 58)	70%
Coordinate service planning with others in order to make service delivery effective. (Task 67)	61%
Service Connection	
Persuade others that people really do qualify for service. (Task 60)	59%
Professional Development	
Take part in discussions with co-workers in order to share experiences or gain insights. (Task 84)	86%
Review your workload in order to plan activities and set priorities. (Task 38)	84%
Evaluate your services in order to see if you are serving clients' best interests. (Task 81)	55%
Evaluate your actions/decisions in order to see if they meet quality requirements. (Task 94)	52%
Delivery System Knowledge Development	
Read administrative literature in order to keep up with policies. (Task 88)	52%

Conclusion

What, then, have these data revealed about baccalaureate-level social workers? As the first part of the chapter showed clearly, there was a considerable amount of homogeneity among them. The typical baccalaureate social worker was a white female in her early to mid-thirties, with relatively few years of practice experience, who worked in a direct service capacity in one of a number of practice settings. The analysis of the task data showed that there were significant differences between the cluster and factor score means in the three major job functions—direct services, supervision, and management/administration. However, it is clear that the delivery of direct services to clients was the primary focus of the BSW workers in the study. More than four out of every five respondents were employed as direct service practitioners. In this capacity, they attempted to change clients or to bring about changes in the clients' immediate environment. To a lesser degree, they were involved in activities that strengthened the organizations in which they worked. They reported regular involvement in professional development and self-monitoring activities that enhanced their ability to serve their clients.

The picture that emerged of the direct service practitioners is one of a versatile, "all-purpose" worker. The clients served by these workers varied greatly from setting to setting and their ages spanned the life cycle. There were also some differences in clients from one region of the country to another. Different employment settings and areas of practice presented the workers with a strikingly different array of client problems and needs; Table 2.3 summarizes this diversity. Despite these differences, it would seem that the workers tried to meet these needs in similar fashion from one setting to another. The BSWs did this most often by using a combination of basic interpersonal helping, counseling, and problem-solving activities. This was done within the framework of a considerable amount of planning and maintenance of cases and case loads. Formal therapeutic techniques and group interventions were used less often.

The consistent pattern of intervention and case management activities from setting to setting supports the notion that the baccalaureate social worker brought to the job situation a set of generalized practice approaches that were not specific to setting or practice area. The BSW social workers were clearly engaged in nonspecialized practice and, in this sense, were practicing as generalists. Curriculum design, therefore, can appropriately focus on the basic skills required for social work practice, and only minimal adaptation is needed to prepare for practice in different settings and practice areas or in indirect services (i.e., supervision and management). That adaptation might most efficiently be provided through in-service training or continuing education programs at the local, regional, or national levels.

Implications

Obviously, the task and cluster data described in this chapter can be of considerable importance in assessing the relevance of and making revisions to existing undergraduate curricula. However, the potential of these data to impact social work goes far beyond the revision of BSW curricula. In Chapter 5, experts in a variety of areas have been asked to examine various portions of the data set and comment on their implications for a number of social work education policies, concepts, and issues. With regard to this BSW material, Leslie Leighninger examines the BSW practitioner findings and indicates what she sees as important to undergraduate social work education. In separate but related discussions, Joseph Anderson comments on implications of the data for the educational continuum and Donald Pilcher describes his thoughts about the study findings and the accreditation process. For an additional assessment of these data and their implications, the reader should consult appropriate sections of Chapter 5.

References

Betty L. Baer and Ronald Federico, *Educating the Baccalaureate Social Worker: Report of the Undergraduate Social Work Curriculum Development Project*, 2 vols. Cambridge, MA: Ballinger Publishing, 1978 and 1979.

Council on Social Work Education, *Handbook of Accreditation Standards and Procedures*. Alexandria, VA: Author, 1994.

National Association of Social Workers, *NASW Standards for the Classification of Social Work Practice*. Silver Spring, MD: Author, 1981.

Mona S. Schatz, Lowell E. Jenkins, and Bradford W. Sheafor, "Milford Redefined: A Model of Initial and Advanced Generalist Social Work," *Journal of Social Work Education*, 26 (Fall 1990): pp. 217-231.

Bradford W. Sheafor and Pamela S. Landon, "Generalist Perspective," in Anne Minahan (ed.), *Encyclopedia of Social Work*, Vol. 1. Silver Spring, MD: National Association of Social Workers, 1987, pp. 660-669.

Robert J. Teare and Harold McPheeters, *Manpower Utilization in Social Welfare*. Atlanta: Southern Regional Education Board, 1970.

Robert J. Teare and Bradford W. Sheafor, "Separating Reality from Fantasy: A Depiction of BSW Practice," in Barbara W. Shank (ed.), *B.S.W. Education for Practice: Reality and Fantasy*. St. Paul, MN: University of St. Thomas, 1992, pp. 1-18.

3

Master's-Level Social Workers: Who Are They and What Do They Do?

T he past two decades have been a time of dramatic change in social work practice and education. Through revisions to its accreditation standards and Curriculum Policy Statement, CSWE has sought to provide master's-level social work education programs with sufficiently flexible guidelines to allow them to adapt their curricula to meet these changing needs. However, the programs have found it difficult to devise this type of curriculum in the absence of a reliable database on social work practice. The data from the national task analyses have the potential to help them devise up-to-date, needs-related curricula.

Three Influences

Three recent developments in the social work profession have had a direct effect on MSW social work education. First, models of social work practice have been modified over the last two decades. For example, the practice methods of casework, group work, and community organization, at least in their traditional forms, have been abandoned. None of these terms appears in the *Encyclopedia of Social Work* (Minahan, 1987) as more than a historical reference. Instead, these models have been replaced by a number of highly specialized practice frameworks aimed at specific client groups and unique practice situations. NASW's *Standards for the Classification of Social Work Practice* (1981) underscores this emphasis by designating the MSW graduate as a "specialized" worker, and agencies employing MSWs expect them to possess the competencies necessary to perform highly specific roles and functions. For schools of social work, this change has meant a demand for more focused curricula at the graduate level.

Second, accreditation standards have increasingly allowed MSW programs to develop multiple identities—each having one or more "tracks." Where once master's-level social work education was almost identical in content from school to school and curricula could be adopted or adapted readily from other schools, now each school is encouraged to develop its own program based on emphases such as "fields of practice, problem areas, populations-at-risk, intervention methods or roles, and practice contexts and perspectives" (CSWE, 1994, M6.21, p.143). Programs offering specialized education have proven desirable among students who can select a program to suit their interests. Students who feel locked into a particular school for personal or financial reasons, however, may find that they need knowledge and skills for practice areas other than those represented by the program's specialization(s). Thus, programs are challenged to design curricula with sufficient generality to serve the educational needs of students with a variety of educational interests while offering courses that equip students with the specialized competencies that agencies have come to expect from MSW graduates.

Third, the re-emergence of baccalaureate social work education has necessitated changes in master's-level education. As their numbers have increased, BSW programs have expropriated much of the introductory content that had long been considered the purview of graduate programs. As a result, MSW programs had to redesign their curricula for two distinct groups of entering students: those with the BSW degree and those with no previous social work education/experience. In MSW programs, students without a BSW degree are required to take foundation content prior to beginning concentrated (i.e., specialized) preparation.

Given these recent influences on social work education, MSW programs can use the data presented in this chapter—data on both the common characteristics of master's-level practice and the uniqueness found in various specializations—to develop curricula relevant to student interests and social needs.[1]

---

[1] In describing these common and unique characteristics of practice, the authors concentrated their attention on major data trends and significant areas of content. However, since the master's data were collected in the mid-1980s, readers are cautioned to be mindful of recent changes in practice approaches or problem areas (e.g., homelessness, AIDS) that might affect areas of specialization.

Demographic Characteristics

Who They Are

As Chapter 1 and Appendix B indicate, the data on the MSW practitioners are based on responses from 5,272 social workers who, at the time the data were collected, had completed a master's degree from a CSWE-accredited school, had been employed in a social work job for at least one year, and were currently working full-time as a social worker. Pertinent demographic information on this diverse group is summarized in Table 3.1.

Just over 60% of the master's-level social workers were female and most were white. Only about 7% were African American, and other minority groups of color comprised only fractions of the sample. The typical respondent was in his or her mid-40s, had nearly 14 years of social work practice experience, and displayed a high level of job stability, as evidenced by an average of 6.7 years in their positions. Respondents lived all over the United States—62% lived and worked in the Northeast and Northcentral states with smaller proportions from the South and West.

What They Do and Where They Work

Table 3.2 describes the employment characteristics of this group. In marked contrast to the BSW practitioners, only about half of the MSWs were direct service practitioners. Using the language of the framework developed in Chapter 1, almost as many respondents were system- or organization-centered as were client-centered. Of the former, 27.5% were in administrative or management positions, about 10%

Table 3.1. **Personal Characteristics of Master's–Level Practitioners**
(*N* = 5,272)

Location		Ethnicity		Gender	
Northeast	33.3%[a]	American Indian	0.5%	Male	39.2%
Northcentral	28.7%	Asian/Pacific Islander	1.5%	Female	60.4%
South	21.3%	African American	7.1%		
West	16.2%	Chicano/Mexican American	0.5%		
		Puerto Rican	0.3%		
		Other Hispanic	0.6%		
		White	88.7%		
Mean Age = 43.8		**Mean Yrs. in Present Position** = 6.7		**Mean Yrs. in Social Work** = 13.7	

[a]Percentages may not total 100% because of missing values on some variables.

were in supervisory roles, and just over 5% were in education and training jobs. Thus, the entire MSW sample was almost equally split between direct and indirect services and more than 95% of them were concentrated in *just four* job functions. In the opinion of the authors, these data speak to the need to revisit the traditional emphasis on clinical preparation of MSW students, especially in the specialized component of training.

The direct service workers had 10.9 years of experience as social workers as compared to 14.8 years for supervisors, 16.3 years for managers and administrators, and 16.6 years for educators and trainers. These data suggest that direct service practice may have been the entry point for new MSWs, but that many opted for or were asked to take on indirect service job functions as they gained experience. The data clearly indicate that the MSW degree is the gateway to supervision and management positions. More will be said later about the strategic significance of this credential with regard to the upward mobility of social work practitioners and access to positions of leadership, power, and authority.

The data reported in Table 3.2 also reveal that more than two-thirds of the respondents were employed in just three *practice settings*: social service agencies, hospitals, and outpatient clinics. The percentage of workers in any one of the other settings was small. Programs that want to develop specializations in the settings that are most likely

---

Table 3.2. **Employment Characteristics of Master's-Level Practitioners**
(*N* = 5,272)

Primary Job Function			
Direct service	53.5%	Education/training	5.1%
Management/administration	27.5%	Consultation	2.1%
Supervision	10.2%	Policy/research/planning	1.5%

Practice Setting		**Primary Practice Area**	
Social service agency	26.7%	Mental health	28.3%
Hospital	21.4%	Family services	13.7%
Outpatient facility	19.4%	Medical and health care	13.5%
Private practice	7.9%	Children and youth	13.1%
Elementary/secondary school	7.2%	School social work	6.3%
College/university	4.8%	Services to the aged	3.7%
Psychiatric institution	3.7%	Dev. disabilities/mental retardation	3.6%
Non-social service organization	3.0%	Education	3.4%
Group home/residential care	1.6%	Alcohol/substance abuse	2.2%
Courts/criminal justice	1.4%	Pubic assistance/welfare	1.5%
Nursing home/hospice	1.0%	Corrections/criminal justice	1.3%
Other	0.7%	Other	11.3%

to employ MSW graduates should consider these data when designing their curricula and field placements. Table 3.2 also shows that, regardless of job function or employment setting, MSW practitioners were more than twice as likely to work in mental health than in any other *practice area.* Family services, medical or health care, and work with children and youth constituted second-tier practice areas but, beyond these, no single area involved a substantial portion of master's-level social workers.

Gender, Ethnicity, and Employment Characteristics

Because a substantial number of MSW practitioners were male, some observations about employment and gender differences are possible.[2] Because African Americans were the only other significantly represented group (7.1%), comments about employment patterns of minority practitioners must be limited to this group.

Job Function

Of special note is the distribution of gender and ethnicity across the job functions. Of the direct service workers, 66.6% were female. This 2:1 ratio was roughly the same for supervision. For administrative and managerial positions, however, the proportion of women dropped to 49.3%. Essentially, men were more likely than women ($p < .05$) to hold managerial and administrative positions.[3] The data also showed evidence that African-American practitioners were more likely than any other group to be found in supervision, management, and administration: although making up 7.1% of the entire sample, African-American social workers held only 5.7% of the direct service jobs while holding 9.1% of the supervisory positions and 8.0% of the managerial/administrative positions.

Job Setting

The proportion of male and female practitioners also varied considerably from one setting to another. Although males constituted only 39.2% of the sample, they comprised 51.3% of those employed in criminal justice settings and 52.8% of those in psychiatric institutions.

---

[2]Whenever differences are discussed, they have been tested and found to be statistically significant ($p < .05$). However, only those differences that are large enough to have practical implications for curriculum decision making have been singled out for discussion.

[3]The implications of these data for women and management were discussed at an invitational presentation at the 1993 CSWE Annual Program Meeting (Bernard, Brandwein, Teare, & White, 1993).

By contrast, males made up only 22.6% of the MSWs working in nursing homes, 28.9% of those in schools, and 33.4% of those in hospitals. African Americans were most likely to be employed in colleges and universities (11.9%) and least likely (1.2%) to be engaged in private practice.

Practice Area

Some rather substantial differences in gender were evident in the various practice areas. Female MSWs were more likely to be working in services for the aged (69.2%), school social work (71.1%), and medical or health-related services (74.0%). Males made up the majority of the MSWs in public welfare (53.1%), substance abuse (58.3%), community organization and planning (59.0%), and corrections (69.6%). These deployment patterns reflect both traditional hiring practices and gender-based job preferences. Race or ethnicity, on the other hand, did not vary to any significant degree among the various practice areas except in education, where African Americans constituted 13.4% of the practitioners.

What Their Clients Are Like

If graduate social work education is to be relevant to the work place, curriculum designers must make some assumptions about the kinds of clients graduates are likely to be serving and the kinds of needs and problems these people will have. The database from the national studies provides much valuable information in this regard. When they filled out the Job Analysis Questionnaire (JAQ), respondents were asked to estimate the percentage of their clientele who were male, indicate as many as three racial/ethnic groups and two age groups they regularly served, and identify the three client needs or problems addressed most frequently in their practice. Their responses to these questions are summarized in Table 3.3.

As a group, the respondents reported that their clientele was almost equally split between females and males. Almost all the workers indicated that white clients were a primary part of their clientele; about half reported that their caseloads included African Americans; and 21.1% reported working with Mexican American or Puerto Rican clients. Only a few workers reported serving American Indian, Asian or Pacific Islanders, or other Hispanic clients. As one might expect, the proportions of respondents serving these minority group clients increased in parts of the United States where these population groups are concentrated (e.g., Mexican Americans in the Southwest, Puerto Ricans in the Northeast). This would suggest that MSW programs planning courses that deal with cultural diversity should emphasize those minorities prevalent in their geographic area. In regard to client age, only a small portion of the MSW practitioners reported that they worked with infants, but substantial numbers indicated working with all other age groups—children, youth, adults, and older persons. These data strongly argue for human behavior content in the graduate curriculum spanning all phases of the life cycle.

As portrayed in Table 3.3, the most prevalent problem of clients served by the MSW respondents was associated with family functioning. Regardless of setting or practice area, almost half of the respondents (45.1%) reported dealing with this problem. The next most prevalent group of problems were those associated with psychological and behavioral dysfunctions, both moderate and severe: Workers reported that their clients had anxiety and depression (30.9%), interpersonal relationship problems (29.8%), mental illness or mental retardation (26.7%), and various types of behavior problems (24.6%). To a lesser extent, respondents reported that their clients had "situation-specific" problems; these were problems related to physical health (18.4%), alcohol and substance abuse (14.8%), school (13.6%), employment (12.4%), and the aging process (10.2%).

Table 3.3. **Client Characteristics and Problems—Master's–Level Practitioners** (N=5,272)

Client Gender		Client Ethnicity[a]		Client Age[a]	
Female (mean)	49.0%	American Indian	3.1%	Infants (0–5)	9.2%
Male (mean)	51.0%	Asian/Pacific Islander	3.0%	Children (6–12)	22.9%
		African American	44.6%	Youth (13–20)	34.0%
		Chicano/Mexican Am.	10.9%	Adults (21–60)	65.5%
		Puerto Rican	8.6%	Aged (over 60)	21.6%
		Other Hispanic	3.8%		
		White	86.1%		

Percentage of Time Each Client Problem Was Cited[a]			
Family functioning difficulties	45.1%	Skill or knowledge development	9.8%
Anxiety or depression	30.9%	Physical disabilities	7.3%
Interpersonal relationship problems	29.8%	Financial problems	7.1%
Mental illness or mental retardation	26.7%	Shelter or housing needs	4.1%
Behavior problems	24.6%	Legal problems	4.0%
Health problems	18.4%	Group interaction problems	3.9%
Alcohol or substance abuse	14.8%	Recreation needs	1.0%
School problems	13.6%	Civil rights or affirmative action	0.9%
Job or work needs	12.4%	Membership development	0.7%
Problems with aging	10.2%		

[a]Percentages total to more than 100% because respondents could name more than one category.

Table 3.4. **Client Problems Addressed in Primary MSW Settings**

Type of Setting	Client Problems Addressed[a]
Social Service Agencies (n = 1,406)	Family functioning (61.0%) Interpersonal relations (34.7%) Character or behavior problems (23.0%) Job or work performance (18.9%)
Hospitals (n = 1,127)	Health problems (49.9%) Anxiety or depression (33.5%) Mental illness or mental retardation (33.1%) Family functioning (31.9%)
Outpatient Psychiatric Facilities (n = 1,026)	Mental illness or mental retardation (55.2%) Anxiety or depression (51.8%) Family functioning (41.1%) Interpersonal relations (34.1%)
Private Practice (n = 416)	Anxiety or depression (74.0%) Family functioning (56.5%) Interpersonal relations (55.5%) Character or behavior disorders (28.1%)
Elementary or Secondary Schools (n = 381)	School related problems (91.6%) Character or behavior disorders (48.6%) Family functioning (48.3%) Interpersonal relations (30.4%)

[a]Percentages total to more than 100% because respondents identified up to three client needs most frequently addressed.

Because unique configurations of client problems were reported in specific settings, programs should consider these configurations when developing setting-specific courses or course content. Table 3.4 summarizes the four most prevalent client problems in the five settings in which MSWs were most frequently employed.

Task Analysis of the Master's Practitioners

Cluster Scores

Up to this point, we have focused on the characteristics and attributes of the workers and their work environments. It is also possible to describe the specific tasks performed by MSW practitioners by look-

---

[4]Respondents rated "how often" they carried out a task by means of a five-point scale. In describing the group cluster data, "almost never" represents an average score ranging from 1.00 to 1.49, "seldom" is from 1.50 to 2.49, "occasionally" ranges from 2.50 to 3.49, and "frequently" ranges from 3.50 to 4.49. None of the cluster means averaged from 4.50 to 5.00 ("almost always").

ing at the frequency with which they carry out each of the 18 clusters of activity displayed in Figure 3.1.[4] Here we see more balance between the client-centered clusters and the delivery system-centered clusters than was the case with the BSW workers. These cluster scores suggest that, as a group, MSW practitioners were "frequently" involved in two clusters of work activity: Interpersonal Helping (Cluster 1), including such tasks as interviewing, listening, and counseling, as well as tasks related to their own professional growth and development (Cluster 9). Figure 3.1 further indicates that, as a group, MSW practitioners "occasionally" engaged in six additional clusters of activity: Case Planning/Maintenance (Cluster 6), Individual/Family Treatment (Cluster 3), Risk Assessment/Transition to other services (Cluster 4), Resource System Knowledge Development (Cluster 15), Staff Information Exchange (Cluster 13), and Staff Supervision (Cluster 11). These data simply reinforce the notion that MSW practitioners were employed in positions with widely differing job functions.

Figure 3.1. **Mean Cluster Scores: All MSW Respondents** (*N*=5,272)

JAQ Clusters

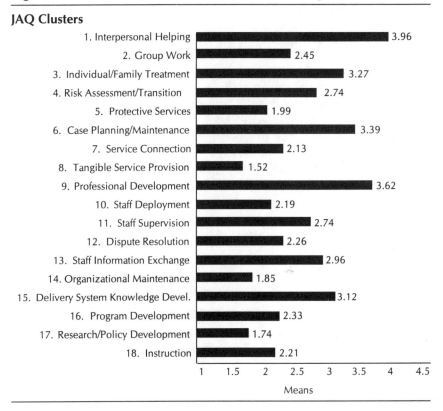

1. Interpersonal Helping — 3.96
2. Group Work — 2.45
3. Individual/Family Treatment — 3.27
4. Risk Assessment/Transition — 2.74
5. Protective Services — 1.99
6. Case Planning/Maintenance — 3.39
7. Service Connection — 2.13
8. Tangible Service Provision — 1.52
9. Professional Development — 3.62
10. Staff Deployment — 2.19
11. Staff Supervision — 2.74
12. Dispute Resolution — 2.26
13. Staff Information Exchange — 2.96
14. Organizational Maintenance — 1.85
15. Delivery System Knowledge Devel. — 3.12
16. Program Development — 2.33
17. Research/Policy Development — 1.74
18. Instruction — 2.21

Means

Factor Scores

The factor score profile in Figure 3.2 presents the same information in a slightly different form—it illustrates the orientation of MSW practice into three primary sets of activity. The first two bars represent client-centered activities—that is, helping clients change their attitudes, skills, knowledge, or insight (Client Change), and the conditions under which they live, work, and interact with others (Client Situation Change). The third emphasis (represented by the fourth bar in Figure 3.2) is system-centered activities—that is, helping to operate and maintain the organizations and agencies delivering these services (Organization/Unit Operation). To a lesser degree, the MSW respondents reported engaging in activities that strengthened their own professional competence (Professional Competence Development), and they reported giving the least attention to bringing about changes in resources, programs, and services (Resource/Service Change). As with the BSW practitioners, whose aggregate patterns were quite similar, this last characteristic again calls into question social work's commitment to its historical mission of facilitating change in both people and society.

Job Function and Practice Activities

In contrast to the undergraduate practitioners, the MSW respondents were almost evenly split between those who reported that they were direct service providers (53.5%) and those who did not (46.5%). Because the social work practice literature is replete with assertions that job functions represent very different spheres of activity, analyses were made to determine whether differing job functions *actually* were associated with different activities. It was important to find out, early

---

Figure 3.2. Factor Scores: All MSW Respondents (*N* = 5,272)

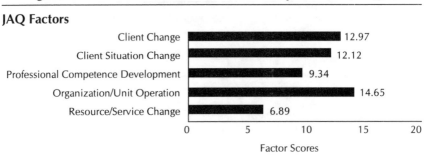

JAQ Factors

	Factor Scores
Client Change	12.97
Client Situation Change	12.12
Professional Competence Development	9.34
Organization/Unit Operation	14.65
Resource/Service Change	6.89

in the analyses, whether composite depictions of the data hid important details about practice differences among subgroups of MSW workers. Accordingly, the sample of 5,272 MSW practitioners was partitioned into the four largest subsamples based on respondent self-reports of primary job function. As an aggregate, the four groups—direct service workers ($n=2,819$), supervisors ($n=536$), managers/administrators ($n=1,451$), and educators/trainers ($n=271$)—accounted for 96.3% of the MSW respondents.

ANOVAs were calculated across the mean cluster and factor scores for each of the four groups to determine if the level of involvement in various types of activity varied significantly from one group to another. Without exception, differences were found among the 4 groups on all 23 variables (18 clusters and 5 factors). To examine these differences further, a total of 138 ex post facto contrasts between means were made (23 variables times 6 pairs of means). Of these, 115 indicated that statistically significant differences ($p<.05$) existed among the 4 subgroups of practitioners.[5] In addition to demonstrating the concurrent validity of the practice framework (see Appendix B for a further discussion of this), the findings clearly indicated that, at least for the MSW practitioners, job-related activities should be seen as distinctly different for each of the four subgroups.

Factor Score Differences

The factor score profiles of each of the four groups, presented in Figures 3.3a through 3.3d, illustrate why the analyses showed statistically significant differences among the groups. All of these differences will not be discussed here. Rather, the text focuses only on those that, in the opinion of the authors, have practical implications for educational policy making.

As expected, the direct service practitioners (Figure 3.3a) were significantly involved in activities intended to change clients (Client Change) and the situations in which they found themselves (Client Situation Change). Somewhat unexpected was the fact that the supervisors (Figure 3.3b), although different from the direct service workers in both of these client-centered factors, still had relatively high loadings on them. The supervisors appeared to be "all purpose" workers—engaged in almost as many client-centered activities as the direct

---

[5] When they did occur, the nonsignificant mean differences were usually associated with the Professional Competence Development factor and/or in contrasts between supervisors and managers.

Figures 3.3a–3.3d. **Factor Scores for Different MSW Job Functions**

Figure 3.3a. **Direct Service Workers (n = 2,819)**

JAQ Factors

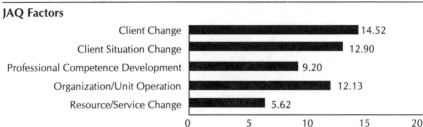

Figure 3.3b. **Supervisors (n = 536)**

JAQ Factors

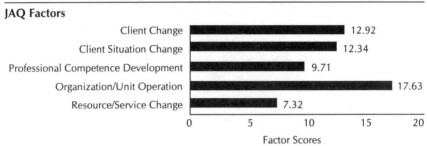

Figure 3.3c. **Managers and Administrators (n = 1,451)**

JAQ Factors

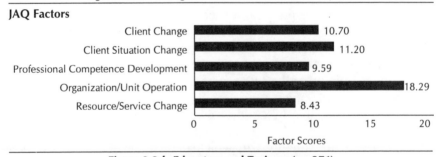

Figure 3.3d. **Educators and Trainers (n = 271)**

JAQ Factors

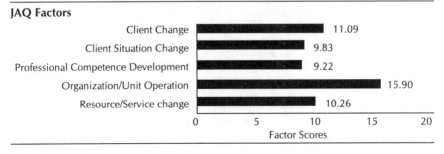

service workers and nearly as much organizational activity as the managers/administrators. Their profiles suggested that they might, in fact, be called the advanced generalists of today's social work practice.

What accounts for the supervisors' high loadings on client-centered activities? Although many of these workers may have had caseloads in addition to their supervisory responsibilities, there is another explanation: Many of the activities associated with the Client Change and Client Situation Change factors are equally relevant to problem solving and behavior change initiatives carried out with colleagues and supervisees. Later in this chapter, when supervisory activities are examined in more detail, this explanation gains plausibility.

As Figures 3.3a–3.3d illustrate, the MSW respondents who were *not* direct service workers were very involved in the operation and maintenance of the organizations in which they worked. This was especially true of the supervisors and managers, but educators and trainers also had a substantial loading on this factor. The fact that a graduate degree greatly increases the probability that social workers will be given supervisory or administrative responsibilities simply cannot be ignored by graduate educators as they prepare their students for practice.

Finally, the factor data clearly indicate that the low score in the Resource/Service Change factor seen earlier in Figure 3.2 was not the result of low scores in one group canceling out high scores in another. With the exception of the educators and trainers, who constituted a small minority of the practitioners, the MSWs simply were not involved in these activities to any great extent.

Cluster Score Differences

As stated earlier, the four work groups all differed among themselves on all 18 clusters. There were, however, some similarities among the differences. Table 3.5 contains a summary of these. The clusters of tasks that, on the average, each group carried out "frequently," "occasionally," "seldom," or "almost never" are listed in four columns in the table. By moving across the columns, one can make comparisons rather quickly. The groups had a common involvement in four areas of work activity, i.e., they were carried out either "frequently" or "occasionally" by all four groups of workers. These clusters (bold-faced in Table 3.5) were Interpersonal Helping (Cluster 1), Professional Development (Cluster 9), Delivery System Knowledge Development (Cluster 15), and Staff Information Exchange (Cluster 13). With the exception of these four clusters, the four groups differed

Table 3.5. Task Cluster Differences by Selected Job Functions (N = 5,077)

	Direct Service (n = 2,819)		Supervision (n = 536)		Administration/Management (n = 1,451)		Education/Training (n = 271)	
Frequently Mean cluster score 3.50–4.49	**Interpers. Helping** Ind/Family Treatment Case Plan/Maint. **Prof. Development**	4.40 3.79 3.79 3.61	Staff Supervision **Interpers. Helping** **Prof. Development**	3.98 3.77 3.63	**Prof. Development**	3.63	Instruction **Prof. Development** **Interpers. Helping**	4.29 3.72 3.54
Occasionally Mean cluster score 2.50–3.49	Risk Assessment **Syst. Knowl. Develop.** Group Work **Staff Info. Exchange**	2.99 2.89 2.58 2.56	Case Plan/Maint. **Staff Info. Exchange** **Syst. Knowl. Develop.** Staff Deployment Ind/Family Treatment Risk Assessment Dispute Resolution	3.45 3.40 3.32 3.18 3.14 2.85 2.71	**Syst. Knowl. Develop.** **Staff Info. Exchange** Staff Supervision **Interpers. Helping** Program Develop. Staff Deployment Case Plan/Maint. Organiz. Maint. Ind/Family Treatment Dispute Resolution Instruction	3.48 3.48 3.37 3.35 3.19 3.14 2.89 2.64 2.62 2.50 2.50	**Staff Info. Exchange** **Syst. Know. Develop.** Group Work Staff Supervision Res/Policy Develop.	3.40 3.04 3.01 2.92 2.63
Seldom Mean cluster score 1.50–2.49	Service Connection Staff Supervision Protective Services Dispute Resolution Program Develop. Instruction Staff Deployment Tangible Services Res/Policy Develop.	2.28 2.20 2.18 2.07 1.82 1.81 1.57 1.56 1.51	Program Develop. Group Work Instruction Service Connection Protective Services Organiz. Maint. Res/Policy Develop. Tangible Services	2.44 2.37 2.32 2.16 2.15 2.00 1.66 1.51	Risk Assessment Group Work Res/Policy Develop. Service Connection Protective Services	2.43 2.16 1.99 1.95 1.71	Program Develop. Case Plan/Maint. Ind /Family Treatment Dispute Resolution Risk Assessment Staff Deployment Organiz. Maint. Service Connection	2.49 2.47 2.36 2.22 1.90 1.88 1.76 1.72
Almost Never Mean cluster score 1.00–1.49	Organiz. Maint.	1.42			Tangible Services	1.49	Tangible Services Protective Services	1.43 1.42

from each other in terms of the emphasis placed on various activities. For this reason, the remaining sections of this chapter will discuss these groups separately.

Activities Reported by Direct Service Workers in Five Practice Settings

Of the 5,272 MSW practitioners in the study, the largest single group characterized themselves as direct service practitioners ($n=2,819$). The factor scores for this group were presented in Figure 3.3a. Their cluster score profile can be found in Figure 3.4. It is clear from looking at the cluster profile that, as a group, they had a high level of involvement in those task clusters associated with the Client Change and Client Situation Change factors. Most especially, they were "frequently" involved with tasks continued in Interpersonal Helping (Cluster 1), Individual/Family Treatment (Cluster 3), and Case Planning and Maintenance (Cluster 6).

This study had enough responses from direct services practitioners in five practice settings to permit a discrete analysis of differences in factor and cluster score patterns. The five settings were social service agencies ($n=501$), hospitals ($n=687$), outpatient clinics ($n=636$), private practice ($n=360$), and schools ($n=330$). Using cluster and factor score means as dependent variables, ANOVAs were calculated across the five practice settings.

Factor Score Differences

Significant ($p<.05$) differences were found between each of the factor scores for the five practice settings.[6] However, only 30 of the 50 possible ex post facto comparisons were statistically significant. Moreover, most of these differences were not as large as one rating scale unit (e.g., from "occasionally" to "frequently"), which indicates that although the direct service respondents displayed some statistically significant variations in their work activity, these variations made little difference in overall activity patterns. As Figure 3.5 shows clearly, the patterns were quite similar from one setting to another.

Stated most simply, direct service workers carried out activities designed to bring about changes in the clients they served; these were

---

[6]As with other analyses described earlier, the statistical significance was due to the large number of observations in the sample.

closely followed by activities designed to alter the situations in which their clients found themselves. All groups manifested some involvement in organizational operation, but these activities were reported with less frequency than client-centered activities. As did almost all of their MSW colleagues, these direct service practitioners devoted little energy to bringing about changes in the resource or service delivery systems of which they were a part. The only group to depart somewhat from this overall pattern were the private practitioners, who devoted significantly less effort to changing their clients' situations and to operating their organizations. In other words, the private practitioners more closely fit the image of a specialized "clinical" social worker.

Figure 3.4. **Mean Cluster Scores, MSW Direct Service Workers**
(*N* = 2,819)

JAQ Clusters

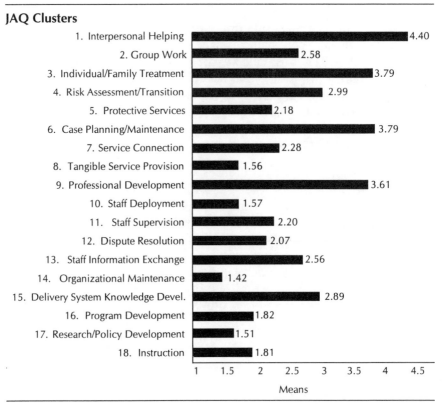

JAQ Clusters	Mean
1. Interpersonal Helping	4.40
2. Group Work	2.58
3. Individual/Family Treatment	3.79
4. Risk Assessment/Transition	2.99
5. Protective Services	2.18
6. Case Planning/Maintenance	3.79
7. Service Connection	2.28
8. Tangible Service Provision	1.56
9. Professional Development	3.61
10. Staff Deployment	1.57
11. Staff Supervision	2.20
12. Dispute Resolution	2.07
13. Staff Information Exchange	2.56
14. Organizational Maintenance	1.42
15. Delivery System Knowledge Devel.	2.89
16. Program Development	1.82
17. Research/Policy Development	1.51
18. Instruction	1.81

Means

Cluster Score Differences

As with the factor scores, the ANOVAs calculated on the mean cluster scores showed statistically significant activity differences among the groups of direct service workers in different settings. The exception to this was the Professional Development cluster (Cluster 9): All of the groups indicated that they frequently engaged in activities designed to maintain or improve their competence as professionals.

As one would expect, all of the direct service practitioners were highly involved in client-centered tasks, frequently carrying out activities associated with Interpersonal Helping (Cluster 1) and Individual/Family Treatment (Cluster 3) to bring about changes in individuals. The private practitioners had the highest ratings on Cluster 1; they almost always reported involvement in interpersonal helping. The use of formal treatment models was lowest among practitioners in hospitals (although frequently reported). The majority of direct service practitioners indicated that they seldom engaged in Group Work

Figure 3.5. **Mean Factor Scores by Practice Settings, MSW Direct Service Workers** (*n*=2,514)

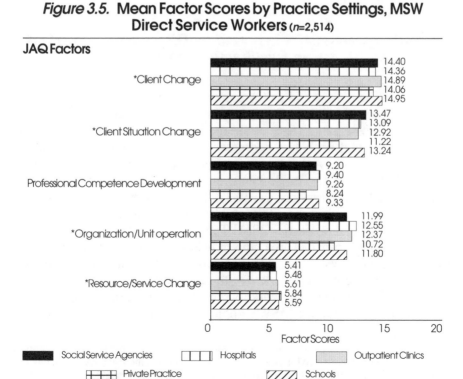

*Indicates significant differences (*p*<.05) between at least one pair of means.

(Cluster 2), but practitioners in private practice, outpatient settings, and schools reported occasionally working with clients in groups. The direct practitioners only occasionally carried out risk assessment activities (Cluster 4); they seldom carried out Protective Services (Cluster 5), except for the agency social workers who occasionally did. Almost all of the workers reported frequent involvement in activities associated with Case Planning and Management (Cluster 6), except for the private practitioners who indicated occasional involvement. Somewhat surprisingly, all of the direct practitioners reported seldom involvement with Service Connection (Cluster 7), and as a group, they almost never delivered Tangible Services (Cluster 8), although social service agency workers "seldom" did.

The picture with regard to the system-centered work clusters (Clusters 10–18) was as one would expect. The activities in these clusters were seldom or almost never performed by the direct service MSWs. Some workers reported occasionally carrying out tasks to get more information about the delivery system in which they worked (Cluster 15) and occasionally taking part in Staff Information Exchange activities (Cluster 13).

Client Characteristics Reported by Direct Service Workers in Five Practice Areas

While the cluster and factor scores showed basically the same activity patterns for the various groups of direct service workers, they indicated substantial differences in the types of clients served and the client needs and problems addressed. These differences were most striking when the workers were grouped by area of practice. In all, 94% of the direct service MSWs were employed in five practice areas—mental health services ($n=983$), family services ($n=385$), medical and health services ($n=398$), children and youth services ($n=322$), and school social work ($n=286$). Table 3.6 lists the percentages of workers in each practice area who indicated they dealt with a particular problem or need. The table also summarizes their descriptions of the types of clients they worked with most often.

The 983 mental health workers represented the largest single practice area specialty in the MSW sample.[7] These workers typically dealt

---

[7]The deployment of a large concentration of workers in this area has been a characteristic of the social work labor force for years, and is also reflected in the 1993 NASW membership data, which constitutes the most complete data set currently available.

with a configuration of problems centered on and exacerbated by mental illness and retardation. They were the only group to deal extensively with the chronic and long-term consequences of these syndromes, including disruptions in family functioning, anxiety, difficulties with interpersonal relations, behavior problems, and alcohol and substance abuse. Although their clients were somewhat diverse in age, they tended to be adults (21 to 60 years of age), and were most frequently female and white.

The family service workers ($n=385$), quite predictably, dealt overwhelmingly with problems experienced by family members of all ages. These workers dealt more frequently with problems that were situational (i.e., externally induced) than did their colleagues in mental health, but the problems were more diverse, including interpersonal relations, behavior problems, school problems, and alcohol and substance abuse. Family service workers reported that their clients were more likely to be female and white; they also reported the lowest percentage of African Americans in their caseloads.

The 398 medical and health workers, like their counterparts in mental health, dealt with a more focused set of problems centering on physical illness and disability. They seemed to help clients with both transitory health problems brought about by illness and injury and chronic, long-term disabilities associated with the aging process. These situations typically required these workers to deal with depleted financial resources and the problems, tensions and anxieties that inevitably followed. The clients of medical and health workers were mostly adults, and were the most ethnically diverse of all the practice areas reported.

The 322 practitioners working in the area of services to children and youth reported serving a clientele mainly between infancy and 20 years of age. These workers were heavily involved in working with families in order to reach young people who were having difficulties with interpersonal relationships, behavioral problems, and problems in school. Mental illness was sometimes involved but, more often, the problems seemed to be situational and age-specific. These workers were most likely to be dealing with young, nonwhite male clients; they reported one of the highest percentages of minority clients among all practice areas.

The school social workers ($n=286$) dealt with clients and problems similar to those of the youth workers, but their efforts were centered on the school environment. Like the youth workers, they focused on behavior problems of young people but also worked with families and interpersonal relationships. Mental illness was sometimes a client problem, but not a dominant one. The clients of these workers were almost twice as likely to be male rather than female and were almost evenly distributed between students in elementary and middle school (6–12 years) and those in secondary school (13–20 years). Their clients were only moderately diverse in ethnicity/race.

Table 3.6. **Client Characteristics Reported by Direct Service Workers in Five Practice Areas**

	% in Mental Health (*n* = 983)	% in Family Services (*n* = 385)	% in Medical/ Health (*n* = 398)	% in Children/ Youth (*n* = 322)	% in School Social Work (*n* = 286)
Client Needs/Problems[a]					
Family functioning	42.9	90.1	27.4	77.0	49.3
Anxiety or depression	69.5	45.2	41.5	19.6	8.7
Interpersonal relations	44.9	49.4	11.8	32.8	33.2
Mental illness/retardation	53.9	4.7	5.3	13.0	12.6
Behavior problems	31.5	28.6	4.3	51.9	51.4
Health problems	4.0	6.2	85.7	7.5	3.1
Alcohol/substance abuse	12.9	18.4	9.0	7.5	5.6
School problems	5.6	11.9	0.5	38.5	93.7
Job/work needs	3.8	2.3	1.8	2.8	1.0
Aging problems	1.9	1.3	25.1	0.0	0.0
Skill/knowledge	0.7	2.6	0.8	4.3	3.5
Physical disability	0.0	1.3	38.2	1.9	3.5
Legal problems	1.1	2.6	0.3	7.5	0.7
Financial problems	2.0	2.9	20.4	0.3	0.7
Client Ages[a]					
Infants (0–5 years)	0.8	9.1	13.1	19.9	7.7
Children (6–12 years)	11.3	22.6	7.8	57.1	76.9
Youth (13–20 years)	36.0	40.5	10.3	60.2	60.8
Adults (21–60 years)	86.4	74.8	74.9	38.2	25.2
Aged (over 60 years)	15.6	3.9	66.6	0.3	0.0
Client Gender					
Male	46.8	47.0	50.8	52.5	62.0
Female	53.2	53.0	49.2	47.5	38.0
Client Ethnicity[a]					
American Indian	2.3	2.3	3.5	5.3	2.4
Asian	1.3	3.1	4.3	3.7	4.2
African American	36.8	27.8	57.5	53.4	44.8
Chicano/Mexican American	10.6	6.5	15.1	13.0	9.4
Puerto Rican	6.1	5.2	7.0	9.0	10.1
Other Hispanic	2.3	2.6	3.8	3.1	6.3
White	91.7	81.0	90.2	91.0	92.0

[a]Percentages total to more than 100% since workers could identify up to three problems, two age groups, and two ethnic groups.

Core Tasks of Direct Service Practitioners

Of the 131 activities on the JAQ, 24 were found to be "core" tasks—that is, those performed either frequently or almost always by at least 50 percent of the direct service workers. They are grouped by cluster area below. To the left of the task statement is the percentage of workers who reported that they performed the task either frequently or almost always; at the end of the task description, in parentheses, is the number of the task as it appeared on the JAQ and as listed in Appendix A.

Interpersonal Helping
(93%) Express and demonstrate an understanding of peoples' points of view, feelings, and needs in order to establish open and trusting relationships. (Task 9)

(93%) Discuss options with individuals in order to help them understand choices and/or resolve a particular problem. (Task 3)

(88%) Talk with individuals and/or their relatives about problems in order to reassure, provide support, or reduce anxiety. (Task 5)

(83%) Encourage and help people to discuss their points of view, feelings, and needs in order to increase their insight into the reasons for their actions. (Task 8)

Individual/Family Treatment
(71%) Use specific intervention techniques with individuals in order to improve behavioral functioning and adjustment. (Task 12)

(63%) Confront individuals about unacceptable behavior in order to bring about changes or promote adjustment. (Task 4)

(58%) Use specific intervention techniques with family members, individually or as a group, in order to strengthen the family unit. (Task 7)

Risk Assessment/Transition
(51%) Observe individuals and gather information from appropriate sources in order to decide whether there is a need for special counseling or mental health services. (Task 20)

Case Planning/Maintenance
(88%) Record or dictate information about individuals, using either prepared forms or narrative, in order to establish or update records, document services provided, or terminate services. (Task 68)

(77%) Discuss proposed actions with individuals in order to provide full information and ensure understanding. (Task 58)

(71%) Analyze case background and consult with appropriate individuals in order to arrive at a plan for services and/or financial help. (Task 64)

(69%) Review case records and consult with appropriate individuals in order to evaluate progress and alter service plans if needed. (Task 65)

(68%) Coordinate service planning with staff, other providers, family members, or significant others in order to make the delivery of services to individuals and groups most effective. (Task 67)

(68%) Review files and records of an individual prior to a contact with that person in order to become familiar with the details of the situation. (Task 57)

(66%) Exchange information about case details with supervisor and/or colleagues in order to get guidance in dealing with an individual or group. (Task 59)

(63%) Carry out appropriate procedures (for example, obtain consent, explain rights, maintain record security, etc.) to ensure that individuals' rights are protected. (Task 62)

(57%) Obtain information from individuals, their relatives, or significant others in order to carry out intake or admission procedures for treatment or services. (Task 39)

(57%) Make contact with other units/agencies by letters, memos, or phone calls in order to refer people to appropriate services. (Task 25)

Professional Development

(72%) Review your workload (appointments, visits, mail, etc.) in order to plan your activities and set priorities for a given period. (Task 38)

(70%) Take part in discussions with co-workers, talking over events or problem situations, in order to share experiences or gain insights. (Task 84)

(62%) Read articles in professional/scientific journals, newspapers, or magazines in order to keep up with developments related to your job responsibilities. (Task 90)

(55%) Evaluate your competence, availability, and feelings about individuals to whom you are providing services in order to decide if you are serving their best interests. (Task 81)

(54%) Evaluate your actions and decisions in order to determine if your professional activities are meeting the standards, values, and ethics required for quality. (Task 94)

(51%) Give information to people, by phone or in person, in order to explain and interpret the programs, policies, or procedures of your organization. (Task 29)

For curriculum development purposes, a school might want to be sure that, at a minimum, it has prepared its graduates who are intending to enter direct service jobs to conduct the kind of practice activities represented by these tasks.

Practice Activities among Supervisors

A total of 536 MSW-level respondents identified their primary job function as supervision. Perhaps the best way to get a feel for the work activities of the graduate level supervisor is to use the factor score profile displayed in Figure 3.3b and the cluster score profile displayed in Figure 3.6 as reference points. Both reflect these practitioners' greater job breadth—that is, more involvement in more activity areas—than did their direct service and management colleagues. In fact, these workers had high levels of involvement in 30 different tasks in 7 different task clusters. As they did for direct service workers, ANOVAs of the factor and cluster scores for supervisors showed some statistically significant differences ($p < .05$) by employment setting and practice area. Three settings—social service agencies ($n=236$), hospitals ($n=122$), and outpatient clinics ($n=92$)—accounted for nearly 85% of these supervisors. On the job factors, the analyses indicated that supervisors in outpatient clinics were slightly more inclined toward client change activities and slightly less involved in delivery system-related activities than supervisors who worked in hospitals and social service agencies.

As Figure 3.6 makes evident, supervisors were typically engaged in ten sets of activity: Staff Supervision (mean cluster score of 3.98), Interpersonal Helping (3.77), Professional Development (3.63), Case Planning/Maintenance (3.45), Staff Information Exchange (3.40), Delivery System Knowledge Development (3.32), Staff Deployment (3.18), Individual/Family Treatment (3.14), Risk Assessment/Transition (2.85), and Dispute Resolution (2.71).

There were a few differences in the activities of supervisors in the three settings (social service agencies, hospitals, and outpatient facilities) with sufficient numbers of workers to warrant analyses. The 92 supervisors in outpatient clinics were slightly more involved in the client-centered activities of interpersonal helping, group work, individual and family treatment, and case planning and maintenance than were those in the other two groups. The 122 hospital-based supervisors reported more involvement in dispute resolution. However, the variations in job activity that showed up in employment settings and practice areas were not deemed large enough to warrant the development of specific curricula.

Figure 3.6. Mean Cluster Scores, MSW Supervisors (*n*=536)

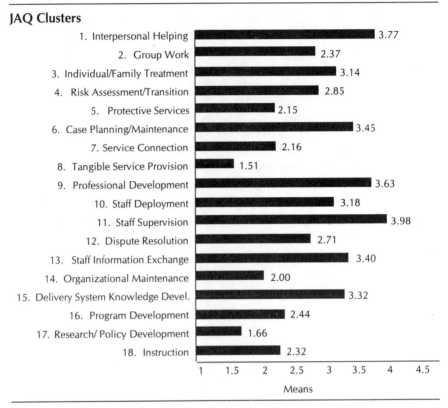

JAQ Clusters

1. Interpersonal Helping — 3.77
2. Group Work — 2.37
3. Individual/Family Treatment — 3.14
4. Risk Assessment/Transition — 2.85
5. Protective Services — 2.15
6. Case Planning/Maintenance — 3.45
7. Service Connection — 2.16
8. Tangible Service Provision — 1.51
9. Professional Development — 3.63
10. Staff Deployment — 3.18
11. Staff Supervision — 3.98
12. Dispute Resolution — 2.71
13. Staff Information Exchange — 3.40
14. Organizational Maintenance — 2.00
15. Delivery System Knowledge Devel. — 3.32
16. Program Development — 2.44
17. Research/ Policy Development — 1.66
18. Instruction — 2.32

Means

Core Tasks of Supervisors

As stated earlier, the job breadth of the supervisors was greater than that of the direct service workers. The 30 core tasks for supervisors—those activities of the 131 on the JAQ that were frequently or almost always performed by at least 50% of the respondents—are grouped by cluster area below. Some are the same as those performed by the direct service workers; others primarily involve internal organizational functions related either to the supervision of people or to the operation of various program units. The system-centered clusters and tasks are listed first, followed by the client-centered activities. To the left of the task statement is the percentage of workers who reported that they performed the task either frequently or almost always; at the end of the task description, in parentheses, is the number of the task as it appeared on the JAQ and as listed in Appendix A.

Staff Supervision

(88%) Go over cases with supervisees (staff, students, or volunteers), recommending methods and approaches in order to instruct them in dealing with various case situations. (Task 97)

(76%) Go over case records of supervisees (including students) in order to ensure that documentation has been carried out according to proper procedures. (Task 99)

(72%) Clarify job duties, roles, and work assignments for supervisees (staff, students, volunteers) in order to increase individual or group effectiveness. (Task 110)

(70%) Discuss your evaluation of a supervisee's performance in order to promote understanding of expectations and/or to work out any differences of opinion. (Task 115)

(67%) Complete rating forms, including narrative if appropriate, in order to evaluate the job performance of staff, students, or volunteers. (Task 114)

(64%) Discuss agency procedures and work expectations with new staff members, students, or volunteers in order to familiarize them with your operations. (Task 113)

(64%) Teach individuals (staff, students, volunteers) how to do a job, helping with tasks when appropriate, in order to provide on-the-job training. (Task 116)

(62%) Go over policies, procedures, or laws with supervisees (staff, students, volunteers) in order to inform them about the material or to alert them to effects on programs. (Task 112)

Staff Deployment

(64%) Schedule/coordinate working hours, vacations, etc., in order to arrange adequate staffing patterns and coverage. (Task 109)

Staff Information Exchange

(63%) Give guidance to staff, students, or volunteers about personal or job-related problems in order to restore job functioning. (Task 10)

(57%) Conduct a meeting (committee, staff, board, students) in order to exchange information, gather opinions, or select courses of action. (Task 124)

Delivery System Knowledge Development

(66%) Read administrative literature (for example, manuals, memos, circulars) in order to keep up with organizational policies and procedures. (Task 88)

(60%) Gather and compile data about services provided to people in order to prepare statistics for various reports. (Task 69)

(55%) Read regulations, guidelines, and other material in order to keep current about federal, state, and local regulations that affect your job. (Task 96)

Professional Development

(79%) Review your workload (appointments, visits, mail, etc.) in order to plan your activities and set priorities for a given period. (Task 38)

(79%) Take part in discussions with co-workers, talking over events or problem situations, in order to share experiences or gain insights. (Task 84)

(61%) Give information to people, in person or by phone, in order to explain and interpret the policies, or procedures of your organization. (Task 29)

(58%) Read articles in professional/scientific journals, newspapers, or magazines in order to keep up with developments related to your job responsibilities. (Task 90)

(53%) Evaluate your actions or decisions in order to determine if your professional activities are meeting the standards, values, and ethics required for quality. (Task 94)

Interpersonal Helping

(84%) Discuss options with individuals in order to help them understand choices and/or resolve a particular problem. (Task 3)

(75%) Express and demonstrate an understanding of peoples' points of view, feelings, and needs in order to establish an open and trusting relationship. (Task 9)

(62%) Encourage and help people to discuss their points of view, feelings, and needs in order to increase their insight into the reasons for their actions. (Task 8)

(54%) Talk with individuals and/or their relatives in order to reassure, provide support, or reduce anxiety. (Task 5)

Case Planning/Maintenance

(72%) Review case records and consult with appropriate individuals in order to evaluate progress and alter service plans if needed. (Task 65)

(66%) Discuss proposed actions with individuals in order to provide full information and ensure understanding. (Task 58)

(65%) Coordinate service planning with staff, other providers, family members, significant others in order to make delivery of services to individuals or groups most effective. (Task 67)

(63%) Analyze case background and consult with appropriate individuals in order to arrive at a plan for services and/or financial help. (Task 64)

(56%) Record or dictate information about individuals, using either prepared forms or narrative, in order to establish or update records, document services provided, or terminate services. (Task 68)

(55%) Review files and records of an individual prior to contact with that person in order to become familiar with the details of the situation. (Task 57)

(55%) Exchange information about case details with supervisor and/or colleagues in order to get guidance in dealing with an individual or group. (Task 59)

Analysis of Core Activities

As the previous listing clearly shows, the MSW supervisors regularly engaged in a wide range of activities as they carried out their jobs. Their core duties spanned 30 tasks and 7 task clusters. Two of these, Interpersonal Helping (Cluster 1) and Case Planning/Maintenance (Cluster 6), were also core activity areas for the direct service providers. Is it possible that these supervisors were also delivering services to a caseload of clients on a regular basis? Although it's possible that supervisors in small service organizations might have been doing this, another explanation for the entire group seems more likely: All of the tasks in Interpersonal Helping and most of those in Case Planning/Maintenance are activities that one would expect supervisors to be engaged in as they provided personal assistance and case-oriented guidance to *supervisees*. Interpersonal helping activities designed to explore options, increase insight, provide support, and resolve problems can apply to situations involving clients in a therapeutic context as well as to workers in a supervisory context. This is also true of case planning activities—that is, supervisors may review their workers' case records, discuss proposed case actions, coordinate service planning, carry out record keeping, review files and records, and exchange case information with colleagues.

The client-centered tasks that were missing from the supervisory core (but appeared in the direct service workers' core) reinforce the assumption that most supervisors were *not* carrying substantial caseloads. In the Case Planning/Maintenance cluster, the tasks that would typically be used only with clients (e.g., obtaining informed consent, carrying out intake, and providing information and referral) were seldom carried out by the supervisors. Furthermore, none of the tasks in Individual/Family Treatment (Cluster 3) and in Group Work (Cluster 2) were part of the supervisory core. Stated another way, this means that the supervisors surveyed rarely used formal therapeutic techniques either with individuals or groups.

Finally, client-centered tasks in two other clusters—Risk Assessment/Transition and Professional Development—did not appear in the array of core supervisory tasks. This overall pattern of task emphasis and omission would be unlikely if the supervisors, as a group, were extensively involved in the provision of direct services to clients.

The data clearly establish the fact that the role of the MSW supervisor is a broad one. Supervisors used an array of interpersonal skills and techniques for providing personal and case-related guidance to supervisees while carrying out a range of supervisory functions necessary to the operation of their organizations. Currently, almost all MSW students receive instruction in interpersonal helping skills. The same cannot be said, however, for supervisory instruction. Because so many MSW practitioners move into supervisory roles, graduate social work education should provide students with the *technical* knowledge and skills required to supervise and manage others: for example, delegation, dispute resolution, accountability, limit and standard setting, performance monitoring and evaluation, deployment, staffing, and the fair application of sanctions.

Practice Activities among Managers/Administrators

A large number ($n=1,451$) of MSW respondents indicated that their primary job function was to serve in a management or administrative capacity.[8] More than 78% of these managers/administrators were employed in just three practice settings: social service agencies ($n=581$), hospitals ($n=293$), and outpatient facilities ($n=263$.) No other setting employed a large enough number of social workers in these positions to warrant a separate analysis. In addition, four practice areas—mental health ($n=330$), family services ($n=222$), children/youth ($n=214$), and medical/health ($n=212$)—accounted for 67.4% of the workers. These deployment distributions were very similar to those of the direct service workers.

As with the data for direct service workers and supervisors, ANOVAs of the mean cluster and factor scores for these settings and practice areas were computed. Although some statistically significant differences ($p<.05$) were found, very few reflected a variation of even one rating point on the frequency scale (e.g., from "occasionally" to "frequently"). Given these findings, the practice activities of the managers will be described as an aggregate and not reported by practice area and employment setting.

The best depiction of the work activities of the managers and administrators can be found in Figure 3.3c and Figure 3.7.

As the figures show, the pattern of activities for the managers was quite similar to that of the supervisors in that the primary emphasis in both jobs was on the provision of indirect services, or system-centered activities. The managers, however, did not have the same job breadth as the supervisors. Managers were typically involved in Professional

---

[8]Although some authors have made a distinction between managers and administrators, we use these terms interchangeably.

Development (3.63), Delivery System Knowledge Development (3.48), Staff Information Exchange (3.48), Staff Supervision (3.37), Interpersonal Helping (3.35), Program Development (3.19), and Staff Deployment (3.14). Both factor score and cluster score patterns suggest that the MSW managers/administrators, on average, had less involvement with "people-oriented" tasks and more involvement with "data-oriented" tasks than did the supervisors. Stated another way, the tasks that the managers typically performed were more abstract, with many involving the compilation of information and the analysis of data and situations in order to arrive at program and personnel-related conclusions. This point is best illustrated by examining the core tasks of the managers.

Figure 3.7. Mean Cluster Scores, MSW Managers/Administrators
(*n* = 1,451)

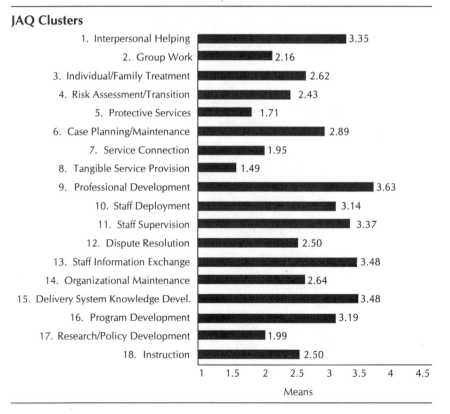

JAQ Clusters

Cluster	Mean
1. Interpersonal Helping	3.35
2. Group Work	2.16
3. Individual/Family Treatment	2.62
4. Risk Assessment/Transition	2.43
5. Protective Services	1.71
6. Case Planning/Maintenance	2.89
7. Service Connection	1.95
8. Tangible Service Provision	1.49
9. Professional Development	3.63
10. Staff Deployment	3.14
11. Staff Supervision	3.37
12. Dispute Resolution	2.50
13. Staff Information Exchange	3.48
14. Organizational Maintenance	2.64
15. Delivery System Knowledge Devel.	3.48
16. Program Development	3.19
17. Research/Policy Development	1.99
18. Instruction	2.50

Means

Core Tasks of Managers/Administrators

The 26 "core" tasks for the managers—those tasks of the 131 on the JAQ that were frequently or almost always performed by at least 50% of the respondents—are grouped by cluster area below. Many are the same as those performed by the supervisors, and some were also carried out by the direct service workers. The system-centered clusters and tasks are listed first and are followed by the client-centered activities. (The format is the same as that for the previous listings of core tasks for the direct service workers and the supervisors.)

Program Development
(66%) Establish and/or write down policies, either for service or administrative functions, in order to provide standard operating procedures. (Task 98)
(57%) Propose a plan to your supervisor(s) or administrator(s) in order to gather needed support for a change in practices, guidelines, or policies within your organization. (Task 50)
(52%) Describe needs to decision-makers (for example, legislators, managers, board members, community leaders) in order to persuade them to initiate, maintain, or restore programs. (Task 48)

Delivery System Knowledge Development
(76%) Read administrative literature (for example, manuals, memos, circulars) in order to keep up with organizational policies and procedures. (Task 88)
(63%) Read regulations, guidelines, and other material in order to keep current about federal, state, and local regulations that affect your job. (Task 96)
(58%) Gather and compile data about services provided to people in order to prepare statistics for various reports. (Task 69)
(57%) Draft, dictate, or proofread letters to various individuals in order to answer inquiries or request specific information or action. (Task 70)
(55%) Contact and/or work with representatives of agencies or other organizations in order to develop cooperative arrangements. (Task 100)

Staff Information Exchange
(74%) Conduct a meeting (committee, staff, board, students) in order to exchange information, gather opinions or select courses of action. (Task 124)
(57%) Give guidance to staff, students, or volunteers about personal or job-related problems in order to restore job functioning. (Task 10)
(56%) Take part in group meetings in order to assist the group in arriving at a decision. (Task 14)

Professional Development
(82%) Review your workload (appointments, visits, mail, etc.) in order to plan your activities and set priorities for a given period. (Task 38)
(70%) Take part in discussions with co-workers, talking over events or problem situations, in order to share experiences or gain insights. (Task 84)
(67%) Give information to people, by phone or in person, in order to interpret the program, policies, or procedures of your organization. (Task 29)
(66%) Read articles in professional/scientific journals, newspapers, or magazines in order to keep up with developments related to your job responsibilities. (Task 90)
(52%) Evaluate your actions and decisions in order to determine if your professional activities are meeting the standards, values, and ethics required for quality. (Task 94)

Staff Supervision
(60%) Clarify job duties, roles, work assignments for supervisees (staff, students, volunteers) in order to increase individual or group effectiveness. (Task 110)
(56%) Discuss your evaluation of an employee's performance in order promote understanding of expectations and/or work out any differences of opinion. (Task 115)
(53%) Complete rating forms, including narrative if appropriate, in order to evaluate the job performance of staff, students or volunteers. (Task 114)
(52%) Discuss agency procedures and work expectations with new staff members, students, or volunteers in order to familiarize them with your operation. (Task 113)
(52%) Go over policies, procedures, or laws with supervisees (staff, students, or volunteers) in order to inform them about the material or to alert them to effects on programs. (Task 112)
(50%) Go over cases with supervisees (staff, students, or volunteers), recommending methods and approaches, in order to instruct them in dealing with various case situations. (Task 97)

Staff Deployment
(57%) Review and analyze data about service needs and demands in order to establish workload and staffing requirements. (Task 78)
(53%) Schedule/coordinate working hours, vacations, etc., in order to arrange adequate staffing patterns and coverage. (Task 109)

Case Planning/Maintenance
(63%) Discuss proposed actions with individuals in order to provide full information and ensure understanding. (Task 58)

Interpersonal Helping

(70%) Express and demonstrate an understanding of peoples' points of view, feelings, and needs in order to establish open and trusting relationships. (Task 9)

Analysis of Core Activities

The core tasks of these managers/administrators suggest that they functioned at what human resources specialists would call the "middle-management" level. The absence of many of the client-centered tasks, so characteristic of the supervisors, clearly supported the notion that they did not have substantial involvement in the day-to-day supervision of front-line caseworkers and service providers, as did the supervisors. Although the managers/administrators reported performing some supervisory activities, they tended to deal as much with procedures as with people. They reported activities related to the internal operation of their organizations at the program or unit level; for example, developing standard operating procedures, communicating policies and procedures to workers, conducting on-the-job orientation and training, and compiling and assimilating certain kinds of information to make operational decisions. In short, they typically functioned as operational managers. Absent from their jobs were the duties typically ascribed to top administrators, such as financial management (Task 131), budgeting (Tasks 122, 127), converting organizational goals into program design (Task 129), assessing program effectiveness (Task 123), and carrying out external organizational functions such as meeting with community leaders, board members, and various constituency groups (Tasks 130, 49, 41).

Characterizing these individuals as middle-managers, however, should in no way diminish their importance to social work. Next to the direct service workers, they represented the second largest functional subgroup. If only for this reason, it is clear that MSW education has an obligation to prepare social workers with the information and skills needed to function effectively in management-level jobs, and to assume leadership roles in those organizations delivering social services to people.[9]

---

[9]The study data suggest that three locations-social service agencies, hospitals, and outpatient facilities-are prime field placements for students with concentrations in planning, management, and administration. The 1993 NASW membership data also support this finding (NASW, 1993).

Practice Activities among Educators and Trainers

Of the four subgroups, the 271 individuals who identified education and training as their primary job function are the easiest to characterize. The factor scores shown in Figure 3.3d and the cluster scores shown in Figure 3.8 indicate that they were the most functionally specialized of the MSW practitioners. Their cluster mean for Instruction (Cluster 18) was 4.29, the highest mean for any group on any cluster. The educators and trainers had high factor scores on Organization/ Unit Operation (Factor 4) and Resource/Service Change (Factor 5) because most of the task clusters in which they were involved—Instruction (Cluster 18), Professional Development (Cluster 9), Staff Information Exchange (Cluster 13), Group Work (Cluster 2), and Delivery System Knowledge Development (Cluster 15)—had high loadings on these two factors (see Table B.4 in Appendix B). Their re-

Figure 3.8. **Mean Cluster Scores, MSW Educators/Trainers** *(n=271)*

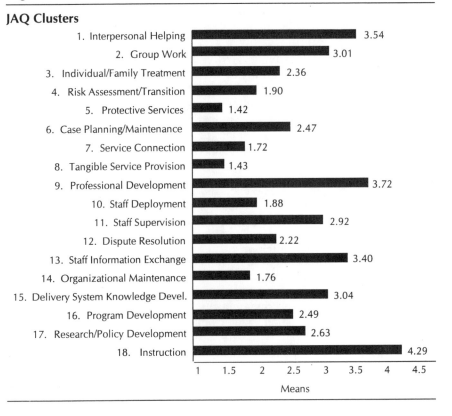

JAQ Clusters

Cluster	Mean
1. Interpersonal Helping	3.54
2. Group Work	3.01
3. Individual/Family Treatment	2.36
4. Risk Assessment/Transition	1.90
5. Protective Services	1.42
6. Case Planning/Maintenance	2.47
7. Service Connection	1.72
8. Tangible Service Provision	1.43
9. Professional Development	3.72
10. Staff Deployment	1.88
11. Staff Supervision	2.92
12. Dispute Resolution	2.22
13. Staff Information Exchange	3.40
14. Organizational Maintenance	1.76
15. Delivery System Knowledge Devel.	3.04
16. Program Development	2.49
17. Research/Policy Development	2.63
18. Instruction	4.29

Means

sponses concerning employment setting and practice area also reflected this emphasis on education and training: Almost 73% of them were employed in college or university settings. The second largest proportion (14.8%) consisted of 40 staff development specialists, 25 of whom worked in social service agencies and 15 of whom worked in hospitals. Of the 271 in this group of educators and trainers, 160 (59%) specified "education" as their primary practice area. No other practice area predominated.

Core Tasks of Educators and Trainers

This highly specialized group of.MSW practitioners was involved in 22 "core" tasks (i.e., frequently or almost always performed by at least 50% of the respondents). They are grouped by cluster area below. The system-centered clusters are listed first, followed by those that are client centered. (The format is the same as for previous listings.)

Instruction
(90%) Teach groups of individuals in a classroom, workshop, or other setting, according to a training plan, in order to increase knowledge and skills. (Task 119)

(86%) Plan a course or training activity, designing a syllabus and making up a schedule, and/or arranging facilities in order to improve skill and knowledge. (Task 117)

(76%) Review courses and/or training programs in order to evaluate whether or not learning objectives are being met. (Task 133)

(71%) Construct and/or give exams, tests, or other measures in order to assess how much each individual has learned. (Task 55)

Group Work
(74%) Teach people (for example, supervisors, parents, students, volunteers) how to listen, negotiate, or understand nonverbal behavior in order to increase their communication skills. (Task 46)

Staff Information Exchange
(60%) Present information to staff, students, or volunteers about confidentiality and the right to privacy in order to protect the rights of individuals. (Task 56)

(54%) Conduct a meeting (committee, staff, board, students) in order to exchange information, gather opinions, or select courses of action. (Task 124)

(50%) Take part in group meetings in order to assist the group in arriving at a decision. (Task 14)

Professional Development
(86%) Read articles in professional/scientific journals, newspapers, or magazines in order to keep up with developments related to your job responsibilities. (Task 90)
(72%) Review your workload (appointments, visits, mail, etc.) in order to plan your activities and set priorities for a given period. (Task 38)
(72%) Take part in discussions with co-workers, talking over events or problem situations, in order to share experiences or gain insights. (Task 84)
(64%) Evaluate your actions and decisions in order to determine of your professional activities are meeting the standards, values, and ethics required for quality. (Task 94)
(52%) Attend workshops, seminars, or programs dealing with topics of interest or need in order to improve your job knowledge and skills. (Task 92)
(52%) Give information to people, by phone or in person, in order to explain or interpret the programs, policies, or procedures of your organization. (Task 29)

Delivery System Knowledge Development
(53%) Read administrative literature (for example, manuals, memos, circulars) in order to keep up with organizational policies and procedures. (Task 88)

Research/Policy Development
(55%) Teach or help individuals with regard to their speaking or writing in order to improve their communication skills. (Task 45)

Staff Supervision
(51%) Go over with supervisees (staff, students, volunteers), recommending methods and approaches, in order to instruct them in dealing with various case situations. (Task 97)
(51%) Teach individuals (staff, students, volunteers) how to do a job, helping with tasks when appropriate, in order to provide on-the-job training. (Task 116)

Case Planning/Maintenance
(55%) Discuss proposed actions with individuals in order to provide full information and understanding. (Task 58)

Interpersonal Helping
(80%) Express and demonstrate an understanding of peoples' points of view, feelings, and needs in order to establish open and trusting relationships. (Task 9)
(72%) Discuss options with individuals in order to help them understand choices, and/or resolve a particular problem. (Task 3)

(65%) Encourage and help people to discuss their points of view, feelings, and needs in order to increase their insight into the reasons for their actions. (Task 8)

Analysis of Core Activities

At first glance, these workers seemed to have a fair amount of job breadth—there were 22 tasks in the core, distributed among 9 task clusters. Closer inspection, however, underscores the specialization inherent in this group. Four of the nine core clusters involved only one task and three of these tasks were informational in nature. Also, involvement in activities in other clusters such as Staff Supervision (Cluster 11) and Staff Information Exchange (Cluster 13) was closely related to the education function. In short, almost everything these practitioners did was related to obtaining and conveying interpersonal and job-related information, formally and informally, in order to improve their own job skills or those of others. They designed courses and curriculum modules and provided instruction according to specific curricular objectives. In the agency settings, these courses were designed to impart skills and knowledge that could be applied immediately to work-related situations. The respondents deployed in colleges and universities provided field liaison and supervision or worked as classroom educators in undergraduate and graduate social work programs.

It is particularly interesting to note that this group of educators and trainers had a significantly ($p < .05$) higher involvement in Group Work activity than any other subgroup of MSW practitioners, primarily because they worked with groups in classroom situations and in task-oriented meetings. The skills required to perform these activities—skills in designing, delivering, and evaluating effective learning experiences, and in shaping, directing, and managing the task-oriented group process in organizational settings—are not typically given a high priority in MSW-level education.

Despite their relatively small numbers, educators and trainers are an important component of the graduate social work labor force, in part because they were the only subgroup with a high involvement in activities related to Resource/Service Change (see Figures 3.3a–3.3d). These MSW practitioners functioned as a potential force for changing the service organizations and systems with which they were involved by working *within* the systems, and by using the tools of learning and personal development to bring about evolutionary change. The data do not permit us to infer whether they tried to change individuals to conform to the organizations and systems, or tried to change organizations and systems to deliver more and better services to clients. One hopes it was the latter. However, if the profession of social work is committed to advocacy and positive social change, social work education must provide students with a clear mandate for change, a supportive set of change-oriented guidelines and policies, and the skills and knowledge required to bring about system change.

Conclusion

Perhaps the most striking impression left by these data is the importance of job function in differentiating specializations of MSW social work practice. Four such specializations emerged: direct service provision, supervision, management/administration, and education/training. Together, they accounted for 96% of the MSW respondents and reflected *fundamental* differences in job activities. In fact, only the following 7 tasks were performed by at least 50% of the respondents from all 4 of the primary specializations:

- Express and demonstrate an understanding of peoples' points of view, feelings, and needs in order to establish open and trusting relationships. (Task 9)

- Give information to people, by phone or in person, in order to explain and interpret the programs, policies, and procedures of your organization. (Task 29)

- Review your workload (appointments, visits, mail, etc.) in order to plan your activities and set priorities for a given period. (Task 38)

- Discuss proposed actions with individuals in order to provide full information and secure understanding. (Task 58)

- Take part in discussions with coworkers, talking over events or problem situations, in order to share experiences or gain insights. (Task 84)

- Read articles in professional/scientific journals, newspapers, or magazines in order to keep up with developments related to your job responsibilities. (Task 90)

- Evaluate your actions and decisions in order to determine if your professional activities are meeting the standards, values, and ethics required for quality. (Task 94)

Direct Service Workers

Although job activities were very different across the four job functions of MSW direct service practitioners, they were very similar across employment settings and practice areas. Apparently, the respondents approached direct practice with a set of rather generic interpersonal helping techniques and treatment models. Therefore, although information related to employment setting or practice area may be a consideration in developing background content on various practice contexts, it apparently has little relevance to the actual job activities workers perform in these various jobs. For direct service workers, the most striking job activity-related variations were associated with the kinds of clients and client problems encountered in their jobs.

The relative importance of employment setting, practice area, clients, and client needs suggests four configurations for MSW-level educational content:

- family services in human service agencies,

- children/youth services in schools and criminal justice settings,

- medical/health-related social services in hospitals and outpatient facilities, and

- social services related to mental illness/retardation in institutional and community-based agencies.

Simply put, these data indicate that MSW programs should devote their primary attention to providing those who plan to enter direct service practice with *fundamental practice competencies* (Morales & Sheafor, 1995; especially see Chapter 8), as opposed to stressing the unique patterns of practice activities in different settings or practice areas. Preparation for specific jobs might better be accomplished through specialized course work in the major areas listed above, accompanied by appropriate field placements (Raymond, Teare, & Atherton, in press).

Indirect Service Workers

The picture is not quite so clear in regard to the indirect service providers. Little information is available about the career patterns of graduate-level social workers, but all available data—the 1988 and 1991 NASW membership data (Gibelman & Schervish, 1993), the composite data from these national studies, and the 1993 NASW membership data (NASW, 1993)—consistently show managers outnumbering supervisors by about 2.5 to 1. Although these data sources do not provide clear information on movement from one job function to another, this ratio makes it unlikely that MSW direct service practitioners are moving into management positions only after they have been supervisors. However, if MSW practitioners are likely, sooner or later, to move into either supervision or management/administration, MSW programs must take steps to provide educational opportunities, either through specialized curricula or continuing education, that help graduates make these transitions.

Social Change Activities

Finally, the data consistently reveal that social workers, with the possible exception of the administrators and educators, devote very little of their work activity to the human service delivery system or the broader society. The master's-level workers tend to take part in either client-centered activities or those focused on organizational change. The scope of their work only minimally extends beyond the immediate environment of their clients or the functioning of the organizations that employ them. This pattern of activity calls into question social work's historic claim that its uniqueness among the helping professions lies in its simultaneous attention to both person and environment.

A challenge for graduate social work programs and the profession itself is to reexamine this claim in light of current social work practice and either strengthen this aspect of graduate education, or abandon the claim.

References

L. Diane Bernard, Ruth A. Brandwein, Robert J. Teare, and Barbara W. White, "Women, Social Work Education, and Management: A View From Three Bridges." Paper presented at the 39th Annual Program Meeting of the Council on Social Work Education, New York, February 1993.

Council on Social Work Education, *Handbook of Accreditation Standards and Procedures.* Alexandria, VA: Author, 1994.

Margaret Gibelman and Philip H. Schervish, *Who We Are: The Social Work Labor Force as Reflected in the NASW Membership.* Washington, DC: NASW Press, 1993.

Anne Minahan, ed., *Encyclopedia of Social Work* (2 vols.). Silver Spring, MD: National Association of Social Workers, 1987.

Armando T. Morales and Bradford W. Sheafor, *Social Work: A Profession of Many Faces*, 7th ed. Boston: Allyn and Bacon, 1995.

National Association of Social Workers, *NASW Standards for the Classification of Social Work Practice*. Silver Spring, MD: Author, 1981.

National Association of Social Workers, *1993 NASW Membership Update Statistics* (Special data run at the request of the authors). Washington, DC: Author, 1993.

Ginny T. Raymond, Robert J. Teare, and Charles R. Atherton, "Is 'Field of Practice' a Relevant Organizing Principle for the MSW Curriculum?" *Journal of Social Work Education*, in press.

4

Comparisons between BSW and MSW Social Workers

T hroughout much of the 20th century, the social work profession has reflected on the similarities and differences among practitioners who work in different regions, employment settings, and practice areas, and who have different job functions, clienteles, and educational credentials. How are social work practitioners alike? How are they different? A review of social work's intermittent efforts to answer these questions (reported in Chapter 1) reveals a variety of assertions from the profession about its common features and its uniqueness at differing education levels or in various job functions, settings or practice areas. The three national studies described in this book represent a breakthrough because they bring together a substantial body of data that can be used to formulate more complete answers to these questions.

Answering the question "How are we alike?" will help the profession identify a common "core" of practice activities. With those common features in evidence, social work can then most effectively differentiate itself from the other helping professions and stake its claim to professional turf.

For CSWE, such data can be most useful in formulating the foundation requirements in the Curriculum Policy Statement. Identifying the elements common to all forms of social work practice, irrespective of setting and practice area, is essential to designing a core curriculum required of all those who become professional practitioners.

Answering the question "How are we different?" will help human service organizations select the most appropriately prepared workers for the positions they have available. Information about the unique features of particular jobs can also aid agencies in developing meaningful job descriptions, promoting workers with the most appropriate educational and job preparation, and planning in-service training to supplement the competencies of variously prepared workers.

For social work educational programs, a clear recognition of any differences in practice activities among the subgroups of social workers is necessary to establish concentrations intended to prepare graduates for specialized practice.

Although the studies described in this book were not originally designed to provide definitive answers to these two questions, they have generated a comprehensive data set that can be brought to bear on the deliberations. As noted in Chapter 1, these data corroborate, at several levels of abstraction, most of the generally accepted conceptions of social work. Therefore, they have the power to clarify and validate our understanding of social work as a profession; they do not, for the most part, demand radically new conceptualizations or practice models.

In this chapter, baccalaureate-level social workers are compared to those practicing with the master's degree. To our knowledge, this is the first time a direct comparison, using a common empirical framework, has been made.

Differences in Worker Characteristics

Gender

The demographic data generated by the national studies highlighted several characteristics on which these two groups of social workers differed significantly. (As in previous chapters, differences between the two groups are not discussed unless they are statistically significant [$p < .05$] as well as practically significant.) Although females were predominant in both groups, they were substantially more prevalent among the BSW practitioners where 90.8% were female, as opposed to 60.4% of the MSW workers.

Age and Experience

The BSW workers were also considerably younger, with an average age of 33.4 years as compared to 43.8 years for the MSWs. Data derived from the BSW screening cards revealed a fair amount of attrition of BSW graduates from the work force.[1] First, 15.7% of the BSW graduates had never worked as social workers; another 16.9% had

---

[1] The screening cards, mentioned as part of the BSW sampling procedure in Appendix B, were used to separate BSW graduates who had entered the labor force as practitioners from those who had not.

worked in the field and then elected to leave it. At the time of the screening, another 29.0% had entered MSW programs and were therefore not included in the BSW study. Taken as a group, five years after graduation, only 38.4% of the 5,228 respondents to the screening cards remained in the work force as baccalaureate-level practitioners. Given that rate of attrition, it is not surprising that the BSW practitioners were not only younger but, on average, had much less job professional experience—5.3 years as compared to 13.7 years for the MSWs.

Geographic Location

In the South and Northeast, the proportions of BSWs and MSWs were almost equal. However, BSWs were much more heavily concentrated in the Northcentral region (38.8% compared to 28.7% of the MSWs), where there are a relative abundance of undergraduate social work programs. In the West, where there has been mixed acceptance of bachelor's-level social work education both as a valid job credential and as eligibility for advanced standing in MSW programs, there were relatively fewer BSW social workers—10.4% compared to 16.2% of the MSW practitioners.

Ethnicity

The racial or ethnic backgrounds of the two groups of social workers were quite similar. White social workers predominated in each group, comprising 87.4% of the BSWs and 88.7% of the MSWs. The proportion of African-American social workers was also almost equal—7.3% of the BSWs and 7.1% of the MSWs. Only small differences between the two groups were found for respondents of other ethnic or racial origins.

Employment Settings

As Table 4.1 reveals, there were considerable differences in the two groups across employment settings.[2] These data, when combined with the data on job function (discussed below), suggest that BSWs and MSWs perform somewhat different jobs. The MSWs dominated the jobs in specialized settings such as mental health clinics, hospitals, schools, colleges and universities, and private practice. The BSWs, on the other hand, were much more likely to be employed in nursing

---

[2]This and subsequent tables place the percentages of BSWs in descending order to allow readers to readily compare the two groups.

homes, group homes, and the many public and private social service agencies that addressed a wide variety of client needs. The only major setting that had a somewhat balanced number of MSWs and BSWs was the psychiatric hospital.

Job Function

The data also suggest that the MSWs, as a group, had considerably more latitude with respect to job choice. The screening card data (see Appendix B, p. 171) indicated that more than 90% of the BSWs who entered the work force started as direct service practitioners, and only 10% subsequently moved into other types of jobs. Although comparable MSW data regarding entry-level jobs were not available, the data in Table 4.2 show that MSWs were much more likely than the BSWs to have something other than direct practice as their primary job function. In particular, more than one in four MSWs had administrative or management responsibilities in the human service organizations where they were employed. This information underscores the point made in Chapter 3 that the MSW degree is the gateway credential into management in the social work profession.

Table 4.1. **Distribution of BSWs and MSWs**
by Employment Setting

Employment Setting	Percent BSWs	Percent MSWs
Social service agency	46.4%	26.7%
Hospital	13.7%	21.4%
Nursing home/hospice	11.5%	1.0%
Outpatient clinic	8.7%	19.4%
Group home/residential care	6.3%	1.6%
Psychiatric institution	4.4%	3.7%
Court/criminal justice	2.8%	1.4%
Elementary/secondary school	2.1%	7.2%
Private practice	0.9%	7.9%
College or university	0.6%	4.8%

Table 4.2. **Distribution of BSWs and MSWs by Job Function**

Job Function	Percent BSWs	Percent MSWs
Direct service	80.9%	53.5%
Administration or management	8.2%	27.5%
Supervision	6.6%	10.2%
Education or training	2.1%	5.1%
Consultation	0.8%	2.1%
Policy/research/planning	0.6%	1.5%

Practice Area

With some notable exceptions, the data on primary practice area reflected more similarity between BSWs and MSWs than did the setting or job function data. As Table 4.3 indicates, the BSWs were considerably more likely than the MSWs to provide services to the aged and developmentally disabled. The biggest difference, however, was in the area of mental health services: only 9.9% of the BSW practitioners reported this as their primary practice area, compared to 28.3% of the MSWs. The MSWs were also considerably more likely to be engaged in school social work or some form of social work education than were the BSW practitioners. However, the two groups were quite similar in the percentages involved in the important practice areas of family services, medical and health care, and alcohol and substance abuse.

Summary analysis of these data suggests that baccalaureate- and master's-level social work education programs are preparing different groups of students for somewhat different jobs. Rather than working as a "junior level" MSW or competing directly with the MSW for the same job at a lesser salary, the BSW practitioner appears to have carved out a distinct niche in the human services. In contrast to graduate-level practice, baccalaureate-level practice involves almost exclusively direct service provision in less-specialized social service agencies and residential facilities such as nursing homes, group homes, and psychiatric institutions. In particular, BSWs are more likely than MSWs to provide direct services to children and youth, older people, and people with handicapping conditions. BSWs appear to be more involved than the MSWs in "caring for" practice areas.

Table 4.3. **Distribution of BSWs and MSWs by Primary Practice Area**

Primary Practice Area	Percent BSWs	Precent MSWs
Children and youth	18.8%	13.1%
Services to the aged	16.5%	3.7%
Family services	13.7%	13.7%
Medical and health care	12.8%	13.5%
Mental health	9.9%	28.3%
Develop. disabled/mentally retarded	9.6%	3.6%
Alcohol and substance abuse	3.2%	2.2%
Public assistance/public welfare	3.1%	1.5%
Corrections/criminal justice	2.7%	1.3%
School social work	1.4%	6.3%
Education	0.6%	3.4%
Community organization	0.5%	1.5%

Differences in Clients Served

Age

The BSW and MSW workers reported some variation in the ages of the clients they served. A greater proportion of BSWs than MSWs worked with children under the age of six; and BSWs were much more likely to work with people over age 60 (34.5% versus 21.6% of the MSWs)—a reflection of the fact that BSWs were much more likely to be found in nursing homes and hospices. MSWs, however, were a little more likely to work with children 6–12 years old and were much more likely to work with adult populations, ages 21–60 (65.5% versus 54.7% of the BSWs).

Ethnicity

There was little difference in the racial or ethnic background of those served by these two groups of workers. The exception was that the BSWs were more than twice as likely to be serving American Indian clients (6.6% versus 3.1% of the MSWs).

Gender

As a group, the MSW respondents estimated that males comprised just over half of their clientele/caseloads (51.0%) as compared to the BSW respondents, who estimated their clientele/caseloads at 42.6% male. This difference may be accounted for by the BSWs relatively higher involvement in service provision to older, and thus predominantly female, individuals.

Client Needs and Problems

Further supporting the conclusion that BSW and MSW workers perform different jobs was data on the client needs and problems each group addressed. The frequency pattern suggests that the MSWs were more likely than the BSWs to provide what are often called "clinical services," such as helping individuals with anxiety and depression, interpersonal relations, and family functioning. The BSWs tended to focus on services that were more concrete, such as health problems, substance abuse, financial assistance, and housing. Table 4.4 compares the two practice levels regarding the client needs and problems addressed.[3]

Table 4.4. Distribution of BSWs and MSWs by Client Needs/Problems

Client Needs/Problems	Percent BSWs	Percent MSWs
Family functioning difficulties	38.6%	45.1%
Health-related problems	26.8%	18.3%
Problems associated with aging	23.6%	10.2%
Character or behavior disorders	23.5%	24.6%
Mental illness or mental retardation	21.6%	26.7%
Alcohol or substance abuse	20.1%	14.8%
Interpersonal relations problems	18.2%	29.8%
Anxiety or depression	15.6%	30.9%
Financial assistance	14.9%	7.1%
Physical disabilities	11.8%	7.3%
Housing or shelter	10.5%	4.1%
Skill or knowledge development	10.5%	9.8%
School-related problems	8.4%	13.6%
Work or job performance	8.1%	12.4%
Law-related problems	6.4%	4.0%

These data indicate that social work practice, at both levels, was quite diversified. A social worker practicing at any level must be prepared to assist with a wide range of client needs. The BSW practitioners would have to possess some clinical skills to address family problems, social problems that arose in the context of providing health care, and some aspects of emotional health. In contrast to the MSWs, however, they seemed to require little in the way of advanced clinical skills. Instead, the BSWs appeared to need skills associated with assisting clients to handle health-related problems, handicapping conditions, financial need, and lack of adequate housing.

Job Activity Comparisons between BSW and MSW Direct Service Practitioners

These data clearly indicate that degree level was associated with differences in respondents' job functions, the client problems they addressed, and the clients they served. The BSW-level practitioners were found in a smaller range of jobs than their MSW counterparts—notably in fewer supervisory, managerial, or administrative positions. Most BSWs reported practicing in direct service positions; in contrast, only about half of the MSW-level practitioners reported such jobs.

---

[3] Readers are again reminded that respondents were asked to identify up to three needs that they most regularly addressed with their clientele. The percentages total to more than 100%, reflecting the proportion of practitioners who identified a need as one of the three most often dealt with in their practice.

Making direct comparisons between the job activities of BSW- and MSW-level practitioners who responded to the JAQ is much more meaningful when the respondents from the two groups have similar job responsibilities. Therefore, the authors aggregated data from the three national studies only for the direct service practitioners. This resulted in samples of 1,172 BSW-level and 2,819 MSW-level direct service practitioners who could be directly compared on their practice activities. These sample sizes yielded sufficient numbers of respondents in several subgroups based on employment setting and practice area to allow meaningful comparisons of their task, cluster, and factor scores, and to answer the overarching question: "Do BSWs engage in different practice activities than MSWs?"

Factor Scores

Looking at factor scores for the two groups—the most abstract level of comparison—shows that only one type of generalized practice activity, client situation change, was markedly different for the BSWs and MSWs. The BSWs were considerably more involved in activities aimed at helping clients address the situations that affected their social functioning than were the MSWs. As Figure 4.1 indicates, the mean factor score for this type of activity was 14.36 for the BSW respondents as compared to 12.90 for the MSWs. Two other factor scores were significantly different ($p < .05$) for BSWs and MSWs, but those differences were not considered to be large enough to be of practical significance in describing practice activities.

There was, of course, the possibility that the requirements of practice in different settings demanded different levels of activity from the practitioners at the two professional levels. The patterns of activity in the three settings where BSWs and MSWs are most likely to both be employed—social service agencies, hospitals, and outpatient clinics— were therefore compared. To do this, ANOVAs were run between the two groups for each of the three employment settings. The results for client-centered activities are depicted in Figure 4.2. In all three settings, the BSWs were more actively involved than the MSWs in efforts designed to change their clients' situations. No significant differences were found for BSWs and MSWs in activities directed toward client change.

In Figure 4.3, differences in the delivery-system factor scores for the BSWs and the MSWs in the three practice settings are displayed. Although statistically significant differences ($p < .05$) were found, they were neither consistent nor large enough to reflect real practice differences.

Four practice areas contained large enough samples of BSW and MSW respondents to make direct comparisons of mean factor scores possible. These areas were mental health, family services, medical and health care, and services to children and youth. As with the previous data, ANOVAs were run between the BSWs and MSWs for each of the four practice areas. The pattern that emerged for employment

Figure 4.1. Mean Factor Scores: BSW and MSW Direct Service Practitioners

JAQ Factors

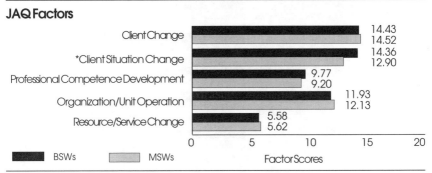

*Indicates a significant difference ($p<.05$) between the factor scores of the two groups of respondents.

Figure 4.2. Mean Factor Scores: Client-Centered Activities of BSW and MSW Direct Service Practitioners, by Setting

JAQ Factors

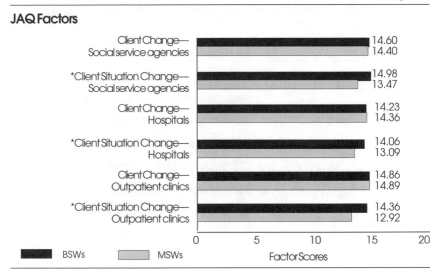

*Indicates a significant difference ($p<.05$) between the factor scores of the two groups of respondents.

settings was repeated here. (See Figure 4.4.) Although small differences were found in the client change factor scores for two areas, family services and services to children and youth, only the differ-

Fig. 4.3. **Mean Factor Scores: Delivery System-Centered Activities of BSW and MSW Direct Service Practitioners, by Setting**

JAQ Factors

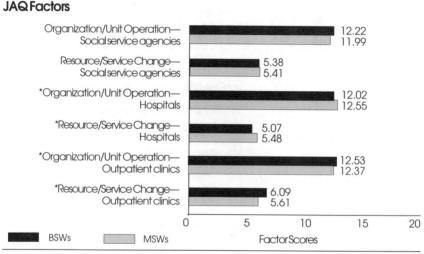

*Indicates a significant difference (p<.05) between the factor scores of the two groups of respondents.

Figure 4.4. **Mean Factor Scores: Client-Centered Activities of BSW and MSW Direct Service Practitioners, by Practice Area**

JAQ Factors

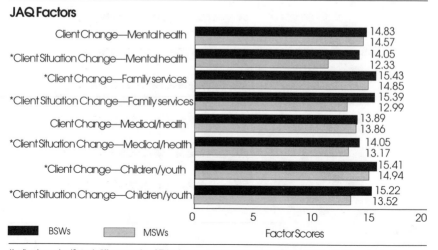

*Indicates a significant difference (p<.05) between the factor scores of the two groups of respondents.

ences in factors scores for client situation change were consistently large across all practice areas. In each of the four practice areas, BSWs substantially exceeded the MSWs in their reported efforts to address clients' problematic situations.

These analyses were also carried out for the two system-centered factor scores. The results, depicted in Figure 4.5, indicate some differences of statistical significance, but none large enough to have clear implications for developing curricula based on job activities. Reinforced again is the finding that, regardless of education level, practice area, and employment setting, relatively little worker effort was directed toward changing service systems and resources.

At the factor level of description, then, these data suggest that social workers perform in remarkably similar patterns regardless of setting or practice area. The one substantial difference between BSWs and MSWs that emerges from these data is the greater likelihood that the BSW-level workers provide services to help clients change their situations. An examination of the "core" tasks performed by the two groups of workers suggests that this difference was due to the greater emphasis among the BSWs on tasks contained in the clusters Risk Assessment/Transition and Service Connection.

Figure 4.5. **Delivery System Factor : BSW /MSW Direct Service**

JAQ Factors

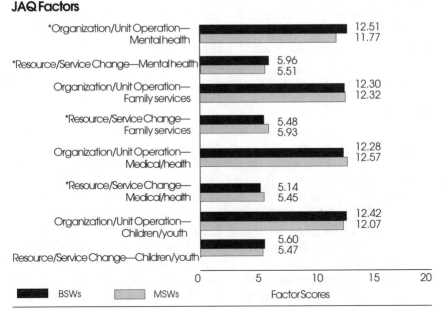

*Indicates a significant difference (*p*<.05) between the factor scores of the two groups of respondents.

Cluster Scores

For the initial comparison, differences between the mean cluster scores of BSW and MSW direct service workers were analyzed. These are depicted in Figure 4.6. Because of the large sample sizes in each group (1,172 and 2,819 respectively), all of the cluster scores differences were significant ($p < .05$). However, only three clusters—Group Work, Individual/Family Treatment, and Service Connection—had scores that were different enough to affect the frequency rating by one level (e.g., from "occasionally" to "frequently"). These data again confirm the notion that the MSWs were more "clinical" in their approach to practice than were BSWs, that is, they typically used more formal therapeutic models and techniques in both individual, family, and group treatment. On the other hand, the BSWs were more frequently involved in activities designed to connect people with services. These data, then, suggest that master's-level social work programs should equip students specializing in direct practice with the knowledge and skills required to conduct advanced clinical practice with individuals, families, and groups.

At the other end of the practice activity scale, it is evident from Figure 4.6 that neither the BSW nor MSW direct service practitioners were involved to any significant degree in activities related to the Staff Deployment, Staff Supervision, Organizational Maintenance, and Program Development clusters; or to the system-change oriented clusters of Research/Policy Development and Instruction. The work of both BSWs and MSWs was clearly focused on their clients. The moderate amount of BSW and MSW activity concerned with the indirect service clusters of Delivery System Knowledge Development, Staff Information Exchange, and Dispute Resolution would all appear to be directed at providing more effective services to clients, as opposed to improving the delivery system.

When the cluster data for the direct service workers was analyzed by employment setting and primary practice area, the results reaffirmed the patterns seen in the factor scores. Figures 4.7a and 4.7b show the pattern of means for the direct service clusters (Clusters 1-8) for these workers in three employment settings: social service agencies, hospitals, and outpatient clinics. Using the criterion that a mean difference must be large enough to change the frequency rating by one level, the authors found that, regardless of setting, MSW practitioners frequently carried out Individual/Family Treatment whereas the BSWs only occasionally performed these tasks. Activities associated with the Protective Services cluster were carried out almost exclusively in social service agencies, and then were carried out only occasionally by the BSWs. Activities associated with Service Connection and Tangible Services were also more likely to be performed by the BSWs than the MSWs. Not portrayed in Figures 4.7a and 4.7b is Cluster 9, Professional Development, where the scores in all three settings were similar for BSW and MSW workers.

The same analysis was carried out for the indirect service clusters (Clusters 10–18). The results are depicted in Figures 4.8a and 4.8b. As can be seen, both BSW and MSW direct service workers were, on

***Figure 4.6.* Mean Cluster Scores: BSW and MSW Direct Service Practitioners**

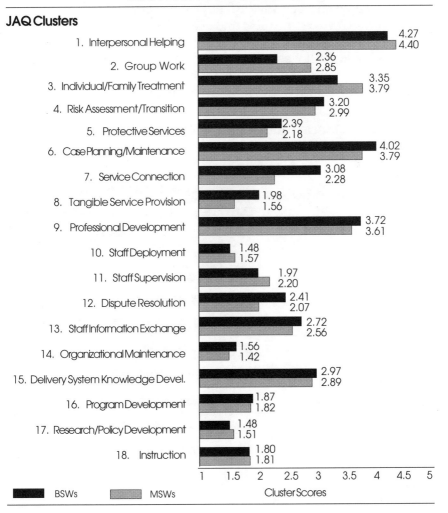

JAQ Clusters

	BSWs	MSWs
1. Interpersonal Helping	4.27	4.40
2. Group Work	2.36	2.85
3. Individual/Family Treatment	3.35	3.79
4. Risk Assessment/Transition	3.20	2.99
5. Protective Services	2.39	2.18
6. Case Planning/Maintenance	4.02	3.79
7. Service Connection	3.08	2.28
8. Tangible Service Provision	1.98	1.56
9. Professional Development	3.72	3.61
10. Staff Deployment	1.48	1.57
11. Staff Supervision	1.97	2.20
12. Dispute Resolution	2.41	2.07
13. Staff Information Exchange	2.72	2.56
14. Organizational Maintenance	1.56	1.42
15. Delivery System Knowledge Devel.	2.97	2.89
16. Program Development	1.87	1.82
17. Research/Policy Development	1.48	1.51
18. Instruction	1.80	1.81

Cluster Scores

average, involved with these indirect service activities only occasionally. For two clusters, however, the differences between BSWs and MSWs merit mention. First, the MSW-level direct service practitioners were more likely than their BSW counterparts to assume some supervisory responsibilities regardless of the setting in which they worked. Conversely, in all settings the BSWs were more likely than the MSWs to be engaged in Dispute Resolution. This was due to higher involvement in activities related to resolving disputes between clients and agencies and to involvement in interdisciplinary work groups. Other than these, the differences from setting to setting and degree level to degree level were small among the direct service workers.

Analyses of the cluster score differences between BSW and MSW direct service practitioners in the four primary practice areas (mental health, family services, medical and health care, and services to children and youth) revealed a pattern similar to that found in the employment setting data.[4] It was evident that in all four practice areas, and particularly in mental health and family services, the MSW respondents were more involved with formal treatment models than were the

---

Figure 4.7a. **Mean Cluster Scores for Direct Service Clusters 1–4: BSW and MSW Direct Service Practitioners, by Setting**

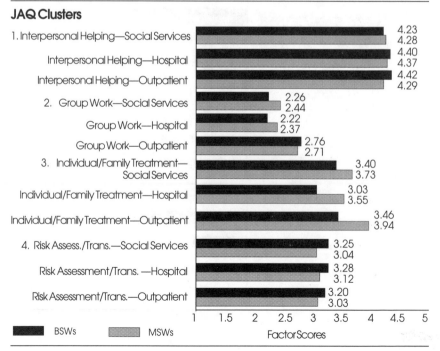

Figure 4.7b. **Mean Cluster Scores for Direct Service Clusters 5–8: BSW and MSW Direct Service Practitioners, by Setting**

JAQ Clusters

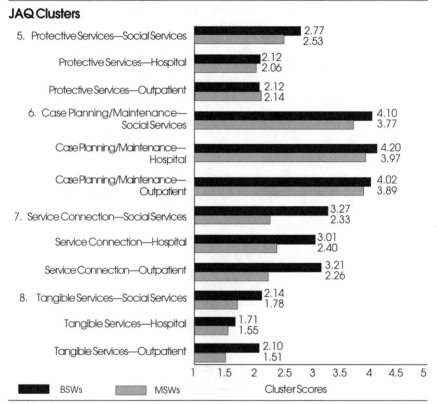

5. Protective Services—Social Services — 2.77 / 2.53

   Protective Services—Hospital — 2.12 / 2.06

   Protective Services—Outpatient — 2.12 / 2.14

6. Case Planning/Maintenance—Social Services — 4.10 / 3.77

   Case Planning/Maintenance—Hospital — 4.20 / 3.97

   Case Planning/Maintenance—Outpatient — 4.02 / 3.89

7. Service Connection—Social Services — 3.27 / 2.33

   Service Connection—Hospital — 3.01 / 2.40

   Service Connection—Outpatient — 3.21 / 2.26

8. Tangible Services—Social Services — 2.14 / 1.78

   Tangible Services—Hospital — 1.71 / 1.55

   Tangible Services—Outpatient — 2.10 / 1.51

■ BSWs   ▨ MSWs   Cluster Scores

BSWs. The data also indicate that practice in hospitals involved much less formal treatment activity with individuals, families, and groups than did practice concerned with mental health, family services, and services to children and youth. As we saw earlier, the BSWs engaged in considerably more protective service activities for children, youth, and families. Also, the BSWs were more likely to make connections with other services and providers, deliver tangible services, and to be involved in dispute resolution. The MSWs, however, were more likely to be involved in staff supervision, regardless of practice area.

The cluster scores and task data allow identification of some important variations within subgroups of direct service practitioners that

---

[4]With a combination of 18 clusters, four primary areas, and two degree levels, the figure would have contained too much information to present in this document. Therefore, we present only a textual analysis.

should be considered in curriculum development. Specifically, educators and curriculum designers should take into account that MSW practitioners reported more formal treatment-orientation and supervisory activities, and BSWs reported more activities related to linkage, tangible service provision, and dispute resolution.

Similarities in Practice Activities, The Generic "Core"

To date, the generally accepted definitions of social work have relied on somewhat abstract statements on the basic purposes and beliefs that characterize the profession. However, as Chapter 1 sets forth clearly, the calls for more precise descriptions of social work practice have persisted. Perhaps one reason the existing definitions have not been fully embraced is that, although a certain level of identification

Figure 4.8a. **Mean Cluster Scores for Indirect Service Clusters 10–14: BSW and MSW Direct Service Practitioners, by Setting**

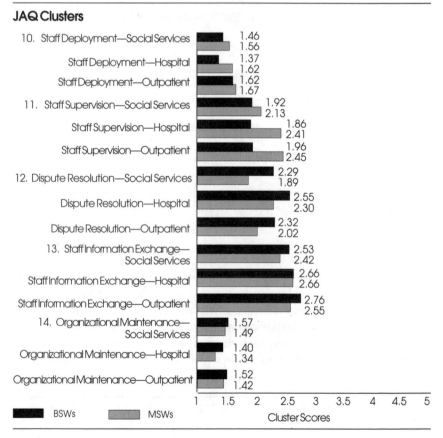

JAQ Clusters

10. Staff Deployment—Social Services: 1.46 / 1.56
Staff Deployment—Hospital: 1.37 / 1.62
Staff Deployment—Outpatient: 1.62 / 1.67
11. Staff Supervision—Social Services: 1.92 / 2.13
Staff Supervision—Hospital: 1.86 / 2.41
Staff Supervision—Outpatient: 1.96 / 2.45
12. Dispute Resolution—Social Services: 2.29 / 1.89
Dispute Resolution—Hospital: 2.55 / 2.30
Dispute Resolution—Outpatient: 2.32 / 2.02
13. Staff Information Exchange—Social Services: 2.53 / 2.42
Staff Information Exchange—Hospital: 2.66 / 2.66
Staff Information Exchange—Outpatient: 2.76 / 2.55
14. Organizational Maintenance—Social Services: 1.57 / 1.49
Organizational Maintenance—Hospital: 1.40 / 1.34
Organizational Maintenance—Outpatient: 1.52 / 1.42

1   1.5   2   2.5   3   3.5   4   4.5   5

■ BSWs   ▨ MSWs   Cluster Scores

with a common mission and values is important, some common activities must also be identified for the wide range of practitioners that comprises the profession. Unless this happens, there is little to bind the profession into a unified group. Many professional groups share a similar ideology with social workers; in fact, ideological overlap can be found among professionals in almost any multi-disciplinary setting, which suggests that at least some aspects of their missions are similar. It is not surprising, therefore, that definitions that do not specify common *practice activities* have been judged inadequate or incomplete.

What practice activities, then, do social workers have in common? The composite data from the three national studies provide a large-scale profile of social work practice. Merging the results from all respondents, however, means that the larger subgroups of social workers (e.g., direct service practitioners) skew mean scores for the total, per-

---

Figure 4.8b. **Mean Cluster Scores for Indirect Service Clusters 15–18: BSW and MSW Direct Service Practitioners, by Setting**

JAQ Clusters

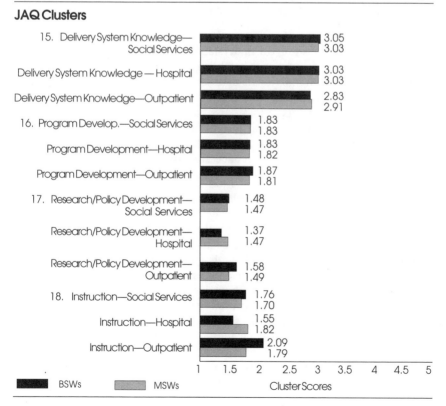

	BSWs		MSWs

Cluster Scores

haps masking the presence of activities peculiar to the smaller subgroups. To search for tasks that were common to all of social work practice, the "core" tasks—those that were performed by at least 50% of the social workers in any subgroup—were examined. A task that was a core task for three of the four largest subgroups (BSW direct practitioners, MSW direct practitioners, MSW supervisors, and MSW administrators/managers) was deemed a "generic" social work task.

Analysis of these data yield 17 generic tasks of the 131 tasks on the JAQ. Six were "core" tasks for all four subgroups and 11 were "core" for three of the four subgroups. Sixteen of these 17 generic tasks were located in just three clusters of practice activity: Interpersonal Helping, Case Planning/Maintenance, and Professional Development. The other was from the Delivery System Knowledge Development cluster.

Through the use of this method of "generic" or common task identification, it is possible to conclude that the following tasks represent the activities that cut across all worker levels, employment settings, and practice areas of social work. (The number in parentheses to the left of each task description below represents the total of the four subgroups in which the task was a core activity.)

Interpersonal Helping
(4) Express and demonstrate an understanding of people's points of view, feelings, and needs in order to establish open and trusting relationships.
(3) Discuss options with individuals in order to help them understand choices and/or resolve a particular problem.
(3) Encourage and help people to discuss their points of view, feelings, and needs in order to increase their insight into the reasons for their actions.
(3) Talk with individuals and/or their relatives about problems in order to reassure, provide support, or reduce anxiety.

Case Planning/Maintenance
(4) Discuss proposed actions with individuals in order to provide full information and ensure understanding.
(3) Analyze case background and consult with appropriate individuals in order to arrive at a plan for services and/or financial help.
(3) Review case records and consult with appropriate individuals in order to evaluate progress and alter service plans if needed.
(3) Record or dictate information about individuals, using either prepared forms or narrative, in order to establish or update records, document services provided, or terminate services.
(3) Review files and records of an individual prior to a contact with that person in order to become familiar with the details of the situation.
(3) Exchange information about case details with supervisor and/or colleagues in order to get guidance in dealing with an individual or group.

(3) Coordinate service planning with staff, other providers, family members, or significant others in order to make the delivery of services to individuals or groups most effective.

Professional Development
(4) Evaluate your actions and decisions in order to determine if your professional activities are meeting the standards, values, and ethics required for quality.
(4) Review your workload (appointments, visits, mail, etc.) in order to plan your activities and set priorities for a given period.
(4) Take part in discussions with co-workers, talking over events or problem situations, in order to share experiences of gain insights.
(4) Give information to people, by phone or in person, in order to explain and interpret the programs, policies, or procedures of your organization.
(3) Read articles in professional/scientific journals, newspapers, or magazines in order to keep up with developments related to your job responsibilities.

Delivery System Knowledge Development
(3) Read administrative literature (for example, manuals, memos, circulars) in order to keep up with organizational policies and procedures.

Examination of these 17 generic tasks suggests three content areas for practice education. *First*, all social workers must possess basic problem-solving skills. They must know how to interview and provide basic counseling—whether to clients, supervisees, or agency staff. These are not the highly specific practice approaches typically taught in clinical practice, supervision, or administration courses, but rather the fundamental helping skills of relationship building, contracting, counseling, etc. *Second*, all social workers must manage their workloads and plan their practice activities. They must be prepared to do recording and other paperwork, consult with colleagues, and approach their practice strategically. *Third*, they must be vigilant about the quality of their practice. They must know how to accurately evaluate their work, study the literature, collaborate with co-workers, and interpret their agency's programs and procedures to maximize their practice effectiveness. In the nomenclature of social work education, these are the "foundation practice skills" that students should master as part of their classroom and field instruction experiences.

Summary of Findings

Since the baccalaureate level of social work practice was reintroduced in 1970, social work has sought to differentiate between the two levels while recognizing the central features that are common to all of social work. Historically, isolating those characteristics has proven difficult.

This study, however, has yielded much useful information on this issue. Additionally, the comparisons made possible by the data provide valuable information for those who develop both job descriptions and program curricula.

Job function is clearly the most important factor that shapes the work of social workers. Although there is some overlap, the tasks performed by those in the two largest job functions, direct service work and management/administration, were distinctly different. Supervisors were the only subgroup of practitioners that maintained a balance between the direct and indirect service activities (although their direct service activities were often focused on supervisees rather than clients).

These data indicate that access to a range of job functions is strongly related to one's level of professional education. MSWs exhibited a much broader spectrum of positions than BSWs, including direct service provision, administration, supervision, education, policy development, and consultation. Occasionally BSWs evolved into other job functions, but virtually all began as direct service workers and most remained in that capacity.

Some employment settings and practice areas tended to be the purview of primarily BSW- or MSW-level practitioners. MSWs tended to be found in mental health clinics, private practice, school social work, and social work education. BSWs tended to be found in public social services and the smaller local agencies, nursing homes, and residential care facilities. The BSWs tended to deal with the more tangible needs of clients, while the MSWs were more likely to address their personal issues. Overall, there appeared to be little overlap between the two professional practice levels.

In direct service practice, the job function where there were significant proportions of both BSW- and MSW-level practitioners, the data revealed remarkably similar activity. (Readers are again cautioned that the data do not provide information regarding practice approaches or practice outcomes; they do show, however, consistent patterns of practice activities that cut across educational level, employment setting, and practice area.) The differences that consistently emerged among the BSW and MSW direct service workers suggested that the BSWs tended to engage in activities that can be characterized as case management responsibilities. The MSWs, by contrast, were more clinically or treatment oriented and had more supervisory responsibilities.

Regardless of job position, educational level, employment setting, or practice area, some activities appear to be common to all social work practice. Further, the overwhelming evidence from these data is that social workers in similar positions perform similar functions. Therefore, in addition to the central purposes, beliefs, and values that have been central to the profession's attempts to define itself, there are common practice activities that clarify and bind together the array of professional roles played by professional social workers, that allow us to view social work as a single profession.

Finally, one activity was lacking among virtually all the social workers who responded to the JAQ. With the possible exception of administrators and managers (see Chapter 3), no subgroup of social workers was more than nominally involved in social service delivery system change activities. Social work's historic claim has been that its uniqueness among the helping professions is its simultaneous attention to both person and environment. An NASW definition of social work, for example, indicates that "social work is the professional activity of helping individuals, groups, or communities enhance or restore their capacity for social functioning and creating societal conditions favorable to that goal" (Barker, 1995). However, these analyses indicate that direct service workers neither engaged in helping communities enhance or restore their capacity nor creating societal conditions favorable to the goal of positive social functioning for people. Prevention, social policy development, and even community education efforts appeared to be virtually nonexistent.

Should social work education programs adjust their curricula to better prepare their graduates to assume practice roles for changing the larger environment? Or, should preparation for these tasks be removed entirely from the curricula for direct service practice in favor of more emphasis on those activities that are actually *used* in practice? To what degree should the schools lead or follow practice? These are questions that the data cannot answer. The answers, however, are crucial to the future of the profession and to the means by which social work education fulfills its mission of preparing effective practitioners.

References

Robert L. Barker, *The Social Work Dictionary*, 3rd ed. Washington, DC: NASW Press, 1995.

5

Implications for Social Work Education and Planning

T hroughout the life of the National Social Work Job Analysis Study, the authors have tried to refrain from inserting their own biases into this analysis of social work practice. Teams of social work educators and practitioners participated in the selection of content to be included in the Job Analysis Questionnaire; statistical analyses were used to group the tasks into the clusters and factors that created the depiction of social work practice; practitioners assisted in formulating the descriptions and titles of the clusters; and the presentation of the findings has been characterized by an effort to present, rather than interpret, these data. The data most relevant for social work education have been presented in previous chapters; it is now possible to turn attention to the implications the data hold for social work education.

Several prominent social work educators were invited to assist in the interpretation in an effort to introduce or amplify implications of the findings for social work education. In his forward to this volume, William Reid pointed to the need to reexamine our generally accepted concept of social work in light of these data. The commentators in this chapter reflect on several ongoing concerns in social work education, such as the similarities and differences in baccalaureate and master's level practice, evidence of the presence of a continuum between these two levels, the need to reconsider the structure of BSW and MSW education, the congruence between social work practice and CSWE's Accreditation Standards and Curriculum Policy Statement, and the congruence of our generalist and specialized practice conceptions with the realities of social work practice. Indeed, these commentators offer considerable food for thought for the profession as a whole, and especially its educational arm. It is hoped that this material will initiate a healthy dialogue.

Those selected for presenting commentary have established records as social work educators, administrators, and authors. Their past or current positions include baccalaureate program directors, deans or directors of master's programs, director of a doctoral program, staff and volunteer members of CSWE's Educational Planning Commission and Commission on Accreditation; one has even served as CSWE's Executive Director. Each was asked to respond to information included in the previous chapters from his or her vantage point.

Readers should also note the commentaries included with Appendices B and C, in which prominent social work educators evaluate and discuss the survey and the data analysis procedures.

Using Practice Data to Inform Curriculum Design

Invited Commentary
by
Charles Guzzetta
Hunter College

The analysis of social work practice reported herein forces social work educators to address a dilemma that social work and, in fact, all of professional education has comfortably ignored for years. This dilemma can be expressed in the form of a question: Should we base our curricula on what we believe ought to be (i.e., our beliefs and values) or on what *is* (i.e., our knowledge of the facts)? Until now, it has not been necessary for social work educators to consider that question seriously because we have not had a sufficiently complete and objective database on current social work practice—a database that would allow us the option of basing our curricula on a sound foundation of knowledge. However, Teare and Sheafor have provided us with an attractive option, if we elect to use it, to inform curriculum design.

Social work education has traditionally operated from the assumption that curriculum design is an exacting and demanding enterprise. Actually, it is the easiest task in education. Anyone can do it and, in fact, everyone who teaches does, in one way or another. When problems arise, they usually involve disagreements about what the design is intended to accomplish and why. There is rarely a debate over the question of using data in curriculum design; without some sort of data there can be no curriculum. The conflicts invariably arise over decisions about which data should be used, in what ways, and to what ends.

In academic disciplines, battles are regularly waged over the selection and interpretation of data that are used to develop curricula. Astronomers quibble over black holes and massless matter; sociologists challenge the accuracy and meaning of census figures; anthropologists build or ruin reputations with a few bones. Data in the academic disciplines are largely a matter of general agreement; the devil is in the details. Needed intellectual and applied skills form a reasonably consistent cluster of activities peculiar to each discipline. The major arena of battle is in scholarly interpretation of the data.

Yet, compared to professional education, academic disciplines are wrapped in a warm blanket of sweet accord. The traditional professions (i.e., medicine, law) have a fairly consistent perspective on curriculum, and agreement over data may be even more consensual than in the academic disciplines. However, in professional education, it is the skills component that rises in importance. Heroic professionals of the public imagination are not admired as intellectuals, but as artful practitioners of their craft. In educating for the traditional professions, then, the greatest controversy lies in selecting which skills and techniques should be taught and which methods work best to teach them.

And then there's social work. In social work education, all curricula are required to address the challenge of imparting knowledge or information (teaching about), developing skills (teaching how), and communicating values (teaching why). It is further required that the curriculum rest on a liberal arts "base" or "perspective," a concept so vague that the profession's Curriculum Policy Statement leaves determination of it "to the judgment of the faculty of each social work program" (CSWE, 1992, p. 138).

Curriculum development in social work is further complicated by the fact that the field did not grow from a single tap root but from the dual traditions of direct service and social reform. The culture of the profession maintains the assumption that education for social work should include the information, skills, and values that will prepare students to be competent in *both* social service and social change.

The findings reported in this book result from a different assumption: that social work curricula should be examined in terms of their consistency with what social workers actually do in their workaday jobs, not just with what educators believe they *ought* to be doing. Amazingly, before the studies reported here, no one really knew with any degree of specificity or reliability what practitioners did. The data they provide should profoundly influence how the social work profession thinks about its programs of education.

A few cautions should be sounded, however, to those who seek to draw definitive conclusions from Teare and Sheafor's exhaustive and impressive analyses. For example, women represent 91% of the BSW graduates and 60% of the MSW graduates in their sample. The actual gender balance is probably somewhat different today. The field always has been predominantly female, and the percentage of women has grown steadily in recent years. In 1989, 85.2% of the BSW graduates were women. By 1993, it was 86.4%. Women graduates of MSW programs increased from 81.6% in 1989 to 83.1% in 1993 (Lennon, 1993). Since the study does not demonstrate differences in the sorts of work done by male and female social workers, certain curriculum questions become obvious. For example, should the field give significant attention to the job tasks that will be performed primarily by men, whose membership in the field is less than 20% and declining? Or should there be a curriculum revision to prepare women to do the work now performed by men? Or is gender irrelevant to this issue? This is a rather simple example of a problem encountered in applying data to curriculum design. The function of developing curriculum in social work is driven not only by information but by intent. Curriculum development is at least as political as it is technical.

Although Teare and Sheafor's research provides important, previously unavailable, objective data to curriculum designers, the inferences drawn from those data will be less objective. In social work, curriculum designers always face the demands of finding a balance between what is, what will be, and what ought to be. While professional education has an obligation to prepare its graduates with relevant competencies for today's practice, it must also provide students with a foundation for the practice needs of tomorrow.

Because it is the responsibility of social work educators to prepare students for competent practice in today's society, it is essential to know what practitioners are *actually* doing right now. However, curriculum designers must also take into account that social work practice does not remain static for long. Practice inevitably is influenced by natural changes, such as the appearance of AIDS and the dramatic extension of life for the elderly; by social changes, such as homelessness, shifting immigration patterns, and the sharp increase in single-parent families; and by ideological changes, such as the demand for welfare reform and national health coverage. Furthermore, the various problems seem increasingly to interact with one another, adding to their complexity. Teare and Sheafor have provided the first sound portrait of the profession at work, but because of the rapid changes in social problems and ideology, their studies will require regular updates.

Choosing between Beliefs and Information

The heart, or major control mechanism, in curriculum design is the interaction between belief and information, or ideology and data, in determining what is "right" and what is "true" for teaching. The balance is constantly shifting, with one side or the other predominating at any given moment. Historically, however, the balance has almost always favored belief over information: data that supported the dominant belief system was held to be "true" and data that did not was viewed as "false." In the act of truth-testing, ideology has had more influence than data. One of the more familiar examples is taken from medieval scholasticism, in the debate over how many teeth a horse has. The successful debater demonstrated mastery of prevailing ideology and skill in formal logic; empirical data were deemed irrelevant in discussing the question and arriving at the truth.

Many academics are ambivalent in addressing the dilemma of belief versus information. This is true even in the "hard sciences," where the accumulation of data has not led to continual, open inquiry, but rather to a succession of scientific orthodoxies. The struggle to increase the influence of data over belief was a kind of guerrilla warfare for centuries, and it broke into an open assault in the 1800s. Accumulating data made many beliefs more and more difficult to sustain, until major changes in ideological systems were required. In science, Kuhn (1970) called this phenomenon a "paradigm shift": that is, the point at which the weight of data that cannot be explained by accepted beliefs forces change in the beliefs or systems of explanation and proof. Drawing a parallel with the professions is risky—Kuhn warned against easy applications to the social sciences—but allusions to Kuhn's thesis nevertheless abound in social work literature.

Both major branches of social work grew out of distinct ideologies. Reform or social change are obvious attempts to make society reflect a model of rightness or goodness. Decisions about service provision are less obviously, but no less significantly, influenced by ideology. Indeed, the movement that sought to replace moral belief with systematic and impersonal use of data in service provision was known as "scientific philanthropy" or "scientific charity." (See discussions in Trattner, 1984; Axinn & Levin, 1975; Handel, 1982.)

In some respects, Mary Richmond (1917) was the Darwin of social work, arguing for social work practice based on objective observations, systematic collection of data, and consistent application of data to policy and provision decisions. It is probably no accident that the author of *Social Diagnosis* had been the first forceful advocate, 20 years earlier, of university education for social workers (Richmond, 1897). It may be a reasonable explanation for her advocacy, but it certainly is an irony that she had not herself been a beneficiary of the enlightenment available from universities of her time.

In the belief-data oscillation, the hard sciences appear to have resolved their ambivalence in favor of empirical data, at least for now. In social work, the ambivalence has never ended, but ideology remains paramount. One of the more dramatic instances in which belief overwhelmed knowledge, to social work's disadvantage, was in Eastern Europe between the end of World War II and the fall of communism. Social work simply disappeared as a professional endeavor because the problems with which it dealt were contrary to the official orthodoxy in those countries and, therefore, were not acknowledged. The actual existence of social problems in communist societies was no more relevant to official reality than the actual number of teeth in a horse's mouth were to the reality of medieval scholasticism.

Although the lines have not been so ideologically clear in American social work, the requirements of the Curriculum Policy Statement demonstrate the profession's tendency to yield to belief over data in curriculum design. Selected populations, lifestyle preferences, and value orientations comprise the menu of mandated instruction, and data are expected to fit this curriculum menu, not to modify it. Certain groups are "officially" oppressed, and data about them are expected to demonstrate this alleged oppression within the context of this accepted ideology, irrespective of contrary information. Similarly, programs are obliged to prepare students for work that official orthodoxy requires graduates to do but which, as shown by Teare and Sheafor's data, they do not appear to be doing. Because data are now available to show what social workers *are* doing in their practice, a need for curriculum revision may be indicated, but whether it will come and the form it will take is certainly not assured. The fact that the authors found their massive sample of social workers engaged almost exclusively in client change and client situation change, but not in resource or system change, would suggest the need for serious realignment. However, these data cannot point to the direction of the change needed; that is dictated by belief.

To illustrate: All programs are obliged to prepare students "to promote social change and to implement a wide range of interventions that further . . . social and economic justice" (CPS, 1992, p. 140). Because the Teare and Sheafor data show that few practitioners reported engaging in that sort of work, one might conclude that the requirement should be dropped from the curriculum. Or, one might conclude that the curriculum should be strengthened in that area. Or, one might conclude that the reporting practitioners were actually engaged in promoting social change but did not recognize it as such. Ultimately, the direction of any change based on these new data will not be specifically designated by these data, which can only point out the discrepancies between social work education and practice. The revisions will be driven by belief.

Possible Influences of Data on Curriculum Design

The potential influence of data on curriculum design arises whenever new empirical data demonstrate the conflict between what social workers are educated to do and what they actually do. Social work curriculum development, however, is so dominated by subjectivity that the debate over the nature of needed changes, regardless of the seriousness of need revealed by empirical data, may result in little or no change. Locked in ideological combat, curriculum designers usually find it easier to stay with the familiar. Thus, the influence of data on curriculum design usually takes the form of noting potential for change, not indicating the substance of the change. All too often, data are merely interpreted to support an established ideology, a danger against which Vigilante (1974) warned with his rhetorical question: "Is proof truth?"

The influence of data on curriculum design is also felt when data show that areas in which social work is active are undergoing fundamental change, or that new areas of activity are emerging. In such cases, the data may document change in either knowledge or belief. For example, Teare and Sheafor found that MSW practitioners were heavily engaged in work with "psychological dysfunctions," as they seem to have been doing at least since the 1920s. But 70 years ago, "psychological dysfunction" had a meaning rather different from today's. Homosexuality, for example, was a deviance to be "treated" through the "casework service" arm of the field; today, it is a gender orientation to be protected through the field's "social action" arm. Unlike some changes, this shift did not result from any new empirical data about homosexuality; it was a consequence of new social attitudes. Gay and lesbian curriculum content changed because of political action, and moved within the social work curriculum, almost imperceptibly, from direct practice to social policy.

Finally, new objective information may have no impact on curriculum design because professional beliefs do not change to accommodate it. Kramer (1981) conducted empirical studies for more than ten years in three countries, examining aspects of the private and the public sectors of social services. In a number of articles and a noteworthy book, he refuted a several common beliefs about the relationship between public and private services. Contrary to conventional wisdom, he found that the private sector tended to be more conservative in making service innovations than the public sector. In fact, he found that the public sector often induced change in the more resistive private sector. No substantive attacks have ever challenged his methodology or his findings, yet there is no indication that these findings have influenced curriculum content or the literature on which it is based. Indeed, numerous authors have continued to present as valid the beliefs Kramer's research effectively demolished.

Curriculum design in social work remains captive to the current orthodoxies of influential special interest groups. Even data that indicate a need for reflection and revision may be used to maintain the status quo or to produce change in a variety of irrelevant directions. In this book, the authors have provided a sound, scholarly description of the field of social work practice as it currently exists and have sought to address the relation between the field's education and its practice. But their work is a diagnosis, not a prescription. They may even have succeeded in providing the first empirical evidence that the patient is very sick, as well as suggestions for further testing, but they have correctly stopped short of recommending a treatment.

In social work education, the treatment comes from struggles over preferences, beliefs, and subjective agendas rather than from an examination and analysis of data. It is a process that is more political than scientific, more personal than objective, more responsive to the demands of pressure groups than to principles of curriculum construction. The main hope that Teare and Sheafor can have is that further diagnostic evidence may have a salutary effect—before the patient dies.

Implications of the National Study for BSW Education

Invited Commentary
by
Leslie Leighninger
Louisiana State University

Brad Sheafor and Bob Teare have undertaken an impressive study that should illuminate our thinking about professional education for social work. They have accurately described their research as permitting "the construction of an empirically based depiction of the framework of social work practice, an analysis of its task activities, [and] a clearer understanding of how the division of labor is influenced by education and work setting." Their work is more comprehensive and more detailed than previous task analyses, which have concentrated on particular fields of practice or areas of the country (see, for example, Green, 1988; Kolevzon & Biggerstaff, 1983; Olsen & Holmes, 1982). Their use of both cluster and factor analysis provides a variety of ways to understand and interpret what social workers do. They have produced, in broad strokes, a picture of today's social workers in action.

The data from this study indicate that social work is a diverse profession, which nevertheless has a dominant job function (direct service to clients) and a core set of activities and skills. Most workers in the field are also involved to a high degree in organizational maintenance and professional development. Interestingly, despite the profession's stress on a dual commitment to social service and social change, the study does not find much evidence of engagement in social action activities. Finally, the research finds both similarities and differences in the work performed by BSW and MSW social workers.

Unanswered Questions

While the study provides detail about what social workers do on the job, limitations were placed on the scope of the study. Consequently, there are questions it does not answer. Some relate to quality; for example, how effectively do workers carry out their various job activities? Do MSW social workers generally offer a more successful version of individual and family treatment than do BSW practitioners, and vice versa for case management skills? Does the fact that social workers use generic skills across settings and with different client groups reflect the demands of the setting and the needs of the clients, or is it simply a matter of practitioners "plugging in" what they've learned, regardless of effectiveness? (The answer may well be a little of each.)

Another set of questions relates to worker potentials that cannot be captured through analysis of current activities. Are there skills that social workers possess that they are not in a position to use? For example, are BSW workers denied access to certain areas of practice and job functions in which they might be able to engage successfully? A broader issue is whether the depiction of present job activities of social workers constitutes a sufficient description of the profession and its potential.

There are further details about the nature of current jobs which would be helpful if known. Each cluster could be broken down into its component tasks to allow a closer inspection of what is involved. (For example, does individual treatment include a psychosocial assessment? Does policy development involve building coalitions?) It would be particularly helpful to view social work job analyses in comparison to those of other professions, in order to draw further conclusions about which activities and emphases are unique to social work. Many, if not all, of these questions have no doubt been raised by the authors themselves. They constitute some of the avenues for future research.

One area of uniqueness claimed by the profession is a focus on the interaction between individual and environment, and a commitment to social change. Yet Teare and Sheafor conclude that the job analysis provides little evidence of social workers' sustained attention to the creation of social conditions that would enhance individual and group functioning. Part of the problem may be definition: Is the dual focus on individual and environment displayed only through social action activities (as contained in the "Resource/Service Change" factor)? The "Client Situation Change" factor, on which respondents, particularly BSWs, scored highly, seems equally relevant, as it includes an emphasis on working with and modifying the client's more immediate environment.

In addition, by its very nature as a job analysis, the study cannot capture the social action and social policy involvement of workers off the job. The research carried out by Reeser (1992), Reeser and Epstein (1990, pp. 17-31), Butler (1990), and others indicates that the majority of social workers not only profess a commitment to social action activities, but also report high levels of involvement in such activities. It is likely that much of this involvement, which includes electoral politics, takes place on the worker's own time. One has only to open an issue of *NASW News* to find evidence of the organized profession's concerted effort to influence policy on many issues, including health care and welfare reform. What the current study *does* suggest is that we might pay more attention to increasing opportunities for policy making and environmental change within social workers' actual work settings.

Findings vs. Expectations/Conceptualizations

Having said all of this, it is important to recognize the many useful implications of the job analysis study for baccalaureate social work education. One area to examine is the fit between the study's findings and historical expectations of the BSW degree. In the 1940s, when undergraduate education first emerged as an alternative to graduate training, proponents lauded its importance in preparing individuals to staff the growing public social service agencies. Given the perpetual shortage of MSWs for these jobs, undergraduate educators, college and university administrators, and many state and local public welfare departments emphasized the utility of a broadly educated BA-level public service worker (Leighninger, 1987, pp. 125-43). However, 50 years later it is clear that this promise of creating a trained staff for the public social services has not materialized. As Teare and Sheafor note, only 3% of BSW respondents identified "public assistance/welfare" as their primary practice area. In addition, protective services, a job activity generally associated with public child welfare work, had a very low frequency score in the cluster analysis. These findings are reinforced in the most recent analysis of NASW membership surveys (Gibelman & Schervish, 1993, p. 57), which indicates that only one in four baccalaureate members of NASW is employed in the local public agency sector.[1]

The Teare and Sheafor study does, however, show a congruence between early conceptualizations of the baccalaureate social worker as a generalist practitioner and the realities of current practice. While the term "generalist" had yet to be coined, supporters of undergraduate social work education in the 1940s visualized broad training in major social work skills coupled with relevant course work in the social sciences. In the 1960s, when undergraduate education began to achieve greater legitimacy, a generic practice model was developed by Teare,

---

[1] This section includes, but is not limited to, public assistance and child welfare agencies. Another 17% of BSW respondents worked under a public state auspice, yet this too includes settings other than public welfare.

McPheeters, and other social work educators, under the rubric of the Southern Regional Education Board (Teare & McPheeters, 1970). The continuing relevance of this model is attested to in the job analysis findings related to the "job breadth" of BSW practitioners. BSWs registered high involvement in all but one factor measure of work activity, and were almost equally involved in "client change" and "client situation change." These findings confirm the need to provide a generalist education at the undergraduate level.[2]

An Appropriate Educational Continuum

Since the study covers both BSWs and MSWs, it has obvious implications for discussion of an appropriate continuum in social work education and practice. The profession has debated the nature of such a continuum, or the relationship between the two educational levels, for almost 50 years. Some educators have even questioned whether a continuum exists, arguing that there are few demonstrable differences between the activities and skills of undergraduate and graduate practitioners. This book's findings help clarify these issues. A comparison of the two levels of practice finds them similar in their dominant emphasis on direct practice, with this emphasis being more pronounced in the activities of baccalaureate social workers. Yet within the area of direct practice, BSWs focus more on case management activities and MSWs on therapeutic interventions. Overall, BSWs are stronger in their orientation toward change in the client's situation, including the connection of clients with relevant services, while MSWs tend to display a more specialized clinical approach to practice. These data add credence to similar conclusions reached in earlier, less comprehensive studies on task differentiation among child welfare workers (Kolevzon & Biggerstaff, 1983; Olsen & Holmes, 1982) and among other social work practitioners (see summary in Anderson, 1985).

Teare and Sheafor's conclusions that BSWs are more generalist practitioners, with an emphasis on service connection and a strong commitment to change in client situations, point to a relevant continuum of education and practice. Based on this continuum, preparation in undergraduate social work should continue to emphasize a broad

---

[2] It is interesting to review Teare and Sheafor's findings in light of the work of Baer and Federico (1978 and 1979), whose conceptualization of what the entry-level practitioner "ought to be prepared to do" avoids the generalist label, but whose list of basic competencies appears to reflect a generalist perspective. In a rough comparison with the job analysis study, there is close to moderate congruence between the job activity reports and 7 out of the 10 basic competencies.

range of skills for work with a variety of populations and human problems, rather than training for specialized practice. More could probably be done in the educational program to enhance skills in service connection, helping clients to build informal support systems, networking with other professionals, and other facets of the case management role.

Another way of interpreting the continuum would be to assign specific work settings and practice areas to each educational level. Teare and Sheafor report, after all, that in comparison to MSWs, BSW practitioners rarely work in private practice, are more likely to be found in group home and nursing home settings, and almost never list school social work as their primary practice area. Partly for this reason, the authors note that "the BSW appears to have carved out a distinct niche in the human services." However, one might argue that this niche is more a matter of exclusion by others than choice on the part of baccalaureate practitioners. School social work, for example, has traditionally been viewed as the province of MSW social workers. In this author's opinion, there has been no definitive study establishing that the skills required for school social work practice can be acquired only through graduate education. It is worth investigating whether a similar situation exists in mental health, which involves many more MSWs than BSWs. Interestingly, among baccalaureate workers practicing in mental health, it seems likely that the majority work in aftercare settings with the chronically mentally ill, suggesting a lack of access to work with acutely ill clients. Such professional deployment patterns, if they are based on "tradition" or stereotypes rather than job research, constitute a poor basis for development of a continuum.[3]

A final issue related to the continuum and relevant educational preparation has to do with the BSWs' apparent low involvement in administration and program development tasks. Other research approaches might reveal a higher level of baccalaureate involvement than that reported here (see, for example, Edelman-Bastian & Leighninger, 1983). Further information would help determine whether the continuum should differentiate between the MSW as the supervisory and

---

[3] Raymond and Atherton (1991) present an interesting discussion of the continuum issue, in which they suggest that MSW and BSW social work should in fact be seen as two different entities. They argue that baccalaureate practitioners should concentrate on case management in the public social services, and that MSW education should provide students with specific skills and knowledge for "advanced practice." Yet, as indicated by Teare and Sheafor, as well as Gibelman and Schervish (1993), BSWs do not have a particularly high representation in the public social services, at least in the areas of public assistance and child welfare.

management director, and the BSW as the front-line worker. However, even if BSWs are not found to perform these functions, the undergraduate curriculum should still cover supervision (from the perspective of the supervisee's involvement in the process) and the organizational policy information necessary for understanding and working effectively within agency programs and structures.

Since a major goal of the job analysis is to inform curriculum decisions, some final words on the relationship between this study and the recently adopted CSWE Curriculum Policy for Baccalaureate Degree Programs (CSWE, 1994) are called for. As should be clear from the reported low involvement in social action on the part of both MSW and BSW practitioners, the policy statement's strong emphasis on social change may be unrealistic. Yet if social change commitment and activities exist in social work in other forms, as argued above, the emphasis remains relevant. The policy statement does concur with Teare and Sheafor's conclusions in its emphasis on a generalist practice model that stresses direct service provision. As the policy statement is reviewed for translation into educational practice, undergraduate programs would do well to ground their deliberations in the comprehensive findings of the job analysis study.

A New Role for Graduate Education

Invited Commentary
by
L. Diane Bernard
Visiting Professor, Smith College

The data and analyses provided herein should encourage social work educators to reexamine the structure and content of our professional degree programs. Teare and Sheafor's picture of what is happening in practice (let alone what *ought* to be happening) suggests that we may have outgrown our existing model of education, and should begin to seriously rethink our position as we approach the 21st century.

Where is social work education today, and how did we get here? At this writing, there were 393 accredited BSW Programs with 28 more in candidacy, and 123 accredited MSW programs with 10 in candidacy (Norlin & Randolph, 1995). The range of social work education encompasses two other levels. The Associate Degree, typically provided by community or junior colleges, prepares students to carry out technical or pre-professional social service tasks. The doctorate (PhD or DSW), provided in graduate schools of social work, prepares students for leadership roles in administration, policy formulation, advanced and specialized practice, research, and teaching. In addition, continuing education programs impart specialized knowledge and skills to those holding any or all of the above degrees.

Emergence of BSW- and Doctoral-Level Education

There is no orderly progression among these degrees. As each developed independently, it affected all the other levels and changed the identification of practice tasks deemed appropriate for each level of preparation. The governmental auspice regulating accrediting bodies has stipulated that only the degree providing entry into a profession should go through formal accreditation. Prior to 1974, only MSW programs were subject to such scrutiny. When the case was made that the BSW degree prepared students for beginning professional practice, CSWE acknowledged both degrees as professional entry points and the accreditation process was expanded to include this BSW programs.

Undergraduate social work had been offered in various formats for many years, beginning when the need arose to train personnel to carry out the provisions of the Social Security Act of 1935. Following World War II, the burgeoning U.S. population and the growing complexity of social problems further increased the demand for social work personnel, and a number of baccalaureate and associate degree programs were developed to meet these needs. During the 1960s, many additional social forces converged to reinforce this need. Student interest in social reform and academic relevancy stimulated the expansion of educational opportunities in the human and applied social services. Increased sensitivity to client rights and greater recognition of the needs and contributions of ethnic minorities triggered the involvement of indigenous and paraprofessional workers. Government support for antipoverty programs, along with expanded interest in career-related training, gave further impetus to developing the levels of social work education.

In 1963, CSWE prepared a guide to appropriate content and learning experiences for BSW programs in accredited colleges and universities. This followed CSWE sponsorship and publication in 1959 of a 13-volume study that recommended the distribution of social work education content over an undergraduate-graduate continuum. By 1970, CSWE was granting approval status to programs fulfilling the suggested content and learning requirements. Concurrently, NASW admitted to full professional membership those practicing in social welfare agencies who held baccalaureate degrees from CSWE-approved programs. This growing recognition of the baccalaureate as the first professional degree led to intensified concerns for quality control and professional accountability. The approval status was upgraded to formal accreditation in 1974 when CSWE secured permission to accredit at more than one entry level.

In 1971, CSWE's Commission on Accreditation adopted a new standard permitting advanced standing of up to one year for MSW students who held a BSW from a CSWE-approved program. A special CSWE committee, as well as a joint CSWE-NASW Committee on Manpower Issues, recommended this action. A major consideration supporting this move was the need to reduce redundancies in the educational process and recognize the linkage between levels. Although granting advanced standing is not a requirement for MSW programs, CSWE does require all accredited MSW programs to focus the first year of the graduate degree on foundation generalist practice, which is equivalent to what students learn in accredited BSW programs.

Although the MSW is acknowledged as the advanced practice degree, it has lost some of its status as the sole professional degree. In addition, its identity has been confounded by an endless array of tracks, concentrations, and specializations. To some extent the MSW degree has lost clarity by virtue of its very diversity. Although the number of MSW programs has continued to grow, they are being overtaken by the more numerous BSW programs and by doctoral programs.

In the past, education beyond the MSW occurred primarily in third-year programs that focused on advanced practice. In 1950, only two programs, at Bryn Mawr and the University of Chicago, offered doctorates in social work. However, as professional schools gained academic recognition, the demand for those who could contribute to theory and knowledge development increased, along with the demand for more faculty for the expanding number of programs. At this writing, the Group for the Advancement of Doctoral Education (GADE) now lists 50 doctoral programs in social work. Currently, two types of doctoral degrees are offered—the PhD and the DSW. The different titles, more often than not, reflect institutional preference rather than a real difference between the subject matter taught. All doctoral programs offer preparation for research and teaching, and many provide preparation for social planning, policy analysis, and administration. Curriculum on advanced direct practice is available in less than 5% of the programs and is not the norm for doctoral-level education.

Other Factors

In addition to the growth of BSW and doctoral programs, other factors have influenced the nature of the curriculum offered at the MSW level. Despite the majority of students (over 80%) in graduate programs opting for direct services, many programs have embraced an advanced generalist model for the second year. There has been increased awareness that social workers employed in rural and vastly under-serviced geographic areas are expected to undertake some planning, evaluating, and management tasks. Although it is clear that new problem areas have emerged (and will continue to emerge) that require specialized knowledge and commitment, the profession faces a concurrent need for more independent practitioners with a broad service perspective and range of skills. The growing complexity of service delivery systems is demanding more flexibility of the social work educational system.

Despite initial student interest in pursuing direct service preparation, the reality is that MSW practitioners are just as likely to be working in supervision and management. The Teare and Sheafor data make this very clear. Given the past 30 years of change and development at the BSW and doctoral levels, it is time for the MSW level to establish an identity based on the actual significance of the degree for both the graduate and the social service delivery system. The second year of the MSW should be spent in preparing students for those areas of supervision, middle management, and administration in which they are expected to function. The ratio of BSW to MSW programs makes it clear that, in the foreseeable future, there will be only one MSW practitioner for every four BSW workers. It would seem that those with advanced degrees will be needed to assume responsibilities beyond that of direct service.

Delineating the Role of MSW Education

Economic and other constraints make extending MSW programs beyond the present two years an unreasonable alternative; and interest in this possibility has been reduced by the increased availability of doctoral education. Recognizing the established credibility of the BSW degree, it would seem an acceptable alternative to require all MSW applicants to obtain the BSW or its equivalent prior to being eligible for graduate admission. This is an accepted expectation in other professional disciplines and would not necessitate tampering with the time dimension of either degree. The role of the MSW curriculum within this new continuum would be clarified: Two years of beginning generalist direct service preparation (the BSW degree) would be followed by two years of advanced indirect service preparation (the MSW degree). Beyond establishing greater relevance for the MSW degree, it would assure more adequate preparation of graduate social workers for the service delivery systems of today and tomorrow.

At least two other issues need to be addressed in support of this proposed continuum. First—perhaps not surprisingly given the present emphasis of MSW programs on a wide range of direct practice specializations—Teare and Sheafor report that MSW practitioners have little professional involvement in social reform and/or delivery system changes. More and more graduate practitioners have settled into private practice and a narrower practice orientation. This increased involvement of MSWs in the private sector has left the public arena almost entirely to BSW graduates. At present, there is little or no emphasis in MSW-level education on preparing graduates for the public sector or for changing the social service system. Reconceptualizing the second year for advanced generalist indirect practice could encompass both the public and private sectors, and place greater emphasis on providing the organizational and legislative tools for bringing about social change.

The second issue centers around the fact that MSW programs offering indirect service tracks tend to attract the male students. While both genders may initially be prompted to choose social work by similar direct service interests, males have been more likely than females to specialize in management and administration. Given the overrepresentation of women in direct practice activities and the profession as a whole, this tendency is especially unfortunate. If both genders received essentially the same graduate education, however, women would be exposed to the same indirect service knowledge and skills as men are, which in turn would give them similar professional options in management and administration.

As the research presented by Teare and Sheafor has revealed, the more social work education a practitioner acquires, the lower the probability that she or he will provide direct services to clients. Furthermore, the graduate degree serves as the "ticket" to the assumption of greater responsibility through indirect services. Since this is what actually occurs, graduate social work education needs to respond to reality. Instead of adding more years to the degree or finding ways to encourage women to opt for a specialized track of indirect service, all MSW programs should offer similar curricula—using the full two years of the program to prepare students for positions they will be expected to perform in the real world.

The National Study and the Educational Continuum

Invited Commentary
by
Joseph D. Anderson
Norfolk State University

The concept of an educational continuum in social work is based on five major assumptions or guiding principles (Anderson, 1985). These are as follows:

1. All levels must include a generic core of knowledge, values, and skills requisite for all social work practice.

2. Each level must have an educational integrity of its own with unique objectives and content requisite for the specific practice for which it prepares.

3. The continuum must have a design which builds on, without repeating, the segments preceding it and prepares its graduates for successful entry into the next higher level.

4. The outcomes and content of advanced levels must be different from and/or more complex than those taught at lower levels.

5. There must be a planned relationship between the educational continuum and an operational practice continuum.

The data presented by Teare and Sheafor directly address this last principle while illuminating aspects of each of the others. If there is a practice continuum between BSW and MSW levels in client-centered or direct service practice, it appears to be one of BSW/case management to MSW/clinical practice. The findings of this ambitious study on the similarities and differences between BSW and MSW practitioners in direct practice contexts support many of those found in earlier studies (reviewed in Anderson, 1985).

Comparing BSW and MSW Practitioners

A summary of the data here reveals that BSWs, as compared to MSWs, were more likely to deal with such problem situations as health, aging, substance abuse, financial assistance, and housing. Their goals were most often related to the factors the authors identified as "client situation change" and "client change." Their tasks involved much more brokerage in conjunction with interpersonal helping activities and the variety of tasks in the Case Planning and Maintenance cluster. Their function was most often one of mediating between client-centered needs and environmental resources in order to sustain social functioning and to ameliorate problem situations.

The MSWs differed significantly from BSWs by virtue of their involvement in mental health services. They focused much more on such problems as anxiety and depression, interpersonal relations, and family functioning. Their goals were related to client "clinical" change. Their tasks involved counseling and therapy related to clients' emotional problems, and entailed frequent use of individual and family treatment techniques (lowest for those in hospitals) and some use of the case planning and management tasks (only "occasionally" for those in private practice). This was true even when they had the major additional function of staff supervision. For those MSWs not primarily in direct service—those whose primary job functions were administration/management or education/training—these clinical tasks, as one would expect, were less central.

On the surface, these data suggest that BSW and MSW direct service practice is very different in nature, which supports principles 2, 4 and 5 above. The data imply the need for a set of competencies for each level of practice. In particular, the data raise a key question about the current continuum proposed in accreditation standards: How does the requirement that BSW programs provide the same foundation as MSW programs affect the preparation of both BSWs and MSWs for the different demands of their practice (Anderson, 1985; Hartman, 1983; Kolevzon, 1977; Raymond & Atherton, 1991)?

The issue is further complicated by the requirement that this foundation be based on a "generalist" conception of practice, that is, that it requires an equal level of competence for work with individuals, families, groups, organizations, and communities. The data from this study, however, suggest that neither BSW nor MSW practitioners needed to function with such job breadth. Rather, both appeared to need a depth of competence for interpersonal helping, especially effective counseling. In addition, BSWs needed special analytical and interactional skills for case management that linked clients to appropriate resources; MSWs needed special skills for influencing clinical change.

Core Skills and Specialized Competencies

These data also have somewhat less direct implications for the application of continuum principles 1 and 3. "Generic," or "core" tasks, common to both groups of practitioners, were identified by Teare and Sheafor. For those in direct services, it was the "direct service" clusters related to interpersonal helping and case planning. For a significant number of MSWs, it was the "indirect services" clusters related to supervision, administration/management, and education/training. This practice core included 17 tasks in four clusters: Interpersonal Helping (requiring relationship, problem-solving, and communication skills); Case Planning/Maintenance (requiring coordination, recording, and monitoring skills); Professional Development; and Delivery System Knowledge Development (requiring skills in understanding and using organizational policies and procedures). The interpersonal helping tasks require foundation practice skills, informed by knowledge and values, that would imply a standardized approach in both the BSW and MSW curriculum. These skills would be integrated and expanded in the advanced practice concentration curriculum in MSW programs. If education followed practice, the BSW and MSW foundations would not be the same, but would have some identifiable similarities in the practice content presented in the curriculum.

In light of the data produced by this study, a conceptualization that appears especially fruitful for articulating the social work continuum has been presented by William Gordon (1965) and others (Anderson, 1985; Gross, 1992). This conceptualization views the social work profession, and social work practice in particular, in terms of a transactional paradigm—that is, a focus on the transactions between people and their environments that attempts to maximize the development of both. The data from this study imply that this paradigm, at least in some form, is applicable to BSW-level practice: BSW practitioners appeared to view clients consistently in their situational contexts in order to change aspects of this transactional relationship. This emphasis on a person-in-environment framework, however, did not appear to mark the practice of MSWs.

To properly define an educational continuum, we need to examine not only what social workers do at various levels but also what they do well and what they intend to accomplish. Gerald Gross (1992) recently identified this combination of purpose and competence in the notion of the "great traditions" that help define social work. To him, these great traditions are tested in our "record of competence in creating social environments and developing forms of exchange between people and environments which support human dignity and social justice" (p. 111). These great traditions generate "little traditions" which recur in the daily lives of social workers, link their specific job tasks to the profession's vision and mission, and provide a key element in any definition of practice competence.

In this respect, the important questions are not just what do social workers do, but what is the vision of the quality of life to which they direct their activities, and how do they contribute to such a quality of life for both their clients and the society at large?

The answer to these questions leads us to one of the most disturbing findings of this research—relatively few of the 7,000 practitioners identified active engagement in prevention, social policy development, or community education tasks as part of their regular work activities. Thus, we must also wrestle with another question posed at the end of Chapter 4 and raised again by Charles Guzzetta in his commentary: To what extent should schools of social work lead or follow practice? To me, the answer seems indisputable: Schools must take the lead in defining and imparting to students a clear vision of purpose and competence. The clear intent must be to promote the human dignity and social justice of those we serve.

The National Study and Curriculum Policy Materials

Invited Commentary
by
Donald Pilcher
University of Maine at Orono

The task analysis data produced by Teare and Sheafor's national study raise several issues for the accreditation process of baccalaureate and master's programs and highlight the need for additional research to inform deliberation about curriculum policies. Discrepancies exist between the curriculum policy statements adopted by CSWE over the years and the activities described by respondents in this study. The language in the Curriculum Policy Statement (CPS) would lead one to expect that both baccalaureate and master's graduates are engaged in a wide range of practice activities and, indeed, this is typically true. However, social and political action and the development of knowledge, clearly prescribed in the CPSs, are only weakly evident in the reports from the field.

Expectations of the 1982 Curriculum Policy Statement

Some might argue that, given the years of education and practice spanned by the sample, an exact correspondence between the CPS and the activities of respondents should not be expected. The respondents varied in age, years of practice experience, and assumedly dates of education. The pool may have included some master's students graduating as early as the 1950s and as recently as the early 1980s. During that period, there were extensive changes in the curricula offered at the master's and baccalaureate levels. Programs, therefore, would have been developed with various course offerings under different versions of the CPS.

Despite variations over the years, the educational expectations expressed in the 1982 CPS probably reflect the predominant philosophy and orientation of social work educators and the majority of their programs at the time the study data were collected. The 1982 CPS, contained in the 1991 revision of the 1988 *Handbook of Accreditation Standards and Procedures* (CSWE, 1991), established comprehensive mandates for both BSW and MSW programs. Although it did not prescribe any particular curriculum design, certain content areas were specified and required. It also identified four related purposes of social work (identical for both the baccalaureate and master's levels) based on transactions between people and their environments "that affect their ability to accomplish life tasks, alleviate distress, and realize individual and collective aspirations" (CSWE, 1991, p. 106). The four were:

1. The promotion, restoration, maintenance, or enhancement of the functioning of individuals, families, households, social groups, organizations, and communities by helping them to prevent distress and utilize resources.

2. The planning, development, and implementation of social policies, services, and programs required to meet basic needs and support the development of capacities and abilities.

3. The pursuit of such policies, services, and programs through legislative advocacy, lobbying, and other forms of social and political action, including expert testimony, participation in local and national coalitions, and gaining public office.[5]

4. The development and testing of professional knowledge and skills related to these purposes.

Three types of task content can be inferred from these statements: client-centered activities and direct service provision; social and political action; and knowledge development. These statements appear in the introductory section of the CPS, which provides elaboration through statements on expectations and mandated curriculum areas. Some of these statements are very specific; others are very general.

The 1982 CPS clearly stated that students receiving a baccalaureate degree were expected to possess the professional judgment and proficiency necessary to apply differentially, with supervision, foundation skills and knowledge to service systems of various sizes and types. The CPS also mandated special emphasis in the baccalaureate and foundation content on direct services to clients, which included

---

[5] The latest Curriculum Policy Statement, adopted in July 1992 and contained in the 1994 *Handbook of Accreditation Standards and Procedures* (CSWE, 1994), made a substantive change in this statement, emphasizing administrative advocacy and social and political action "so as to empower groups at risk and promote social and economic justice." The other three purposes were changed slightly but not substantively from the 1982 CPS.

organizing and securing resources. This language was not as strongly stated as it was under the purposes of social work, listed above. It really called for a "generalist" practice—one embracing a wide range of practice including advocating for legislation, participating in local and national coalitions, and engaging in other forms of social and political action. In short, each program was expected to explicate the ways in which students were being prepared for generalist practice (p. 109).

Students receiving an MSW degree, in addition to the skills and competencies expected in the generalist foundation, were expected to be prepared in a concentration organized by field of practice, population group, problem area, professional role, or interventive modes, or for advanced general practice (p. 110). However, the related sections of the CPS (6.11-6.12) did not strongly reflect the need for social and political action.

Congruence Between the CPS and the Activities of Practitioners

A careful review of the curriculum policy statements and the data from the study reveals some areas of congruence between preparation expectations, as expressed in the CPS objectives, and the activities reported by the baccalaureate and master's level practitioners. Client-centered activities and direct services clearly engaged practitioners.

However, there were also some major differences. In the areas of social and political action, the findings suggest that social workers were only nominally involved in service delivery system change activities, and that prevention, social policy development, and community education efforts were conspicuously absent. Very few practitioners reported taking part in or testifying in legislative forums or hearings, providing technical assistance and support to community self-help groups, or taking part in campaigns or demonstrations to persuade public officials to establish or change policies or laws. Furthermore, very few practitioners were engaged in the development of knowledge; few practitioners at either level reported conducting research, publishing or presenting findings, or carrying out surveys.

This lack of congruence could well be due to ambiguity and inconsistency in the 1982 CPS itself. In the section on purpose and structure, the CPS emphasizes *both* direct and indirect services, including social and political action (CSWE, 1991, p. 107). In addition to the sections of the CPS cited above, the mandate on foundation content would be the logical place to include an emphasis on social and political action (pp. 112-114). However, it can be argued that the five foundation content areas do not strongly and consistently suggest such a mandate for social and political action. In a general way, the section on human behavior encompasses content related to both direct and indirect practice. The section on social welfare policies and services stresses content related to change in social policies and programs. The section on practice content implies the inclusion of content on organizations and communities, and practice with all size systems. The section on field emphasizes direct practice and states that the instructional focus of the field practicum "must be consistent with the purposes of the professional foundation curriculum" (p. 12). The mandated research statement at the foundation level prescribes content on research methodologies and systematic evaluation of practice. As one can see, the language is not very specific.

The 1992 Curriculum Policy Statement

The revised 1992 CPS, unlike the 1982 version, has a section that specifies competencies (CSWE, 1994).[6] These competencies, which are expected of both baccalaureate and master's level graduates, include social change and development of knowledge. Graduates are expected to:

1. understand the forms and mechanisms of oppression and discrimination, and apply the strategies and skills of change that advance social and economic justice;

2. apply the knowledge and skills of a generalist social work perspective to practice with systems of all sizes;

3. analyze the impact of social policies on client systems, workers, and agencies and, at the master's level, demonstrate skills for influencing policy formulation and change;

4. evaluate relevant research studies and demonstrate skills in research design, data analysis, and knowledge dissemination; and

5. conduct empirical evaluations of their own practice interventions.

---

[6] The Commission on Educational Policy of the Council on Social Work Education has responsibility for revision of the CPS. The 1992 CPS is included in the CSWE's 1994 *Handbook of Accreditation Standards and Procedures.*

As evidenced in these new guidelines, the social work education community continues to believe that professional social work preparation should include content on social action and knowledge development. Thus, the same inconsistencies between curriculum policy and on-the-job practice exist for today's practitioners. In spite of the mandates in the curriculum policy statements, both old and new, this study shows that practitioners have minimal involvement in tasks designed to bring about changes in resources and services. As pointed out in earlier chapters, this is in sharp contrast to the image of social workers as "social change agents." Similarly, the cluster scores for research and policy development tasks indicate that they were seldom performed by the respondents. MSWs were somewhat more likely than BSWs to engage in research and policy development and in changes in resources and services, but these activities again engaged very few workers.

In the realm of direct practice, the most frequent activities reported by all MSW and BSW respondents were the tasks contained in the Interpersonal Helping cluster. In addition to this, three other clusters—Case Planning/Maintenance, Professional Development, and Individual/Family Treatment—were most frequently identified by respondents. It is reassuring that the basic skills stressed in most social work programs were clearly evident in the responses of practitioners. BSW practitioners reported a predominance of client-centered activities and few indirect service tasks. Although MSW workers also reported a predominance of client-centered activities, many also reported functioning as supervisors and administrators.

The 1992 CPS requires content on the systematic evaluation of practice in the foundation research segment of the curriculum. The foundation social work practice sequence of the 1982 CPS contained a passing reference to practice assessment and the use of appropriate research to monitor and evaluate outcomes, but not a strong mandate.

Evidence of the respondents' efforts to evaluate actions, decisions, competence, and availability in relation to individuals to whom they were providing services (the highest loading in professional development) suggests congruence of intent with expectations of the CPS. The tools for such self-evaluation may, at this point, be crude and generally unspecified. The lower loadings on other components of professional development (using journal articles, setting priorities, sharing insights with colleagues, and interpreting programs and policies) indicate less emphasis in these areas. In part, this may suggest either a lack of time/accessibility to professional journals or the perception that there is little of relevance in the professional literature. It may also suggest that social work practitioners are not yet convinced of the importance of specifying what they do and why they do it, as reflected in Kadushin's (1959) observation that social workers "know more than they know they know." Practitioners seem reluctant to discuss and explore their knowledge, often underestimating the importance of explicating what they do.

With some striking exceptions, there *is* congruity between what practitioners say they do and what is required by the Curriculum Policy Statement. The diversification of activities, practice settings, job functions, and primary practice areas reflected in the responses of practitioners are mirrored in the CPS. However, the *emphasis* in activities is decidedly different. Whereas practitioners, regardless of educational level, report that they direct relatively little effort toward changing social service systems and resources, the CPS mandates that both graduates and undergraduates be prepared to "function as informed and competent practitioners in providing services . . . in efforts to achieve change in social policies and programs" (CSWE, 1991, p. 112).

The preparation for direct services in the foundation curriculum, emphasized in most social work programs, is consistent with the activities reported by most of the baccalaureate-level workers and many of the master's-level workers, even those devoting substantial effort to supervision. It is likely that many of those with predominantly administrative responsibilities at the time of the survey have gone through a direct service phase in their careers. More emphasis on administration, especially in the MSW curriculum, may be indicated for students or practitioners who are headed for that area; and for the many practitioners who eventually assume supervisory roles, it must be said that the CPS places very little emphasis on this aspect of social work practice.

At the baccalaureate level, the CPS expectations are that students will attain the judgment and proficiency to apply, with supervision, foundation skills and knowledge to service systems of various sizes and types. It is therefore surprising to discover that baccalaureate-level workers report a very high degree of autonomy. Nearly one-fifth report almost complete autonomy, another two-fifths report considerable autonomy, and an additional one-fourth report a moderate level of autonomy. Only slightly more than 10 percent report little or almost no autonomy. Since some setting and practice areas tended to be primarily occupied by either BSW or MSW workers, it may be that many baccalaureate workers are in agencies that do not employ master's-level workers, and vice versa.

Over the decades, arguments have often been made that a two-year graduate curriculum is inadequate preparation for the tasks faced by social workers. The Commission on Educational Policy may soon want to consider the alternative proposed in Diane Bernard's commentary (earlier in this chapter) to require a BSW degree for entry into master's-level education and to focus, at the MSW level, on indirect services. The continuum issue is not dead!

Further Research

As with much research, the findings presented here may raise as many questions as they answer. In particular, these data raise questions about the relationships between social work curriculum and post-graduate practice. Do available practice settings limit the possibility of engaging in social change and research activities? Has the implementation of the curriculum failed to provide the necessary skills, knowledge, and sense of responsibility for engaging in social action and/or research? Is it realistic to expect practitioners to engage in social change activities and the development of knowledge *in addition to* meeting the needs of clients?

The anomaly between the prescription for social work education and the activities of graduates is clear. What is not clear is why the anomaly exists. A follow-up analysis of those who *are* engaged in social change activities may be warranted—where do they come from (schools, region, agencies)? Is it possible that some schools, or some geographic areas, or some agencies provide opportunities for social action while others do not? What are the determinants of engagement in social change activities?

The data in this study describe on-the-job activities. What do professional social workers do outside the work setting? Are they engaged in legislative advocacy, lobbying, participation in local and national coalitions, or other forms of social and political action outside their immediate employment? A more disturbing question is whether or not there are social problems, central to social welfare and the profession, so intractable as to be beyond the profession's capabilities, even in collaboration and coalitions with other groups and professions.

Implications

The results of this national study spotlight the stark choices outlined by both William Reid and Charles Guzzetta in their commentaries. Guzzetta calls into question whether the profession is capable of assimilating practice information from the field into curriculum design and policy formulation. Reid and his co-authors ask, "To what extent should the schools lead or follow practice?" The crucial and immediate question for CSWE's Commission on Educational Policy is: Should the curriculum policy statement be strengthened, or should we abandon the notion that we can prepare social workers to engage in social action and development of knowledge?

It is heartening to note that the new CPS does not diminish its emphasis on social change and development of knowledge. Apparently educators are still convinced that these elements should be part of the curriculum and should be expectations of the professional social worker. The task for the Commission on Educational Policy is to determine how the CPS can be modified to enhance the likelihood that graduates are prepared for social and political change activities and knowledge development; the task for the Council on Social Work Education and the National Association of Social Workers is to determine how their combined efforts can enhance the likelihood that practitioners will engage in these important activities.

References

Joseph Anderson, "BSW Programs and Continuum in Social Work," *Journal of Social Work Education*, 21 (Fall 1985): pp. 63-72.

June Axinn and Herman Levin, *Social Welfare: A History of the American Response to Need*. New York: Harper & Row, 1975.

Betty L. Baer and Ronald Federico, *Educating the Baccalaureate Social Worker: Report of the Undergraduate Social Work Curriculum Development Project*, 2 vols. Cambridge, MA: Ballinger Publishing, 1978 and 1979.

Amy Butler, "A Reevaluation of Social Work Students' Career Interests: Grounds for Optimism," *Journal of Social Work Education*, 26 (Winter 1990): pp. 45-56.

Council on Social Work Education, *Directory of Colleges and Universities with Accredited Social Work Degree Programs*. Alexandria, VA: Author, 1993.

Council on Social Work Education, *Handbook of Accreditation Standards and Procedures*. Alexandria, VA: Author, 1988.

Council on Social Work Education, *Handbook of Accreditation Standards and Procedures*. Alexandria, VA: Author, 1991.

Council on Social Work Education, *Handbook of Accreditation Standards and Procedures*. Alexandria, VA: Author, 1994.

Natalie Edelman-Bastian and Leslie Leighninger, "The Value and Marketability of Undergraduate Social Work Education," *The Journal of Applied Social Sciences*, 7 (Fall/Winter 1983): pp. 147-162.

Margaret Gibelman and Philip H. Schervish, *Who We Are: The Social Work Labor Force as Reflected in the NASW Membership*. Washington, DC: NASW Press, 1993.

William E. Gordon, "Toward a Social Work Frame of Reference, *Journal of Education for Social Work*, 1 (Fall 1965): pp. 7-15.

Charles Green, "What Social Workers Do: Implications for the Reclassification Debate," *Journal of Sociology and Social Welfare*, 15 (June 1988): pp. 97-112.

Gerald Gross, "A Defining Moment: The Social Work Continuum Revisited," *Journal of Social Work Education*, 28 (Winter 1992): pp. 110-118.

Gerald Handel, *Social Welfare in Western Society*. New York: Random House, 1982.

Ann Hartman, "Concentration, Specialization, and Curriculum Designs in MSW and BSW Programs," *Journal of Education for Social Work*, 19 (Spring 1983): pp. 16-25.

Michael S. Kolevzon, "The Continuum in Social Work Education: A Destiny Not So Manifest," *Journal of Education for Social Work*, 13 (Winter 1977): pp. 83-89.

Michael S. Kolevzon and Marilyn A. Biggerstaff, "Functional Differentiation of Job Demands: Dilemmas Confronting the Continuum in Social Work Education," *Journal of Education for Social Work*, 19 (Winter 1983): pp. 26-34.

Leslie Leighninger, *Social Work: Search for Identity*. Westport, CT: Greenwood Press, 1987.

Todd N. Lennon, ed., *Statistics on Social Work Education in the United States: 1992*. Alexandria, VA: Council on Social Work Education, 1993.

Alfred Kadushin, "The Knowledge Base of Social Work," in Alfred J. Kahn (ed.), *Issues in American Social Work*. New York: Columbia University Press, 1959.

Ralph Kramer, *Voluntary Service in the Welfare State*. Berkeley: University of California Press, 1981.

S. T. Kuhn, *The Structure of Scientific Revolutions*, 2nd ed. Chicago: University of Chicago Press, 1970.

Julia Norlin and Nancy Randolph, "Accreditation Update," *Social Work Education Reporter* (Spring/Summer 1995): p. 4.

Lenore Olsen and William M. Holmes, "Educating Child Welfare Workers: The Effects of Professional Training on Service Delivery," *Journal of Education for Social Work*, 18 (Winter 1982): pp. 94-102.

Ginny T. Raymond and Charles R. Atherton, "Blue Smoke and Mirrors: The Continuum in Social Work Education," *Journal of Social Work Education*, 27 (Fall 1991): pp. 297-304.

Linda Cherrey Reeser and Irwin Epstein, *Professionalization and Activism in Social Work*. New York: Columbia University Press, 1990.

Linda Cherrey Reeser, "Professional Role Orientation and Social Activism," *Journal of Sociology and Social Welfare*, 29 (June 1992): pp. 79-94.

Mary Richmond, "The Need for a Training School in Applied Philanthropy," in *Proceedings of the National Conference of Charity and Corrections*. Boston: George H. Ellis, pp. 181-188, 1897.

Mary Richmond, *Social Diagnosis*. New York: Russell Sage Foundation, 1917.

Robert J. Teare and Harold L. McPheeters. *Manpower Utilization in Social Welfare*. Atlanta: Southern Regional Education Board, 1970.

Walter Trattner, *From Poor Law to Welfare State*. New York: Free Press, 1984

Joseph Vigilante, "Between Science and Values: Education for the Profession During a Moral Crisis or Is Proof Truth?" *Journal of Education for Social Work*, 10 (Fall 1974): pp. 107-115.

Appendix A

Personal History Variables and Task Cluster Descriptions

Personal History Variables

Name: (write-in)[a]   **Preferred Mailing Address:** (write-in)

Year of Birth: (write-in)   **Gender:** Male Female

Ethnic Origin:
American Indian or Alaskan Native
Asian or Pacific Islander
African American (not Hispanic in Origin)
Chicano/Mexican American
Puerto Rican
Other Hispanic
White (not Hispanic in origin)
Other

Academic Degrees Earned:
BA/BS   BSW   AM/MA   MSW
MBA/MPH/MPA[b]   PhD/EdD   DSW

Current Enrollment in Degree Program: Yes   No[c]

If So, What Type? (write-in)

NASW Membership: Yes   No   **ACSW Membership:** Yes   No[d]

Current Licenses Held: (write-in)[b]

Job Title: (write-in)   **Department Title:** (write-in)

Location (State) of Primary Employment: (write-in)

---

[a]Write-in responses were content analyzed and categories were formed and coded. All other variables used pre-coded value labels for analysis.
[b]Occupational Social Worker Survey only
[c]BSW Survey only
[d]ACSW and Occupational Social Worker Surveys only

Population of Community in Which Currently Employed:[c]
fewer than 10,000 people
10,001 to 40,000 people
40,001 to 100,000 people
100,001 to 500,000 people
more than 500,000 people

Current Employment Setting:
Social service agency/organization
Private practice–Self employed (solo)
Private practice–Partnership/group
Membership organization
Hospital
Institution (non-hospital)
Outpatient facility: Clinic/health or mental health center
Group home/residence
Nursing home/hospice
Court/criminal justice system
College/university
Elementary/secondary school system
Non-social service organization
 (e.g., business, manufacturing, consulting/research firm, etc.)

Current Employment Function:
Direct service
Supervision
Management/administration
Policy development/analysis
Consultant
Research
Planning
Education/training

Employment Function in First Job:[c]
(same choices as for Current Employment Function)

Current Employment Practice Area:
Children and youth
Community organization/planning
Family services
Corrections/criminal justice
Group services

---

[c]BSW Survey only

Medical/health care
Mental health
Public assistance/welfare
School social work
Services to the aged
Alcohol/drug/substance abuse
Developmental disabilities/mental retardation
Other disabilities
Occupational
Education
Other (write-in)

Current Employment Auspice:[b]
Private/for-profit (proprietary)
Private/nonprofit (sectarian)
Private/nonprofit (nonsectarian)
Self-employed
Public sector–Local
Public sector–State
Public sector–Federal
Military

Predominant Ethnicity of Clientele:[e]
American Indian/Alaskan Native
Asian/Pacific Islander
African American (not Hispanic)
Chicano/Mexican American
Puerto Rican
Other Hispanic
White (not Hispanic)

Predominant Client Needs or Issues:[e]
Job/work performance
Family functioning
Anxiety/depression
Civil rights/affirmative action
Membership participation
School-related problems
Substance/alcohol abuse
Health-related problems
Interpersonal relations

---

[b] Occupational Social Worker Survey only
[e] As many as three could be selected. The same pre-coded value labels were used for each.

Physical disabilities
Group functioning/development
Character/behavioral problems
Mental illness/mental retardation
Law-related problems
Financial assistance/management
Aging
Recreation/leisure
Skill/knowledge development
Housing/shelter

Predominant Age Groups of Clientele:[f]
Infants (under 6 years)
Children (6–12 years)
Youth (13–20 years)
Adults (21–60 years)
Aged (over 60 years)

Sex Distribution of Clientele: % Female   % Male

Amount of Control Exercised in Job:[c]
Almost complete
Considerable
Moderate
Little
Almost none

Use Computer on Present Job?[c] Yes   No

If Yes, in What Way(s)? (write-in)

Disciplines of People Worked With:[b] (write-in)

Total Annual Income:[g]
Less than $10,000
$10,000–$14,999
$15,000–$19,999
$20,000–$24,999
$25,000–$29,999
$30,000–$34,999
$35,000–$39,999
$40,000–$44,999

---

[b] Occupational Social Worker Survey only
[c] BSW Survey only
[f] As many as two could be selected. The same pre-coded value labels were used for each.
[g] BSW and Occupational Social Worker Surveys only

$45,000-$49,999
$50,000-$54,999
$55,000-$59,999
$60,000-$64,999
$65,000 or more

Years in Present Position: (write-in)

Years of Social Work Experience: (write-in)

Years Experience as an Occupational Social Worker:[b] (write-in)

Tasks Associated with Each of the Clusters[h]

1. **Interpersonal Helping** (.81)[i]
    3. Discuss options with individuals in order to help them understand choices and/or resolve a particular problem. (.71)[j]
    8. Encourage and help people to discuss their points of view, feelings, and needs in order to increase their insight into the reasons for their actions. (.71)
    5. Talk with individuals and/or their relatives about problems in order to reassure, provide support, or reduce anxiety. (.67)
    9. Express and demonstrate an understanding of peoples' points of view, feelings, and needs in order to establish open and trusting relationships. (.66)

2. **Group Work** (.68)
    15. Work with people in a small group in order to teach them how groups work and how to act as a member of a group. (.55)
    16. Use a specific therapeutic method in a group situation in order to improve the adjustment and functioning of group members. (.50)

---

[b] Occupational Social Worker Survey only

[h] The content of the task statements and the cluster definitions have been copyrighted (1984, 1989, 1995) by Robert J. Teare. Reproduction of any kind, in whole or in part, without the express written permission of the author is not permitted.

[i] The number in parentheses to the right of each cluster label is the internal consistency reliability (Cronbach's alpha) for that cluster. Its technical definition and use is explained in Appendix B.

[j] The number in parentheses at the end of each task statement is the task-to-total cluster score correlation coefficient for that task. It is analogous to a factor loading. The closer its value is to 1.00, the more influence it has had in defining the cluster. Items in each cluster are arranged in descending order of coefficient size.

46. Teach people (for example, supervisors, parents, students, volunteers) how to listen, negotiate, or understand non-verbal behavior in order to increase their communication skills. (.45)

54. Teach parents, volunteers, and other individuals about basic principles, such as child development or aging, in order to increase their skills in dealing with problems in these and related areas. (.35)

3. Individual/Family Treatment (.84)

12. Use specific intervention techniques with individuals in order to improve behavioral functioning and adjustment. (.73)

7. Use specific intervention techniques to work with family members, individually or as a group, in order to strengthen the family as a unit. (.64)

4. Confront individuals about unacceptable behavior in order to bring about changes or promote adjustment. (.60)

4. Risk Assessment/Transition (.79)

20. Observe individuals and gather information from appropriate sources in order to decide whether there is a need for special counseling or mental health services. (.63)

66. Work with hostile or uncooperative clients in order to gain their cooperation in working toward service goals. (.57)

21. Determine the urgency or risk in an individual's situation in order to decide if emergency services or routine handling and referral are required. (.56)

22. Observe individuals and gather information from appropriate sources in order to establish the existence of substance/alcohol abuse problems. (.54)

6. Talk with and counsel individuals and/or relatives in order to prepare for the termination of services or financial help. (.53)

2. Work with individuals, family members, or significant others in order to prepare them psychologically and socially for movement from one living arrangement to another. (.48)

42. Review service plans and procedures in order to assure that clients' rights are protected. (.34)

13. Mediate in a dispute between various individuals (for example, clients and your agency, parents and children, workers and supervisor) in order to achieve a satisfactory solution. (.33)

5. **Protective Services** (.79)

    18. Observe children and adults and gather information from appropriate sources in order to determine whether physical/ psychological abuse or neglect has taken place. (.72)

    19. Observe children and adults and gather information from appropriate sources in order to determine whether sexual abuse has taken place. (.72)

    85. Testify or participate in court hearings in order to provide information on which legal decisions (for example, custody, competence, outplacement, institutionalization) can be based. (.53)

    61. Start a legal process (including referral to a lawyer) in order to protect the rights of an individual (for example, client, worker, student). (.45)

6. **Case Planning/Maintenance** (.90)

    64. Analyze case background and consult with appropriate individuals in order to arrive at a plan for services and/or financial help. (.76)

    65. Review case records and consult with appropriate individuals in order to evaluate progress and alter service plans if needed. (.71)

    68. Record or dictate information about individuals, using either prepared forms or narrative, in order to establish or update records, document services provided, or terminate services. (.70)

    57. Review files and records of an individual prior to contact with that person in order to become familiar with the details of the situation. (.66)

    25. Make contact with other units/agencies by letters, memos, or phone calls in order to refer people to appropriate services. (.64)

    59. Exchange information about case details with supervisor and/ or colleagues in order to get guidance in dealing with an individual or group. (.63)

    39. Obtain information from individuals, their relatives, or significant others in order to carry out intake or admission procedures for treatment or services. (.63)

    67. Coordinate service planning with staff, other providers, family members, and significant others in order to make the delivery of services to individuals or groups most effective. (.62)

62. Carry out appropriate procedures (for example, obtain consent, explain rights, maintain record security, etc.) in order to ensure that individuals' rights are protected. (.62)
28. Tell people about services and/or places where they can get help in order to promote their use. (.51)
58. Discuss proposed actions with individuals in order to provide full information and ensure understanding. (.51)

7. Service Connection (.75)

60. Advocate on behalf of individuals in order to persuade others that those people do qualify for services or financial help. (.59)
27. Provide or arrange for transportation in order to get people to needed services or treatment. (.56)
30. Follow up on individuals who have been referred, discharged, or relocated in order to ensure that services are being received and/or progress is being made. (.55)
53. Visit and/or investigate potential service resources or providers in order to assess their suitability for use by your organization. (.48)
23. Interview people, review applications and/or complete paperwork in order to determine initial or continued eligibility for services or financial help. (.45)
37. Make contact with people by phone, letter, or home visit in order to remind them of a previously scheduled appointment. (.44)

8. Tangible Service Provision (.75)

51. Observe individuals' living settings and evaluate security, hazards, and resources in order to assess the suitability of living arrangements. (.49)
26. Talk with individuals, by phone or visiting where they live, in order to locate people who might need services or financial help. (.48)
31. Put individuals in touch with people of similar backgrounds cultures, or ethnicity in order to make a move or change easier for them. (.48)
43. Teach people about money and budgeting in order to develop skills in the management of personal finances. (.48)

40. Assist individuals to find or obtain supportive papers (for example, birth records, letters, licenses, naturalization papers) in order to help them become eligible for services. (.43)

24. Collect information and follow up leads in order to locate missing individuals. (.43)

35. Describe and explain cultural patterns, job situations, service options to people who are new to or unfamiliar with your community. (.42)

52. Visit day care, foster homes, or other outplacements in order to solve problems associated with the delivery of services. (.41)

17. Take part in leisure activities with individuals in order to provide recreation or reduce loneliness. (.36)

1. Ask about and discuss job opportunities with employers in order to help people find jobs. (.29)

44. Instruct individuals in food preparation and/or housekeeping skills in order to improve homemaking capabilities. (.28)

107. Bargain or negotiate with union (or employee association) representatives in order to represent management/administration interests. (.06)

9. Professional Development (.65)

94. Evaluate your actions and decisions in order to determine if your professional activities are meeting the standards, values, and ethics required for quality. (.49)

92. Attend workshops, seminars, or programs dealing with topics of interest or need in order to improve your job knowledge and skills. (.41)

81. Evaluate your competence, availability, and feelings about individuals to whom you are providing services in order to decide if you are serving their best interests. (.40)

90. Read articles in professional/scientific journals, newspapers, or magazines in order to keep up with developments related to your job responsibilities. (.38)

38. Review your workload (appointments, visits, mail, etc.) in order to plan your activities and set priorities for a given period. (.33)

84. Take part in discussions with co-workers, talking over events or problems situations, in order to share experiences or gain insights. (.33)

29. Give information to people, by phone or in person, in order to explain and interpret the programs, policies, or procedures of your organization. (.24)

10. Staff Deployment (.88)

78. Review and analyze data about service needs and demands in order to establish workload and staffing requirements. (.74)

109. Schedule/coordinate working hours, vacations, etc., in order to arrange adequate staffing patterns and coverage. (.73)

132. Review reports of various personnel actions (for example, leave, performance evaluation, staffing) in order to ensure adherence to policy guidelines. (.70)

75. Assemble or record staff information (for example, attendance, leave, travel, compensatory time) in order to report activities, prepare payrolls, or summarize staff status. (.67)

108. Recruit and/or screen applicants (including students and volunteers) in order to fill the staffing needs of your organization. (.65)

101. Review case records and workload information in order to assign or reassign cases to staff members or units. (.63)

11. Staff Supervision (.94)

115. Discuss your evaluation of an employee's performance in order to promote understanding of expectations and/or to work out any differences of opinion. (.84)

110. Clarify job duties, roles, work assignments for supervisees (staff, students, volunteers) in order to increase individual or group effectiveness. (.81)

114. Complete rating forms, including narrative if appropriate, in order to evaluate the job performance of staff, students, or volunteers. (.81)

99. Go over case records of supervisees (including students) in order to ensure that documentation has been carried out according to proper procedures. (.78)

102. Review case records of supervisees (including students) in order to ensure that practice standards are being met. (.78)

112. Go over policies, procedures, or laws with supervisees (staff, students, volunteers) in order to inform them about the material or to alert them to effects on programs. (.77)

113. Discuss agency procedures and work expectations with new staff members, students, or volunteers in order to familiarize them with your operations. (.76)

116. Teach individuals (staff, students, volunteers) how to do a job, helping with tasks when appropriate, in order to provide on-the-job training. (.72)
97. Go over cases with supervisees (staff, students, volunteers), recommending methods and approaches, in order to instruct them in dealing with various case situations. (.66)

12. Dispute Resolution (.54)

63. Advocate on behalf of a staff member, student, or volunteer in order to protect that person from pressure or attacks from insider or outside of your organization. (.38)
91. Listen to or negotiate with dissatisfied clients, workers, students, or other consumers in order to reduce the likelihood of lawsuits or litigation. (.36)
121. Meet with members of an interdisciplinary work group in order to make them aware of the type of expertise social workers can provide and to clarify the roles of various group members. (.28)
83. Meet with or talk to your supervisor in order to get guidance on how to deal with a staff member you supervise. (.28)

13. Staff Information Exchange (.66)

10. Give guidance to staff, students, or volunteers about personal or job-related problems in order to restore job functioning. (.49)
124. Conduct a meeting (committee, staff, board, students) in order to exchange information, gather opinions, or select courses of action. (.49)
56. Present information to staff, students, or volunteers about confidentiality and the right to privacy in order to protect the rights of individuals. (.41)
14. Take part in group meetings in order to assist the group in arriving at a decision. (.38)

14. Organizational Maintenance (.91)

131. Review program financial materials (for example, policies, budgets, expenditures) in order to ensure compliance with accepted accounting procedures and organizational guidelines. (.73)
122. Estimate or analyze funding requirements in order to prepare budgets for new or existing programs. (.72)
76. Record or verify transactions in order to document expenditures and/or balance accounts for programs or other organizational units. (.67)

79. Initiate, sign off on, or approve payment vouchers in order to pay vendors, suppliers, or other providers. (.67)
104. Collect status information relating to the condition of your building/unit and equipment in order to document the need for repairs or replacement. (.64)
105. Keep track of the distribution and use of supplies, equipment, furniture, and other consumables in order to ensure an adequate supply. (.62)
103. Inspect your building or unit in order to assess security, evaluate hazards, and monitor its status. (.60)
106. Deal with or mediate differences between staff and management/administration representatives, discussing solutions to problems, in order to resolve work issues and/or prevent strikes. (.59)
111. Describe and discuss safety/security regulations with staff, volunteers, or students in order to ensure safe operations. (.57)
127. Prepare and/or submit a program proposal or grant application to the appropriate funding source in order to secure approval and/or funding for needed services. (.57)
47. Work with managers and/or supervisors, individually or in groups, in order to correct inappropriate supervisory behaviors or styles. (.54)
135. Review progress and financial reports from vendors or providers in order to ensure compliance with contract terms. (.53)
118. Teach staff how to make personnel evaluations in order to ensure accurate data on staff performance. (.52)
77. Fill out requisitions and/or vouchers in order to purchase supplies and other items. (.51)
33. Observe people as they work, giving instruction when needed or appropriate, in order to promote effective work habits. (.48)
72. Use standard forms or methods in order to compile data for billing, reimbursement, cost analysis or other purposes. (.30)

15. Delivery System Knowledge Development (.74)
95. Visit agencies/organizations, attend meetings, and make other contacts in order to keep up to date on services that can be provided in your area. (.52)
100. Contact and/or work with representatives of agencies or other organizations in order to develop cooperative arrangements. (.50)

96. Read regulations, guidelines, and other material in order to keep current about federal, state, and local regulations that affect your job. (.49)
88. Read administrative literature (for example, manuals, memos, circulars) in order to keep up with organizational policies and procedures. (.47)
36. Visit agencies, organizations, and other resource locations in order to become acquainted with the service they can provide. (.46)
70. Draft, dictate, or proofread letters to various individuals in order to answer inquiries or request specific information or action. (.43)
69. Gather and compile data about services provided to people in order to prepare statistics for various reports. (.35)

16. Program Development (.93)
129. Convert program goals and concepts into specific plans, including staffing and funding, in order to get a program started. (.76)
123. Gather information from various sources in order to assess the effectiveness of a program or organizational unit. (.72)
130. Meet with employers, administrators, or other organizational decision-makers in order to explain your program and "market" your services. (.72)
128. Develop the basic design and goals of a new program in order to meet various needs for service. (.70)
48. Describe needs to decision-makers (for examples, legislators, managers, board members, community leaders) in order to persuade them to initiate, maintain, or restore programs. (.67)
74. Compile and/or analyze available data in order to describe characteristics or establish relationships about programs, service recipients, or facilities. (.67)
98. Establish and/or write down policies, either for service or administrative functions, in order to provide standard operating procedures. (.67)
125. Get information from community leaders, client groups, community agencies, or other sources about the need for new programs. (.66)
134. Review and analyze available information about programs in order to assess the effectiveness of service being provided. (.66)

126. Meet with staff or co-workers in order to plan and develop a new or expanded service program or administrative unit.
87. Write or supervise the writing of news releases, stories, brochures, and publications in order to provide information to the public. (.63)
71. Summarize data about individuals and services, in tables or graphs, in order to present information about services. (.62)
89. Explain program or organizational needs to people, individually or in groups, in order to encourage them to contribute their time and/or to donate other resources. (.61)
50. Propose a plan to your supervisor(s) or administrator(s) in order to gather needed support for a change in practices, guidelines, or policies within your organization. (.60)
82. Explain service programs or policies to people in public appearances of various kinds in order to inform the general public about issues and programs. (.59)

17. Research/Policy Development (.75)
93. Present and/or publish findings from studies or analyses in order to share your information with appropriate audiences. (.54)
49. Take part or testify, as a professional or technical representative, in legislative forums or hearings in order to explain or advocate a position on pending social welfare legislation. (.50)
86. Provide technical assistance and support to community self-help groups in order to get them organized or achieve their objectives. (.47)
73. Carry out surveys (for example, interviews or questionnaires) with specific groups of people in order to get their opinions about services or service needs. (.46)
41. Organize or take part in a campaign or demonstration in order to persuade public officials or other decision-makers to establish or change policies or laws on behalf of individuals. (.43)
120. Conduct workshops or training sessions with members of various organizations in order to help them cope with stress or boredom on the job and to get along better with others. (.41)
45. Teach or help individuals with regard to their speaking or writing in order to improve their communication skills. (.36)

18. Instruction (.81)

117. Plan a course or training activity, designing a syllabus, making up the schedule, and/or arranging facilities in order to improve skills and knowledge. (.72)

119. Teach groups of individuals in a classroom, workshop, or other setting, according to a training plan, in order to increase knowledge and skills. (.65)

133. Review courses and/or training programs in order to evaluate whether or not learning objectives and needs are being met. (.62)

55. Construct and/or give exams, tests, or other measures in order to assess how much individuals have learned. (.55)

Appendix B

Data Collection and Data Analysis Procedures

Constructing the Composite Sample

The ACSW National Survey

When planning for the ACSW study began in 1981, no definitive, detailed information was available about the demographics of social work practitioners and the settings in which they worked. That situation changed in July 1982 when NASW distributed, for the first time, the NASW Data Bank Questionnaire to its entire membership. By the late fall of 1982, 48,319 members had responded, supplying information about personal history, education background, major work function, practice area, and practice setting. Since NASW membership was a requirement for taking the ACSW examination and since the data elements in the data bank were relevant stratification variables, it seemed most appropriate to use the Questionnaire respondents as the sampling frame and the database as the source of the validation sample. To be included in the ACSW sample, practitioners had to hold at least an MSW degree and be employed full-time in a social work position (self-defined) for at least two years.

The first step was to select from the Questionnaire respondents only those who met the eligibility criteria. This process resulted in a pool of 15,604 eligible respondents, from which a stratified random sample was drawn. Those eligible were categorized into five strata based on geographic region, primary practice function, primary practice setting, gender, and ethnicity.[1] The eligible respondents were then

This technical appendix is included for the benefit of those readers who wish to have more details about the compilation and representativeness of the sample as well as the methodologies used in data reduction.

[1] The value labels under each of these correspond to those detailed for the personal history variables of the JAQ described in Appendix A.

cast into a five-dimensional grid and the proportions in each cell were precisely determined. Within each cell, members were randomly selected to constitute a sample of approximately 7,000 potential respondents. Each stratum in the sample contained the proportion of its corresponding stratum in the population.

Between April and October 1983, three separate mailings were sent to everyone in the sample. Because response rates for whites (83%) were higher than for nonwhites (53%), a fourth non-overlapping mailing was sent to 836 members of the National Association of Black Social Workers (NABSW). By the time data collection was ended, the overall response rate was quite gratifying. Of the 7,901 total surveys mailed, 5,397 usable surveys were returned for a net response rate of 75%. The demographic characteristics of this group of respondents can be found in Table B.1.

The Occupational Social Work Survey

The sampling problems associated with this second study were much different from those in the ACSW validation study. Because this was a relatively new practice area, little was known about the characteristics of its work force. Furthermore, no sampling frame existed for use in drawing a sample of practitioners. The members of the NASW planning group took these factors into consideration and decided, at the outset, to obtain information from social workers in a broad range of practice settings regardless of whether or not they were members of NASW. A variety of sources were used, including NASW chapter Occupational Social Work Committee rosters, membership lists from the Association of Labor/Management Administrators and Consultants on Alcoholism (ALMACA), lists of military social workers, lists of practitioners who served as vendors, lists of people who had requested information about an upcoming national conference, lists of educators with expertise in the area, and lists of individuals who had requested information from NASW national or chapter offices about the field of occupational social work. These lists were combined to form a pool of approximately 2,000 unduplicated names. This was the sampling frame on which this study was based.

Two mailings of the JAQ were made early in 1985. Because the sample was a composite, many different types of individuals were surveyed. Screening criteria, based on respondents' answers to specific questions in the JAQ Personal History section, were used to eliminate respondents who were not occupational social workers. Respondents were left in the sample if (1) they made no major omis-

Table B.1. JAQ Study Samples

	ACSW Study (N = 5,397)	BSW Study (N = 1,363)	Occupational Social Work Study (N = 499)	Composite Sample (N = 7,000)	NASW Data (N = 134,240)[a]
Location:					
Northeast	1,707 (31.6%)[b]	403 (29.6%)	224 (45.0%)	2,264 (32.2%)	38,954 (28.8%)
Northcentral	1,624 (30.1%)	531 (39.0%)	91 (18.2%)	2,136 (30.5%)	34,709 (25.6%)
South	1,179 (21.8%)	281 (20.6%)	91 (18.2%)	1,505 (21.5%)	31,106 (23.0%)
West	862 (15.9%)	143 (10.5%)	85 (17.0%)	1,060 (15.1%)	21,444 (15.8%)
Other	—	—	—	—	9,144 (6.8%)
Ethnicity:					
African American	393 (7.3%)	105 (7.7%)	33 (6.6%)	527 (7.3%)	6,885 (5.8%)
White	4,756 (88.1%)	1,186 (87.0%)	449 (90.0%)	6,361 (88.0%)	103,529 (88.0%)
Hispanic	82 (1.5%)	30 (2.2%)	11 (2.2%)	123 (1.7%)	3,170 (2.7%)
Asian	91 (1.6%)	8 (0.6%)	2 (0.4%)	101 (1.4%)	1,815 (1.5%)
Other	56 (1.1%)	25 (1.9%)	4 (0.8%)	85 (1.2%)	1,580 (1.3%)
Gender:					
Female	3,260 (60.4%)	1,244 (91.3%)	256 (51.3%)	4,606 (65.8%)	100,236 (77.6%)
Male	2,119 (39.3%)	113 (8.3%)	241 (48.4%)	2,366 (30.8%)	28,952 (22.4%)
Employment Function:					
Direct service	2,879 (60.4%)	1,106 (81.1%)	200 (40.1%)	4,053 (57.9%)	65,286 (47.4%)
Supervision	552 (10.2%)	91 (6.7%)	17 (3.4%)	640 (9.1%)	5,984 (4.3%)
Management	1,428 (26.4%)	104 (7.6%)	174 (34.9%)	1,639 (23.4%)	15,739 (11.4%)
Policy/planning	62 (1.1%)	9 (.6%)	19 (3.8%)	83 (1.2%)	3,335 (2.4%)
Consultation	71 (1.3%)	12 (.9%)	56 (11.2%)	128 (1.8%)	1,589 (1.2%)
Education	385 (7.1%)	30 (2.2%)	27 (5.4%)	420 (6.0%)	4,450 (3.2%)
Non-social work	—	—	—	—	2,619 (1.9%)
Current Employment Setting:					
Social services	1,471 (27.2%)	647 (47.5%)	53 (10.6%)	2,107 (30.1%)	21,970 (15.9%)
Private practice	406 (7.5%)	13 (1.0%)	76 (15.4%)	472 (6.8%)	15,432 (11.2%)
Membership	38 (.7%)	9 (.7%)	45 (9.1%)	76 (1.3%)	715 (.5%)
Hospital	1,131 (20.9%)	171 (12.5%)	96 (19.4%)	1,354 (19.3%)	18,820 (13.7%)
Institution	195 (3.6%)	60 (4.4%)	18 (3.6%)	266 (3.8%)	2,738 (2.0%)
Outpatient facility	1,048 (19.4%)	122 (9.1%)	30 (6.0%)	1,171 (16.7%)	15,310 (11.1%)
Group home	92 (1.7%)	90 (6.7%)	—	178 (2.5%)	2,311 (1.7%)
Nursing home/ hospice	65 (1.2%)	155 (11.4%)	—	220 (3.0%)	2,343 (1.7%)
Courts/ criminal justice	84 (1.6%)	38 (2.8%)	—	118 (1.7%)	1,311 (.9%)
College/univ.	384 (7.1%)	8 (.6%)	22 (4.4%)	390 (5.6%)	4,374 (3.2%)
Elem/secondary school	405 (7.5%)	27 (2.0%)	4 (.8%)	418 (6.0%)	5,790 (4.2%)
Other (business/ government)	56 (1.0%)	17 (1.2%)	150 (30.4%)	181 (2.6%)	2,095 (1.5%)
Education Level:					
Graduate	5,238 (97.0%)	—	469 (94.0%)	5,551 (79.3%)	122,125 (92.6%)
Undergraduate	125 (2.3%)	1,363 (100%)	11 (2.2%)	1,449 (20.7%)	9,799 (7.4%)

[a] Based on the 1991 NASW membership data as reported in Gibelman and Schervish (1993).
[b] Percentages are based on sample sizes indicated at the top of each column. Frequencies and percentages may not always add up because of missing cases on some variables.

sions in their data; (2) they possessed an undergraduate or graduate degree in social work; (3) they stated they were currently earning a percentage of their income as an occupational social worker; (4) their job title and organizational affiliation indicated a probable association with occupational social work; (5) they had been employed for six months or more as an occupational social worker; (6) the focus of their clients' problems was on job-related issues such as stress, job security, or substance abuse; and (7) their write-in comments indicated an occupational social work connection. As a final check, the questionnaires of those who were initially excluded were reviewed individually by NASW staff. In many of these cases, a final screening decision was based on personal knowledge of the respondent. When screening was completed, 499 individuals remained in the data file. This group represented 47% of the 1,068 respondents who replied to the survey. The demographic characteristics of this group can also be found in Table B.1.

The BSW National Study

The problems of drawing a sample for a national study of undergraduate practitioners were formidable. As with the occupational social worker survey, no existing list of individuals could be used as a sampling frame. Historically, graduates of BSW programs had not joined NASW because of the expense of membership and their perception that the organization stressed the interests of graduate practitioners. In 1988, only 1,200 of the 105,000 NASW members were baccalaureate-level members, which meant that the NASW membership list, by itself, would not yield a representative sample. Furthermore, although the potential was quite large—Rubin (1986) estimated that there were approximately 95,000 BSW graduates at the time—the whereabouts, current educational level, and job descriptions of these individuals, except for recent graduates, were largely unknown.

In the absence of a single comprehensive list, a multi-stage sampling procedure was used. In late 1988 NASW contacted all of the 349 CSWE-accredited undergraduate social work programs, requesting mailing lists of their graduates. Lists were supplied by 149 schools, with some including those who had graduated as far back as 1971. Combining these names with NASW's BSW membership list yielded an unduplicated primary sample of 22,075 BSW graduates. This was the sampling frame to be used in the second stage of sampling.

To be included in the job analysis sample, BSW graduates had to meet a number of criteria: (1) graduation from a CSWE-accredited undergraduate program; (2) a full-time job in social work, and (3) no further graduate training. In other words, the sample was to include only those whose entry into practice was based solely on their BSW degree. To ensure that these criteria were met in the job analysis sample, and to reduce data collection costs, two mailings of a preliminary screening card was sent to the 22,075 BSW graduates in the spring and summer of 1989. Because many of the addresses supplied by the schools were not recent, the response rate was limited: only 5,228 (24%) of the BSW graduates returned completed screening cards.

To assess the extent to which these respondents were representative of the overall population, several checks were made against the limited demographic data collected from accredited BSW programs by CSWE (CSWE, 1987). The screening card asked for information about the program from which the graduate received a degree (region of the country, size of the program, and program autonomy). Although ethnicity and gender were not queried on the screening card, investigators could infer gender (in most cases) from the respondents' names. The sample (screening card respondents) and the larger population (349 CSWE-accredited BSW programs) were compared on these 4 variables using the chi-square "goodness-of-fit" procedure (Spatz & Johnston, 1984). To a great extent, the results suggest that a reasonably representative sample of graduates returned the cards.

In the sample, the proportionate distribution of programs by region of the country—northeast, northcentral, south, and west—did not differ significantly from those in the population of 349 programs (chi-square $= .672$, $p > .10$). The distribution by size of program—small, medium, or large—also did not differ statistically from the proportions in the population (chi-square $= 2.56$, $p > .10$).[2] Although male BSW graduates were a distinct minority in the population (14.7%), the sample appeared to overrepresent female graduates (chi-square $= 79.2$, $p < .001$). The authors speculated that the male graduates might have been more mobile and thus harder to track down over time. It also appeared that graduates of free-standing programs were more prevalent in the sample (chi-square $= 11.91$, $p < .01$). It was deemed likely that autonomous programs would have more resources to track down graduates and better access to university-generated alumni

---

[2] Size was defined in terms of number of graduates in a given year with "small" programs having 0-19 graduates in 1987, "medium" having 20-49, and "large" having 50 or more.

lists by program (rather than lists that combined all social science graduates).[3]

Satisfied that the sample of screening card respondents was sufficiently representative of the practice population, the investigators identified a subsample of practitioners that met the practice criteria described earlier. Of the 5,228 respondents who returned cards, 2,488 were eligible to receive the JAQ. Four mailings were sent out during the summer and fall of 1989. Of these, 1,480 usable surveys (59.5%) were returned. Figure B.1 illustrates the flow of the sampling processes that resulted in the composite database.

The Composite Sample

The three national surveys resulted in an aggregate data set comprising 7,259 respondents. At the time of the surveys, all were trained social workers actively involved in the full-time practice of social work. Due to differences in variables and incomplete data, some records had to be deleted, resulting in a composite sample of 7,000 respondents. The major demographic characteristics of this group are also described in Table B.1. Since the composite sample has been discussed in some detail in Chapter 1, we will give only an overview here.

Probably the best template to use for assessing the representativeness of the composite sample is the data set compiled from NASW membership renewal forms each year. The far right column in Table B.1 contains the most recent (1991) membership data available from NASW. Since these data contain missing entries on some variables, exact goodness-of-fit tests could not be calculated.[4] However, it is possible to use the overall characteristics of these data as a general blueprint for assessing the match between the composite sample and the national membership data.

The most striking characteristic is the predominance of women. They constitute the majority of the individuals making up each group. Over the years, social work labor force analyses have consistently confirmed this characteristic (Bureau of Labor Statistics, 1991; Fanshel, 1976; Siegel, 1982). NASW membership data indicate that the number of women joining the association increased dramatically between 1972 and 1982 (Hopps & Pinderhughes, 1987; NASW, 1983). Whites

---

[3]For a more detailed discussion of the sampling procedures used in the BSW survey, the reader should see Teare, Shank, and Sheafor (1989a, 1989b, 1990a, 1990b).

[4]It is common for respondents to personal history questionnaires to withhold information about certain demographic variables. This is particularly true with regard to gender and ethnicity.

predominate in both groups but, because of the intentional targeting of African-American respondents in the ACSW study, the composite sample contains a significantly larger percentage of this group than that reflected by the NASW membership data. The same is true for education level. As noted earlier, undergraduate social workers have not joined NASW in great numbers. Since the BSW sample was identified primarily through schools, the composite sample has more baccalaureate workers—almost four times as many as the NASW membership database.

Figure B.1. **Sampling Frames and Processes for the Composite Sample**

ACSW Validation Study (Mar. 1983–May 1984)	Occupational Social Work Study (Nov. 1984–Dec. 1985)	ACBSW Validation Study (Dec. 1988–Feb. 1990)
Sampling Frame: NASW Data Bank Questionnaire (July, 1980) (N = 48,319)	**Sampling Frames:** Occupational Social Worker source lists (e.g., NASW committee rosters, practitioner lists, vendors, ALMACA (N = 2,220)	**Sampling Frames:** 349 accredited BSW programs (Mailing lists of graduates, NASW BSW lists) (N = 22,075 BSW grads)
Screening	Job Analysis Questionnaire (Two mailings)	Screening Card (Two mailings)
(N = 15,604)	Returns: N = 1,068 (48%)	Returns: N = 5,228 (24%)
Selection	Screening	Screening
(N = 7,901)[a]	(N = 499 [47%])	(N = 2,488)
Job Analysis Questionnaire (Three mailings)		Job Analysis Questionnaire (Four mailings)
Complete returns: N = 5,397 (75%)		Returns: N = 1,488 (60%)

Master Database
N = 7,000

---

[a] This includes a nonrandom sample of 836 members of the National Association of Black Social Workers.

Social work is a profession in which the most frequent job function is the provision of direct services to clients. In each data set, the composite sample and the membership data, direct service practitioners are in the majority. Management and supervision are next in prominence, but occur with much higher frequency in the composite sample. This is probably due to the requirement that all respondents in the three studies had to be working full-time at the time they were surveyed. In both samples, the most frequent job setting is in social service agencies, with hospital and institution-based practice following relatively close behind. In the national data bank, there are considerably more private practitioners than in the composite sample. This probably reflects the fact that some NASW members engage in private practice on a part-time basis.

In summary, the most rigorous comparisons permitted by the data strongly suggest that the composite sample reflects the salient characteristics of the labor force of trained, professional social workers who belong to the national association. With regard to the BSW practitioners, the composite is thought to be more representative of practice than the NASW membership list. In those areas where the fit with national data is not exact, the differences can be explained and, in most instances, one can take the position that they enhance the diversity of the composite sample as a platform for generating data about the domain of social work practice.

Generating the Practice Framework

The data generated by the 7,000 respondents in the composite sample yielded considerable detail about the nature of their practice activities. Respondents rated how often, in the course of their jobs, they carried out each of the 131 tasks in the JAQ.[5] The task data provided so much detail, in fact, that the researchers felt overwhelmed by the sheer volume of information. To be able to describe the data and make useful inferences about its curricular implications, a framework involving a smaller number of components had to be developed. From the begin-

---

[5]The respondents actually made two ratings for each task. The first dealt with the frequency of occurrence of each task (How often?) and the second with its importance (How important?). Previous work with the JAQ had shown that there was a high correlation between frequency and importance. In the composite sample, the correlation between the two scales was .99. This confirmed that the two variables were redundant and little information would be lost by deleting one of them from the analysis. Consequently, only the frequency data were used for generating the practice framework.

ning, the researchers felt strongly that they should allow the data to define the practice framework rather than imposing one on the data. To permit "natural" subgroups of practice activity to emerge, a statistical procedure called cluster analysis was used.

Cluster Analysis

"Cluster analysis" is simply a generic name for a variety of statistical procedures that can be used to create a classification scheme (Aldenderfer & Blashfield, 1984). In this study, the tasks were grouped using a hierarchical cluster analysis developed by Ward (1963).[6] The first step in the cluster analysis involved the calculation of a 131 by 131 proximity matrix in which each cell contained a number measuring the dissimilarity between each pair of tasks.[7] This matrix was the data on which Ward's procedure, in successive stages, was used to make comparisons among all the tasks and combine those that were the most similar. The process began by treating all 131 tasks as independent clusters and iteratively decreased the number of clusters until all tasks were combined into a single cluster. The "ideal" solution, from a statistical point of view, was at the point where differences *between* clusters were maximized and differences *within* clusters were minimized. A number of criteria were used to arrive at this solution. Since clusters of job activities are key components of the practice framework used in this book, it is important to understand how they were identified and characterized.

Determining the Number of Clusters

Both theoretical and empirical precedent suggested that any classification scheme derived from the data would contain multiple dimensions, i.e., several clusters of work activity. For example, earlier formulators of various theoretical models of social work practice (Baer & Federico, 1978 and 1979; Dolgoff, 1971; Minahan, 1981; Teare & McPheeters, 1970) have all asserted that the practice content of social work is multidimensional. Furthermore, results of previous cluster analyses of smaller, more homogenous JAQ data sets had invariably

---

[6] The software used to carry out the analysis was the Statistical Package for the Social Sciences (SPSS$_x$).

[7] The similarity measure used was the squared Euclidean distance. This number was the sum (across all 7,000 respondents) of the squared differences between the frequency ratings for the two tasks. The smaller the number, the more similar the pattern of responses for the two tasks.

generated frameworks containing multiple clusters (Teare, 1979, 1981, 1987a, 1987b; Teare & McCummings, 1984). Because previous empirical studies of JAQ data consistently yielded between 10 and 23 clusters, it was felt that this larger, more heterogeneous data set would produce a framework containing between 15 and 25 clusters.

Determining when to stop forming new clusters, that is, the point at which the "ideal" solution was reached, was a bit of a problem. Most of the literature on clustering methods has been written within the past 15 years and methods are still evolving.[8] As Aldenderfer and Blashfield (1984) point out, most methods, including stopping rules, are still heuristics, or simple "rules of thumb." Recognized methodologists in this area (Aldenderfer & Blashfield, 1984; Everitt, 1979; Lorr, 1983) suggest using a blend of statistical and judgmental criteria to decide on the ideal number of clusters and their identifying labels. That approach was taken in this study.

Criteria for Establishing the Clusters

A mix of conceptual and statistical criteria, focused on the stability, meaningfulness, and homogeneity of each cluster, was used to evaluate the classification scheme formed by Ward's analysis.

Stability

One desirable attribute of any statistically derived framework is stability, that is, the assurance that one would get the same results from repeated analyses of independent samples. If the same cluster solution is repeatedly observed across independent samples from the same general population, it can be assumed to have generalizability. The very large sample of data generated by the three studies permitted some unique approaches to be taken. To assess the stability of the clusters, the 7,000 records in the composite data set were randomized and five independent subsets were created. Four consisted of 1,500 records each and the fifth contained the remaining 1,000 respondents.[9]

---

[8] The increasing availability of high-speed computers with large RAMs has spurred interest in cluster analysis. That this interest can be found in disciplines as diverse as anthropology, biology, political science, psychology, and sociology has resulted in nonstandardized methods and terminology, as well as the slow diffusion of new developments (Niemi, 1984).

[9] The sample size of 1,500 was selected because of memory limitations of the mainframe computer available to the researchers. Ward's procedure was iterative and required a tremendous amount of memory. A sample of this size, with 131 variables to be grouped, represented the maximum data set that could be processed by the computer.

By carrying out a separate cluster analysis on all five subsamples, each served as both a derivative and a confirmatory sample for the others.[10]

As with most multivariate procedures, one can decide in advance how many dimensions one wishes to examine. In this regard, eleven different cluster solutions, ranging from 15 to 25 clusters, were plotted out and carefully examined for each of the five samples. Only clusters that were repeated in at least three of the five subsamples were considered stable enough to be included in the final classification; 18 clusters met this criterion.

Meaningfulness

In addition to stability, a good classification scheme should "make sense" within the context of the discipline or general population from which it has been derived. In the present study, this meant that the clusters should contain only tasks that, from a practice perspective, could be connected logically to one another. If this sort of "conceptual internal consistency" is present, it becomes a relatively straightforward task to assign labels to the clusters that will be meaningful to the intended audience. The meaningfulness of the labels is particularly important because they become the shorthand for communicating about the set of activities represented by that cluster. Throughout this book, the cluster labels and definitions are important designations that describe the content of social workers' jobs and delineate ways this content varies among groups.

The authors took great care in developing cluster labels and descriptions. Once the stopping point was determined and the 18 clusters were identified, the tasks in each cluster were studied carefully. A definition that represented a capsule summary of the content in each cluster was written, and a two- to four-word label, intended to capture the central meaning of the cluster, was assigned. To increase the likelihood that the language used would communicate clearly to other social workers, the authors, whenever possible, relied on terms and definitions that were consistent with those contained in *The Social Work Dictionary* (Barker, 1987) and *The Encyclopedia of Social Work* (Minahan, 1987). However, if the tasks that fell into a cluster did not fit the generally accepted labels, an effort was made to introduce an entirely new label that would not be confused with existing ones.

---

[10]This procedure was essentially the same as that demonstrated by Goldstein and Linden (1969) in their study of alcoholics.

To evaluate how well the definitions reflected the task content, a process known as "retranslation" was employed.[11] If the cluster definitions and labels were clear, it was logical to assume that practitioners who had no previous experience with the material would be able to match the labels and definitions with the list of tasks from which they had been originally derived. To that end, 13 full-time social work practitioners were asked to test the meaningfulness of the authors' scheme.

The practitioners selected (or judges) were highly experienced; 11 of the 13 had more than ten years of practice experience. The majority (10) were female. Three had BSW degrees, 9 had MSWs, and 1 had a DSW. Seven were engaged in direct service provision to clients, 2 were supervisors, and 4 were administrators. They worked in a variety of practice capacities including private practice, social action, planning, industry, hospitals, mental health facilities, and social service agencies.

In their initial orientation letter, the judges were given a list of the 18 cluster labels and definitions and were asked to become familiar with them. When they were convened, they were given a more detailed orientation, some guidelines for making their judgments, and a list of the 131 tasks grouped into 18 unlabeled clusters.[12] The judges were told to examine the task groups carefully and then to assign to each the definition and label that best fit it. Of the 234 possible correct matches (13 judges x 18 clusters), the judges made 197 (84.2%) of them. Incorrect associations were carefully analyzed, discussions were held with the judges to identify problems, and, in several cases, language changes were made to the cluster labels and definitions.

Homogeneity

In a good classification scheme, clusters are distinguished not only by their inter-cluster differences, but by their intra-cluster similarities. This within-cluster similarity, or homogeneity, can be measured statistically. A frequently used index of homogeneity is Cronbach's alpha (Cronbach, 1951). It is classified as a measure of internal con-

---

[11] Retranslation was first described by Smith and Kendall (1963) as part of the development of behaviorally anchored rating scales. It is designed to enhance content validity by identifying unintended meaning that is present in derived verbal material. The process greatly resembles one used with language translation. Material in one language is first translated into another. An independent translator then retranslates it back into the original. Where differences are found, they are corrected.

[12] The task groups were presented to the judges in random order and contained no information as to cluster identity.

sistency reliability because it focuses on the consistency of responses to a set of items.[13] The alpha scores indicated a high level of homogeneity within the 18 clusters. Only the Dispute Resolution cluster ($\alpha = .54$) fell below the generally acceptable level of $\alpha = .60$ for use in research.

Concurrent Validity of the Cluster Framework

While the derivation of the clusters from five independent random samples was certainly clear evidence of the stability of the cluster solution, it should not be mistaken as evidence of the validity of the framework. To establish framework validity requires an evaluation of the cluster framework against *external* variables (Aldenderfer & Blashfield, 1984). Stated another way, the clusters should correspond to related variables that played no role in cluster formation. In this case, concurrent validity could be established if the classification scheme was shown to relate to real-life social work practice variables.

Such variables were defined within the data set generated by the JAQ—the current primary employment function reported by the respondents at they time they were surveyed (see Appendix A). These are the categories used by NASW to describe its members and, over the years, have become the standard language for classifying types of social workers. Abundant evidence of the cluster classification scheme's relation to different functions in the social work labor force is presented in chapters 2, 3, and 4. At both the BSW and MSW levels, the categories developed from the self-reported job function data are invariably associated with significant differences in task and cluster means.

The Practice Clusters

Using the process described above, the 18 task clusters were identified, defined, and labeled. The cluster definitions and labels can be found in Chapter 1, sequenced as they are discussed in the book. A list

---

[13] Cronbach's alpha is probably the most popular measure of internal consistency reliability (Carmines & Zeller, 1979). It is used with continuous data and is the average of all split-half coefficients resulting from all possible splitting of the item pool. The logic behind it is simple. If the responses to a group of items, e.g., task statements, are similar, the total scores calculated from all possible combinations of half of these items will be essentially the same. Thus, all possible resulting pairs of scores will be highly intercorrelated. If they are not similar, the intercorrelations will be low. The value of alpha ranges from a low of .00 to a high of 1.00. An alpha value of .60 or larger is considered to indicate quite an acceptable level of homogeneity for scientific purposes (Nunnally, 1978; Nurius & Hudson, 1993).

of the actual task statements in each cluster is contained in Appendix A. In addition to the task statements, the task-to-total cluster score correlation for each task is presented, which indicates the relative influence each task had in defining the cluster in which it is found. The internal consistency reliability (alpha coefficient) of each cluster is presented in both Chapter 1 and Appendix A. All of the coefficients are statistically significant ($p < .01$) and, with the exception of one cluster (Dispute Resolution), they are quite high.

Understanding the content of each task cluster is critical if one is to follow the descriptions of practice and their educational implications. The reader is encouraged to study the task and cluster materials carefully and refer to them whenever necessary.

Relationships among Clusters

One has only to read through the definitions of the clusters to come away with an appreciation for the wide range of activities carried out by social workers. The content of the clusters is indeed quite varied, but underlying this diversity are some systematic relationships. One can get a feel for some of these underlying relationships by examining the correlations among the various clusters.[14] In a sense, it is really a way of looking at the division of labor within the field of social work. For example, if two clusters are positively correlated, it means that workers who engaged in one cluster of tasks also tended to be involved in the other. The higher the intercorrelation, the more likely they were to be carried out by the same practitioners. Conversely, a negative correlation between two clusters would indicate that involvement in one area of activity reduced the likelihood of being involved in the other. Those that are independent of one another (zero correlation) had no systematic pattern of appearance in the jobs of the practitioners. As part of the cluster analysis, the correlations among all pairs of clusters were obtained. This matrix is presented in Table B.2. The clusters are arrayed so that the relationships among them can be seen more readily. Visual inspection shows two major groups of clusters; these are denoted by two triangles. The one in the upper left hand corner encompasses Cluster 1 (Interpersonal Helping) through Cluster 8 (Tangible Service Provision). The correlations among these clusters are all relatively high positive numbers. The nature of the tasks contained in these clusters require that the practitioners, more

---

[14]In hierarchical cluster analyses, the clusters do not have to be independent of, that is, uncorrelated with, one another.

Table B.2. Cluster Intercorrelations

	Help	Group	Treat	Risk/T	Protec	CPI/Ma	SConn	Tang S	ProfDv	Deploy	Super	DisptR	S.Info	OrgMi	S.Know	PrgDv	R/Pol	Inst
1. Interpersonal Helping		0.42	0.75	0.63	0.37	0.65	0.38	0.30	0.32	-0.22	-0.09	0.11	-0.03	-0.27	-0.03	-0.27	-0.13	-0.11
2. Group Work			0.49	0.37	0.26	0.29	0.17	0.27	0.34	0.06	0.20	0.28	0.32	0.07	0.10	0.12	0.33	0.34
3. Individual/Family Treatment				0.65	0.47	0.59	0.30	0.29	0.26	-0.14	-0.03	0.12	-0.02	-0.20	-0.40	-0.22	-0.13	-0.10
4. Risk Assessment/Transition					0.64	0.78	0.63	0.56	0.38	-0.02	0.07	0.35	0.13	-0.07	0.25	-0.08	-0.09	-0.12
5. Protective Services						0.52	0.45	0.48	0.23	-0.02	0.03	0.24	0.05	-0.05	0.19	-0.06	-0.02	-0.09
6. Case Planning/Maintenance							0.88	0.48	0.38	-0.11	0.00	0.25	0.02	-0.21	0.24	-0.21	-0.20	-0.20
7. Service Connection								0.70	0.33	-0.04	-0.01	0.31	0.11	-0.03	0.35	-0.01	-0.01	-0.10
8. Tangible Service Provision									0.31	0.05	0.05	0.33	0.19	0.14	0.32	0.14	0.21	0.07
9. Professional Development										0.21	0.27	0.40	0.37	0.21	0.50	0.30	0.29	0.24
10. Staff Deployment											0.76	0.47	0.59	0.76	0.48	0.70	0.39	0.36
11. Staff Supervision												0.52	0.63	0.57	0.44	0.55	0.35	0.41
12. Dispute Resolution													0.57	0.42	0.48	0.46	0.35	0.29
13. Staff Information Exchange														0.57	0.50	0.64	0.50	0.48
14. Organizational Maintenance															0.47	0.79	0.52	0.40
15. Delivery System Knowledge Development																0.60	0.40	0.25
16. Program Development																	0.88	0.52
17. Research/Policy Development																		0.66
18. Instruction																		

often than not, come into direct contact with clients in providing services. These were labeled "client-centered" clusters. The triangle in the lower right corner encompasses Cluster 10 (Staff Deployment) through Cluster 18 (Instruction). The intercorrelations here are also quite high and positive. Activities in these clusters were carried out on behalf of clients, but were focused on the delivery system and its resources. These have been labeled "delivery system-centered" clusters. A most interesting feature of this scheme is that the two sets of clusters are relatively independent of one another. The rectangle in the upper right-hand corner of the matrix contains the correlations between the two sets of clusters, which, for the most part, show little if any relationship between the two sets.[15] In a number of instances, the intercorrelations are negative.

An exception to the overall pattern is Cluster 9 (Professional Development) which is essentially "practitioner-centered." It correlates to the same degree with both the client-centered and the delivery system-centered cluster sets.

The arrangement of the clusters in Table B.3 highlights these patterns even more dramatically. The first column contains the average intercorrelation of each cluster with those in the client-centered array. The second column lists the average intercorrelation with those in the delivery system-centered array. As expected, the cluster relating to self-development and professional growth seems to stand alone.

Factor Analysis of the Clusters

Most depictions of social work practice suggest that a characterization relying on only two major streams of activity—client-centered and delivery system-centered activity—would be an oversimplification. (Chapter 1 presents an overview of these depictions.) Indeed, the pattern of relationships in Table B.2 strongly suggests that there is more to these data than just two components. To explore this further, a factor analysis was carried out using the 18 cluster scores for each of the 7,000 practitioners.[16] It is not uncommon, in exploratory situa-

---

[15]Because the composite sample is so large, even a correlation as low as $\pm.08$ would be statistically significant. However, it is too low to be of practical use. With the composite data set, it is better to consider only those variables whose intercorrelation exceeds $\pm.20$ as really being related to one another.

[16]Because there were differing numbers of tasks in the various clusters, mean cluster scores were used instead of total scores. Thus, regardless of size, the score for each cluster ranged from 1.0 to 5.0. Using $SPSS_x$, a principle components factor analysis was run using a varimax rotation of an orthogonal factor structure. Orthogonal rotation was used to arrive at a mathematically unique solution.

Table B.3. Average Cluster Intercorrelations with Cluster Sets

Clusters	Correlation with Client-Centered Set	Correlation with System-Centered Set
1. Interpersonal Helping	.50	-.12
2. Group Work	.32	.20
3. Individual/Family Treatment	.51	-.08
4. Risk Assessment/Transition	.61	.04
5. Protective Services	.45	.00
6. Case Planning/Maintenance	.57	-.04
7. Service Connection	.47	.06
8. Tangible Services	.44	.17
9. Professional Development	.32	.31
10. Staff Deployment	-.06	.56
11. Staff Supervision	.09	.53
12. Dispute Resolution	.24	.47
13. Staff Information Exchange	-.06	.57
14. Organization Maintenance	.06	.56
15. Delivery System Knowledge Development	.17	.45
16. Program Development	-.08	.61
17. Research/Policy Development	.00	.48
18. Instruction	-.04	.42

tions, to request a range of factor solutions and examine each one to better understand the data. Therefore, factor solutions ranging from two to eight factors were requested. The two-factor solution yielded a rotated factor matrix with two clear-cut factors. Clusters 10 through 18 loaded heavily on Factor 1. It clearly dealt with delivery system-centered activities. Clusters 1 through 8 loaded heavily on Factor 2 and was clearly the client-centered dimension of work activity. Cluster 9 (Professional Development) had equal loadings on each of the two factors. The accepted statistical criteria suggested, however, that more than two factors were needed to explain the common variance in the data. Using a graphic plot of the eigen values (the "scree" plot) and the magnitude of the eigen values as criteria, the authors found a clear indication that *five* factors should be extracted and examined.[17] The loadings of each of the clusters on these five factors can be found in Table B.4. As can be seen, the 18 clusters array themselves rather clearly over the five factors.

Factor 1 was defined by clusters that have a common focus on the provision of direct services to clients, individually and in groups, by means of a combination of formal intervention strategies and more

[17]The criteria for stopping the extraction of factors in factor analysis are more refined than those used in cluster analysis to determine the number of clusters.

generalized techniques of problem solving and helping. Since the emphasis seemed to be on bringing about changes in the clients themselves, the factor has been labeled "Client Change."

Factor 2, which was also client-oriented, contained clusters that focused on situations that impinged on clients and on the resources that were brought to bear in dealing with their problems—such as Protective Services (Cluster 5), Service Connection (Cluster 7), and Tangible Service Provision (Cluster 8). Because this factor described a domain of activities associated with reducing risks and marshalling resources for clients, it was labeled "Client Situation Change." Since both Factors 1 and 2 deal with the change process as it pertains to clients, it is not surprising that Risk Assessment\Transition (Cluster 4) and Case Planning/Maintenance (Cluster 6) have substantial loading on the two factors.

Factor 3 was defined almost entirely by Cluster 9 (Professional Development). It was the only factor that seemed to focus on the practitioner-centered activities associated with growth, self-awareness, and evaluation. Given this orientation, it is not surprising that it also derived its meaning from the cluster associated with Delivery System

Table B.4. Rotated Factor Loadings of the JAQ Clusters

Clusters	Factor I Client Change	Factor II Client Situation Change	Factor III Professional Competence Development	Factor IV Organization and Unit Operation	Factor V Resource/ Service Change
Interpersonal Helping	**.81**	.22	.19	-.16	-.07
Group Work	**.68**	.08	.02	.10	**.53**
Individual/Family Treatment	**.86**	.23	-.02	-.06	-.06
Risk Assessment	**.62**	**.63**	.15	.10	-.16
Protective Services	.39	**.68**	-.16	.08	-.06
Case Planning	**.57**	**.55**	.34	-.03	-.28
Service Connection	.15	**.82**	.32	-.01	-.08
Tangible Service	.11	**.86**	.08	.06	.22
Professional Development	.30	.15	**.78**	.22	.20
Staff Deployment	-.10	-.04	-.01	**.92**	.06
Staff Supervision	.12	-.10	.05	**.87**	.08
Dispute Resolution	.18	.28	.23	**.64**	.12
Staff Information Exchange	.09	.04	.20	**.72**	.34
Organization Maintenance	-.23	.08	.00	**.78**	.28
Delivery System Knowl. Devel.	-.14	.39	**.56**	**.54**	.11
Program Development	-.27	.06	.17	**.71**	.45
Research/Policy Development	-.12	.08	.11	.34	**.82**
Instruction	.10	-.12	.08	.32	**.78**

Note. Factor loadings in **bold** type indicate the primary clusters defining a given factor. Those in **bold underlined** type indicate a cluster that loads on more than one factor. Generally speaking, only a factor loading greater than ±.40 should be considered of interest.

Knowledge Development (Cluster 15). It has been labeled "Professional Competence Development."

Factor 4 was defined by most of the clusters that dealt with the management of organizational units and the deployment and supervision of staff. With the exception of Program Development (Cluster 16), this factor's emphasis was on the operational maintenance of delivery system units. Accordingly, Factor 4 has been labeled "Organization/Unit Operation."

Factor 5 contained those clusters that focused more on the community and the larger service delivery system. It encompassed activities associated with needs analysis, social action, and the provision of expert technical assistance to various groups outside of the organization (Cluster 17), and the development and evaluation of programs of formal instruction to a variety of individuals (Cluster 18). Given this emphasis on both formal and informal group interaction, it was not surprising that Group Work (Cluster 2) also loaded substantially on Factor 5. This factor was labeled "Resource/Service Change."

Conclusion

When the task analysis instrument, the Job Analysis Questionnaire, was conceived, it was intended that its task content would cover a wide range of social work activities. However, that content was not designed to reflect any formal models of practice intervention or any inherent organization of the domain of practice. As this monograph has demonstrated, the development of the JAQ was an evolutionary process in which successive panels of subject matter experts contributed task content and edited task statements. In the formulation of task statements, panel members were consistently told to avoid language that suggested particular treatment models or theoretical orientations. Despite this, the data analysis produced an ex post facto framework of clusters and factors that "made sense" and was consistent with a number of theoretical formulations of social work practice.

References

Mark S. Aldenderfer and Roger K. Blashfield, *Cluster Analysis*. Beverly Hills: Sage, 1984.

Robert L. Barker, *The Social Work Dictionary*. Silver Spring, MD: National Association of Social Workers, 1987.

Betty Baer and Ronald Federico, eds., *Educating the Baccalaureate Social Worker*, 2 vols. Cambridge, MA: Ballinger, 1978 and 1979.

Bureau of Labor Statistics, *Household Data Survey: Employed Civilians by Detailed Occupation, 1983-1991*. Washington, DC: Author, 1991.

Edward G. Carmines and Richard A. Zeller, *Reliability and Validity Assessment*. Beverly Hills and London: Sage Publications, 1979.

Council on Social Work Education, *Statistics on Social Work Education in the United States*. Washington, DC: CSWE, 1987 (updated annually).

Lee J. Cronbach, "Coefficient Alpha and the Internal Structure of Tests," *Psychometrika*, 16 (September 1951): pp. 297-334.

Ralph Dolgoff, "Basic Skills for Practice in the Human Services: A Curriculum Guide," in Frank Loewenberg and Ralph Dolgoff (eds.), *Teaching of Practice Skills in Undergraduate Programs in Social Welfare and Other Helping Professions*. New York: Council on Social Work Education, 1971, p. 25.

B. S. Everitt, "Unresolved Problems in Cluster Analysis," *Biometrics*, 35 (March 1979): pp. 169-181.

David Fanshel, "Status Differentials: Men and Women in Social Work," *Social Work*, 21 (November 1976): pp. 448-454.

Margaret Gibelman and Philip H. Schervish, *Who We Are: The Social Work Labor Force as Reflected in the NASW Membership*. Washington, DC: National Association of Social Workers, 1993.

Samuel Goldstein and J. D. Linden, "Multivariate Classification of Alcoholics by Means of the MMPI," *Journal of Abnormal Psychology*, 24 (December 1969): pp. 661-669.

June Gary Hopps and Elaine B. Pinderhughes, "Profession of Social Work: Contemporary Characteristics," in Anne Minahan (ed.), *Encyclopedia of Social Work*, Vol 2. Silver Spring, MD: National Association of Social Workers, 1987, pp. 351-366.

Maurice Lorr, *Cluster Analysis for Social Scientists*. San Francisco: Jossey-Bass, 1983.

Ann Minahan, "Purpose and Objectives of Social Work Revisited," *Social Work* (January 1981): pp. 5-6.

Ann Minahan, ed., *Encyclopedia of Social Work*, 2 vols. Silver Spring, MD: National Association of Social Workers, 1987.

National Association of Social Workers, "Membership Survey Shows Practice Shifts," *NASW News* (November 1983): pp. 6-7.

Richard G. Niemi, "Series Editor's Introduction," in Mark S. Aldenderfer and Roger K. Blashfield, *Cluster Analysis*. Beverly Hills: Sage, 1984.

Jum C. Nunnally, *Psychometric Theory*, 2nd ed. New York: McGraw-Hill, 1978.

Paula S. Nurius and Walter W. Hudson, *Human Services Practice, Evaluation, and Computers*. Pacific Grove, CA: Brooks/Cole, 1993.

Allen Rubin, "Current Statistical Trends in Social Work Education: Issues and Implications," in *Social Work Education Monograph Series #4*. Austin: University of Texas School of Social Work, 1986.

Sheldon Siegel, "Graduates in the Labor Force." Paper presented at the annual meeting of the National Association of Deans and Directors of Schools of Social Work, New York, November 15, 1982 (unpublished manuscript).

Patricia Cain Smith and L. M. Kendall, "Retranslation of Expectations: An Approach to the Construction of Unambiguous Anchors for Rating Scales," *Journal of Applied Psychology*, 47 (April 1963): pp. 149-155.

Chris Spatz and James O. Johnston, *Basic Statistics: Tales of Distributions*. Monterey, CA: Brooks/Cole, 1984.

Robert J. Teare, "An Empirical Analysis of Social Work Practice in a Public Welfare Setting," in Frank Clark, et al. (eds.), *The Pursuit of Competence in Social Work*. San Francisco: Jossey-Bass, 1979.

Robert J. Teare, *Social Work Practice in a Public Welfare Setting*. New York: Praeger, 1981.

Robert J. Teare, *Validating Social Work Credentials for Human Service Jobs: Report of a Demonstration*. Silver Spring, MD: National Association of Social Workers, 1987a.

Robert J. Teare, *National Survey of Occupational Social Workers*. Silver Spring, MD: National Association of Social Workers, 1987b.

Robert J. Teare and LeVerne McCummings, "Validation of the ACSW Examination: Implications for Education and Practice." Roundtable presented at the 30th Annual Program Meeting of the Council on Social Work Education, Detroit, MI, March 12, 1984.

Robert J. Teare & Harold L. McPheeters, *Manpower Utilization in Social Welfare*. Atlanta: Southern Regional Education Board, 1970.

Robert J. Teare, Barbara Shank, and Bradford W. Sheafor, "The National Undergraduate Practitioner Survey: A Status Report." Paper presented at the 7th Annual Conference of the Association of Baccalaureate Social Work Program Directors, San Diego, September, 1989a.

Robert J. Teare, Barbara Shank, and Bradford W. Sheafor, "The BSW Graduate: What Happens After Graduation?" Paper presented at the 18th Annual Alabama-Mississippi Social Work Education Conference, Vicksburg, MS, October, 1989b.

Robert J. Teare, Barbara Shank, and Bradford W. Sheafor, "The National Undergraduate Practitioner Survey: Practice Content and Implications for Education and Certification." Paper presented at the 36th Annual Program Meeting of the Council on Social Work Education, Reno, NV, March, 1990a.

Robert J. Teare, Barbara Shank, and Bradford W. Sheafor, "The National Survey of BSW Practitioners," in Kenneth J. Kazmerski (ed.), *New Horizons: Expanding Directions for Baccalaureate Education*. Orlando: University of Central Florida, 1990b, pp. 97-102.

Joe H. Ward, "Hierarchical Grouping to Optimize an Objective Function," *Journal of the American Statistical Association*, 58 (March 1963): pp. 236-244.

An Evaluative Assessment of Methodology Used in the National Study

Invited Commentary
by
Walter Hudson
Arizona State University

It is a maxim of applied science that no study is perfect. However, the work of Teare and Sheafor in their investigation and description of practice-sensitive social work education comes enviably close. From conception to measurement, from data gathering to data cleaning, from statistical analysis to report writing—through all phases of this work—the authors have provided two treasures: a wealth of valuable information and a splendid exemplar of how rigorous investigation should be conducted.

It has been a pleasure and a privilege for me to have watched, from afar, a good portion of this work at nearly all stages of its development and completion. Near the end of the data analysis phase and well into the report writing, I was asked to read, comment on, and offer advice about the methodology of this research. At that time I indicated I did not think this was *good* work—it was *outstanding* work. It has continued to be so. The final product is one that readers can rely on to provide the best such information about social work education than has ever before been made available.

When I was asked to provide commentary about the research methodology, I assumed the authors wanted a critical review. Unfortunately, from my point of view, they have made that task extremely difficult. The work is so solid that it becomes difficult to be critical of it and to do so would likely detract from its value. Thus, rather than attempt to draw attention to trivial considerations that would contribute little if anything to an understanding and use of the information, I would like to note, from a methodological perspective, some perspectives and interpretations that readers might find useful to consider. In most instances, they are simply suggestions for alternative or supplemental approaches to data analysis that will enhance the interpretability of the data. In framing my comments about methodology, I will be drawing most heavily on Chapter 1 and Appendix B. My more general comments will relate to material throughout the book.

Methodology

Sampling

Any study of this magnitude must be examined from the standpoint of the adequacy of the sampling process and the representativeness of the sample. The authors have been very careful to describe the strengths and limitations of the various sampling frames (e.g., NASW and NABSW membership lists, BSW graduate screening cards) from which respondents were selected. Sources of attrition have been described; the resulting samples have been compared to the most recent aggregate demographic data on social workers; and disparities have been noted. In short, the sampling procedures and resulting samples have been very well described in this Appendix B. The narrative is clear and lucid, and Table B.1 and Figure B.1 are masterful summaries of the sampling procedures used in the study.

Data Reduction and Cluster Reliability

As noted in Chapter 1 and Appendix B, the major data reduction tool for the study was a form of hierarchical cluster analysis. It resulted in 18 clusters (they can be viewed as constructs) for which a separate cluster score could then be computed for each respondent. The cluster score was the sum of the frequency score given for each task contained in the cluster. Stated differently, cluster analysis was used to produce 18 subscales from the research instrument, and each subscale score was a simple summated score.

In Chapter 1, the internal consistency reliabilities (alpha coefficients) are reported to range from .54 to .94. Even in large sample studies such as this, subscales with internal consistency reliabilities less than .60 should be used and interpreted with caution. Cluster 12 (Dispute Resolution), with an $\alpha = .54$, falls into this category. The remaining 17 clusters are strong enough with respect to measurement error characteristics to be quite useful, although three other subscales had reliabilities below .70. In developing revised versions of the JAQ, researchers might consider adding some task items to these subscales, which could increase their reliability.[1] The task analysis instrument is

---

[1] The lower reliability of Clusters 2 (Group Work), 9 (Professional Development), 12 (Dispute Resolution), and 13 (Staff Information Exchange) is due primarily to lack of variance rather than lack of task items. Clusters 2, 12, and 13 were infrequent activities for all respondents, while almost everyone reported being engaged in professional development activities. This reduced variability limits the size of the intercorrelations among items and, consequently, the alpha coefficients, in these clusters.

so strong, however, that it warrants only minor additional work that could result in substantial improvement.

Construct Validity of the Clusters

In deriving the 18 clusters on which the practice framework is based, the authors randomly split the entire sample into 5 data sets. Each was used to generate clusters independently of the others. Only clusters that emerged in three out of the five solutions were retained. In a Chapter 1 footnote, the authors state that this type of finding speaks to the convergent validity of the derived subscales. It does, but in a somewhat limited manner. More compelling evidence of the construct validity of the clusters, expressed in terms of divergent and convergent relationships, can be found in Table B.2, which presents the intercorrelations among all possible pairs of clusters and clearly suggests that a large group of clusters (Clusters 1 through 8) are related to one another (i.e., convergent). As the authors point out, these "client-centered" clusters correspond rather closely to the type of activities various theorists have subsumed under the construct of "direct practice." By the same token, these same clusters are relatively independent (i.e., divergent) of another large group (Clusters 10 through 18) of intercorrelated "system-centered" clusters. This latter group contains activities that various theorists have traditionally labeled "indirect services." Differences in the work content of these two practice areas is taken as a given in the practice literature. Thus, as representatives of these constructs, the clusters "behave" as they should.

Furthermore, the authors have done a superb job of demonstrating the stability of the subscales (clusters) across different large samples. This demonstration is important because it illustrates clearly that the obtained clusters are not an artifact of sampling error. Best yet, such stability speaks directly to the generality of the subscales when the JAQ instrument is used with different groups.

Some Suggested Analyses

The authors have generated a rich and very useful data set. Because of its size and complexity, it could serve as an interesting educational tool for exploring alternative approaches to the analysis of large data sets. Several alternatives come to mind.

As the authors noted, their use of cluster analysis was essentially a post hoc procedure for determining how many and what kinds of subscales existed for the 131 items they analyzed. The cluster analysis was superbly executed, providing the 18 subscales that became the major focus of the report. At this point, it would be interesting and worthwhile to use a form of confirmatory factor analysis to determine how well the data conform to the obtained subscale definitions. One could use a device as simple as the Thurstone Multiple Group Method of factor analysis, or the confirmatory factor analysis within the LISREL program. If the confirmation was substantial, that finding would lend further support to the definition of the 18 clusters as types of subscales.

It would also be interesting to carry out a factor analysis using the task data rather than the clusters as input to the correlation matrix. To be sure, the tasks are inherently less reliable than the clusters, but using them would shed further light on the dimensionality of the data set. The use of factor scores rather than cluster scores to create profiles would, however, be more complicated to interpret since the factor scores would contain contributions from all the factors identified in the analysis.

It is understandable that the authors elected to use orthogonal rotation in their factor analysis; this is a mathematically unique solution and minimizes disputes about findings based on methodological concerns. It does, however, assume that all of the factors are independent of one another. It would be interesting to determine whether or not these practice dimensions are indeed uncorrelated. If they are, that could be disclosed from the results of an oblique rotation which would permit the construction of a factor correlation matrix. Orthogonality is much more informative when it is a finding rather than a requirement that is imposed on data. It is hoped that some future analysis of the data might shed additional light on this feature of the data.

Values and Perspectives

Teare and Sheafor have worked very hard, as noted in the preface, to present the findings in a manner that allows the data to "speak for themselves." Of course, data rarely speak with complete clarity. What has been well accomplished, however, is a presentation of the methodology and the findings in a manner that puts the onus of interpretation and application of these data on those who would shape educational policy informed by the realities of professional practice.

In this regard, it strikes this reviewer as critical to highlight yet another point that was also made in the preface to this book. It is one that may be read and forgotten by many. Nowhere have Teare and

Sheafor suggested that these findings about "what we are doing" in the world of practice can replace the value judgments concerning "what we should be doing" in social work education. The critical issue at hand here is to recognize that the authors have done an outstanding job of describing "what is." They have also been clear about their refusal to be prescriptive and have admirably resisted the impulse to tell the reader "what should be." In some instances, their findings are congruent with historical perceptions; in others, they are considerably at odds. How the profession will ultimately react to these data remains to be seen. This is a theme elaborated upon by Charles Guzzetta in his commentary in Chapter 5.

Up to now, it has been difficult to rationally advance or oppose any educational policy in the absence of knowing what we are currently about. Chapters 2 and 3 of this book shed enormous light on the nature of undergraduate and graduate social work practice. Chapter 4 is a superb beginning in the comparison of the two levels of practice and is a mine of information to help guide best choices about where to reconcile the similarities and differences between these two levels of practice and education. For the first time in a quarter-century we can begin with a solid grasp of how they are alike and how they are different. That will help greatly in deciding how they *should be* alike and how they *should be* different.

Despite the enormous and admirable efforts of the authors in presenting the findings of this research, it is all but impossible to fully treat so large a body of information in a single volume such as this. While it is not ageless, it is the first and best of its kind and it is hoped that additional reports will emerge from the data as the authors and others further explore the information that lies within.

Appendix C

A Technique for Establishing the Practice Relatedness of Social Work Curricula

As William Reid stated so aptly in his foreword to this book, "If social work were a city, you might be hard put to find it. The directions you would get would be contradictory." Similarly, if you were to ask a number of social work educators the objectives of social work education, you would get a variety of answers. Yet however they phrased them, somewhere in that mix of motives you would find a common theme—the preparation of students for the world of practice. This appendix focuses on that commonality. It describes a process for assessing the relationship between a program's curriculum and a quantitative depiction of practice exemplified by the task clusters that emerged from the national job analysis study. Stated most succinctly, the process is linked to the central theme of this book—establishing the "practice relatedness" or practice sensitivity of a curriculum.

Four Rationales

At first glance the task can seem daunting. There is no doubt that if a study of the practice relatedness of a curriculum is done properly, it can be a complex and time-consuming activity, but it also offers a number of important benefits.

First of all, empirical evidence regarding the relative fit between practice and education can become a powerful political tool in negotiations with university administrators. The ability to demonstrate "curriculum relevance" from hard data is something that few, if any, other disciplines can match. Coupled with favorable statistics on the projected demand for social workers (U.S. Bureau of Labor Statistics, 1992) and the expansion of student interest in social work education programs (Lennon, 1993), these data should help both BSW and MSW programs at least sustain their level of financial support in an era of cost cutting, strategic planning, and budget reallocation.

Second, social work education programs and practice are inseparably linked. Schools depend on agencies for field placements and agencies depend on the schools for providing their next generation of social workers. Collaborative efforts between these two important constituents of the social work community can only be enhanced by using empirical data that inform each about the other. If a school's practice community has greater confidence that education really prepares graduates to perform needed practice activities, agencies are more likely to invest their resources in providing academic leave to employees and developing high-quality field instruction opportunities.

Third, as a school prepares for accreditation review, a clear assessment of the school's curriculum in relation to the clusters generated from this national task analysis can be valuable. These data can serve both as a basis for curriculum assessment in the self-study phase and as a means of demonstrating the validity of a curriculum as practice preparation when data are presented to CSWE's Commission on Accreditation.

Fourth, and perhaps most important, the task analysis data provide an important base for examining and revising the curriculum of a social work education program. A school can surely benefit simply from using the data as a general background for discussing its curriculum, and thus increase the likelihood that it will prepare its graduates to perform the appropriate job functions. In such cases, the comprehensive picture of social work practice presented herein can help to expand the inherently limited views of social work practice held by any small group of faculty members, students, or practice representatives.

Yet, applying this study's quantitative depiction of practice to a program's qualitative understanding of its curriculum fails to maximize the data's usefulness for curriculum development. Completing an empirical comparison of *both* practice and a curriculum can help those involved in curriculum development to set aside their personal biases, at least temporarily, and consider the aspects of practice for which their graduates are either overprepared or underprepared.[1] With that foundation knowledge in place, schools can (perhaps more rationally) establish a curriculum that represents practice-sensitive social work education.

---

[1] In the authors' view, achieving a perfect match between practice and education is not in itself a desirable goal. Rather, it is our contention that, backed by data about the relative fit between the content of practice and education, schools can best make decisions about what curriculum content to offer, where it should be provided (i.e., the classroom, field instruction, or agency training), and in how much depth.

A Brief History

The process described in this appendix was originally developed as a component of NASW's Curriculum Validation Project (Teare, Sheafor, & Gauthier, 1984).[2] That project reflected NASW's and the profession's deep concern over the phenomenon of "reclassification/declassification," that is, the systematic erosion of the use of social work credentials as minimum requirements for hiring individuals to fill social work positions. Although employers had a variety of motives, some of them far from clear, the end result was the same—the hiring of fewer applicants with social work degrees to fill positions traditionally held by social workers. The phenomenon persists to this day, and is decried because of an underlying belief within the profession that social service and social work interventions require considerable skills and that such skills are imparted only by social work education.

Whether the motive is university-level accountability, program accreditation, agency relations, or curriculum improvement, the need that existed more than a decade ago remains the same today—to demonstrate that the types of skills and knowledge taught in social work curricula have a clear relationship to the activities graduates will be expected to perform in practice.

Job Relatedness and Validity

At the heart of this demonstration of the link between education and practice is the assumption that a professional curriculum prepares its graduates, at least to some degree, to carry out the tasks performed on the job. This presumed job relatedness is called validity. The basic concepts of validity and validation have been described by Nunnally and Bernstein (1994) and Hudson (1982), and their role in personnel decision making has been amply covered by Gatewood and Feild (1994). Validity may be established for educational credentials by linking them to job performance (Cronbach, 1971).

---

[2] It has been applied on three occasions with outcomes that, in broad terms, corroborate the linkage between the curricula of the schools examined and the practice of social workers (Shank, 1993; Sheafor, Teare, Hancock, & Gauthier, 1985; and Teare, 1987). However, each study identified important areas where the curricula could (and should) be fine-tuned to better serve the needs of graduates and the social work profession. The evidence to date indicates that this procedure can become a valuable tool for strengthening social work education.

Four types of validity have been identified over the years—concurrent, predictive, construct, and content validity. The relative strengths and limitations of each have been widely discussed in the literature (American Psychological Association, 1985; Anastasi, 1976; Cronbach, 1971; Gatewood & Feild, 1994; Nunnally & Bernstein, 1994) and need not be recounted here. Establishing construct validation is appropriate when one is interested in validating a measure of an abstract property by showing that it behaves in ways consistent with expectations derived from theory. Establishing predictive and concurrent validity require that an external "criterion" be used as the standard against which the measure is evaluated. No single, agreed-upon measure of job performance in social work is available.

It was decided that establishing content validity was the best way to assess the job relatedness or "practice relevance" of social work curricula (Teare, Higgs, Gauthier, & Feild, 1984a). In this case, content validity involves identifying a domain of job-related activities (practice content) and making a judgment about whether or not the selection device (curriculum experiences) adequately covers the components of the domain. Judgments of "subject matter experts" are used to determine the degree to which the selection device covers the content domain of the job. The steps for carrying this out this procedure will now be described in some detail.

The Practice Validation Model

The major steps in establishing the job relatedness of a curriculum are depicted in Figure C.1. As the figure clearly shows, two major areas of activity are involved: the identification and depiction of the job component (i.e., practice content) to which the selection process is targeted and the identification and depiction of the curriculum component (educational content) on which the selection process is based. As Figure C.1 shows, several steps are involved in the process and the number (in parentheses) above each box indicates the sequence in which they should be carried out. It is assumed that the sequence of steps (1 through 5) resulting in the depiction of practice content would proceed before the curriculum description (steps 6 through 12) is obtained,[3]

---

[3] It should be remembered that the methodology developed for the original NASW Classification Validation Study was designed to assist a *particular* school in a *particular* labor market area in demonstrating the content validity of its curriculum for *specific* strategic jobs, that is, those for which it provided a significant number of applicants.

Figure C.1. Conceptual Framework for the Content Validation of a Curriculum

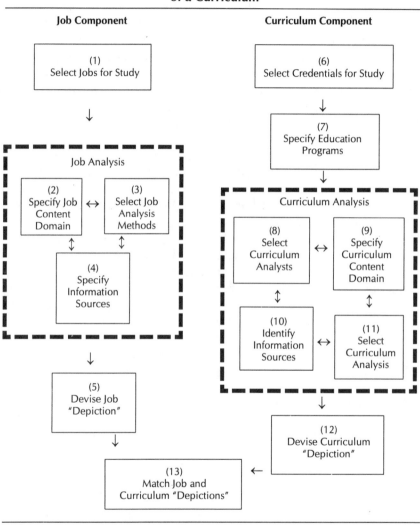

and that the curriculum should be relevant to the practice requirements of the job and not the other way around.[4]

---

[4]The case is often made that the preparation provided by a job-related educational experience may very well be broader than the boundaries of a particular job. This is certainly true. The case cannot be made, however, for the job-relatedness of an educational experience for a particular job if the credential is deficient in providing its holder with important areas of job content.

The Job Component

In an actual validation study, job analyses would be carried out on one or more jobs felt to be within the purview of the curriculum. A "depiction" of the job(s) would result from these analyses. This depiction obviously reflects the method used by the analysts. In this validation effort, the job depictions reflect the format and content of the Job Analysis Questionnaire and are described in terms of an array of tasks and task clusters, along with an indication of the frequency with which they are carried out and their importance to the performance of the job in question.

In this appendix, a particular job in a labor market will not be used as the job component. Instead, the 18 task clusters described in chapter 1 will be used as the framework for constructing job and practice depictions. As has already been seen, these data make it possible to construct a both a characterization and a profile for the BSW practitioners in direct services (Figure 2.5) and for MSW practitioners in direct services (Figure 3.4), supervision (Figure 3.6), management and administration (Figure 3.7), and education (Figure 3.8). If desired, depictions could also be constructed for typical positions in a variety of job settings and practice areas. The particular practice depictions selected—for example, BSW or MSW; direct services, supervision, or administration—would depend on the nature of the jobs to be targeted by the curriculum. In any event, once these depictions have been completed, the next step is to analyze the curriculum.

The Curriculum Component

There is an old adage that states, "The last thing the fish is aware of is the water in which it swims." Because most educators have been immersed in the educational process for some time, they tend to take many things for granted and find it difficult to step back and analyze what they do in an objective fashion. For this reason, when the curriculum analysis methods were being developed, the educational consultants on the task force felt that a number of assumptions had to be made explicit. These became the guidelines for carrying out the curriculum analysis.[5]

---

[5]The authors are indebted to members of the original NASW project Advisory Committee and the Job and Curriculum Analysis Task Forces who played a major role in the early formulation of these guidelines. These educators and administrators included Michael Austin, Betty Baer, Jeanne Bowman, Kirk Bradford, Clifford Brennan, Patricia Ewalt, Hubert Feild, Charles Guzzetta, Dorothy Harris, Catherine Higgs, Herbert Jarrett, Paul Keys, Dorothy Pearson, Peter Pecora, Sheldon Siegel, Dutton Teague, and Henrietta

Emphasis on common experiences. When an academic credential is talked about as a job requirement, it is generally treated as if it were an indivisible entity. Thus, one tends to hear about a BSW or an MSW degree as the necessary educational preparation. In some instances a specialization or practice area, such as child welfare, is designated, but beyond that, uniqueness in educational background is not typically taken into consideration. Since highly individualized preparation is typically not recognized, the depiction resulting from the curriculum analysis reflects only those experiences shared by all (or the great majority of) students who complete the degree requirements in a given program. Thus, the curriculum analysis concentrates on required courses. This point is especially important in the analyses of BSW curricula.

Development of an Additive Model. In a typical academic program, some courses serve as building blocks for others and are thus designated as prerequisites. Other courses serve to reinforce material presented previously. Such interdependency, although widely recognized by educators, is difficult to measure reliably. Rather than make complex assumptions about nonlinear combinations of such interactions, the curriculum analysis reflects a simple "additive" model. That is, every course is viewed as an independent entity and is not assumed to interact with previous or subsequent offerings. Thus, when the construction of the curriculum depiction is described later, the reader will see that it is simply the weighted summation of the individual courses.[6] It is felt that this approach is more defensible than the use of an elaborate scoring rationale for which verification might be hard to obtain.

Emphasis on learning expectations. The Curriculum Task Force consistently emphasized that the curriculum analysis should focus on that which was expected to be *learned* rather than on that which was purported to be *taught*. The methodology emphasizes this in two ways. First, the analysis is predicated on the belief that learning certain content is more likely to occur if it is reinforced. Such reinforcement would occur if mastery of the content is evaluated and reflected in the grades given in the course. Consequently, the scrutiny of examinations, evaluations, and grading procedures is an integral part of the analysis. Second, the Level of Preparation Rating Scale (described in the next section) places a high value on learning experiences that are

---

Waters. It should be pointed out, however, that the procedures presented here have been developed beyond those initial guidelines, and responsibility for their quality and utility therefore rests with the authors.

[6]The weights are the number of credit hours associated with each course.

practice sensitive. Thus, application and utilization of content is rated higher than content which is merely presented to the students (Gordon & Gordon, 1982).

Description rather than evaluation. The curriculum analysis methodology makes no attempt to evaluate the curriculum; it is designed solely to depict the content and not to assess the appropriateness of the material, its internal consistency, or how well it is taught. Student performance is not assessed either. Examinations and grading practices are looked at simply to find out which content areas are reinforced by being evaluated.

Avoidance of inference. Materials describing courses in a curriculum will always have limitations. Sometimes the materials will be too abstract or leave out certain details. In these instances, it is always tempting to "read in" content or make inferences about what really takes place. When analysts make such inferential leaps, they often do not land in the same place. In a rating process, the result can mean low interrater reliability.[7] When experienced social work educators or practitioners are used as analysts, they may infer content because of the similarity between the course being analyzed and another with which they are familiar. Sometimes the course title suggests content that may or may not be present in the course. To minimize unwarranted inferences, several safeguards are recommended. First, the analysts should be sensitized to this problem when they are trained. Second, courses titles and numbers should be masked, and not analyzed in a fixed sequence. Finally, the rating scales used by the analysts should require that the basis for their judgments be clearly in evidence in the materials under review.

Contrast with accreditation. The prospect of a curriculum analysis such as this can generate considerable anxiety and defensiveness among the faculty of a school. This will be even more likely if it is perceived as being similar to the site visit associated with an accreditation review by CSWE. This validation process bears little resemblance to such a review. In accreditation, the emphasis is on quality. The entire accreditation process is oriented toward evaluating how well the teaching program is planned, administered, supported by resources, and implemented. By contrast, this curriculum analysis is concerned only with describing course content.

---

[7] In recognition of this potential problem, it is recommended that analysts, working independently of one another, rate three courses in common. Ratings are compared and agreement levels are established. This is more fully described later in the procedures section of this appendix.

A curriculum validation study also has a much narrower focus than an accreditation review. The latter is concerned with a wide range of academic phenomena: the teaching process, admissions, advisement, the grievance apparatus, administration, and internal and external resources. In short, it is a review of the total program. On the other hand, the curriculum analysis described in this appendix concentrates only on the content of the coursework taken by all the students in the program. Course content is assessed *only* with regard to its relevance to specific job, task, or practice content.

The Curriculum Analysis

Up to this point, the curriculum analysis has been talked about in fairly general terms. This section describes the basic tools and procedures involved in the analysis. Stated most simply, each course is scrutinized in detail and, using a standardized approach, assessed in terms of the extent to which it prepares a student to engage in various types of practice activities. In an undergraduate program, all courses required of social work majors (by virtue of being majors), regardless of the department in which the courses are offered, would be analyzed.[8] This includes field practicum courses. In a graduate program, the required courses in the foundation year (including field practicum) would be analyzed. Depending on the nature of the validation, courses and field experiences in the second year would be analyzed and combined according to the ways in which the specialties in the curriculum are "packaged." (This aggregation at the curriculum level is discussed in more detail below.)

Describing Classroom Instruction

To describe the courses accurately, source materials are required. The analysis makes use of course outlines and syllabi, handouts, tests and examinations, and grading procedures. An important source of descriptive information is the syllabus and/or outline associated with each course, which usually establishes the objectives for the course, describes the topics covered, and lists the texts and reading materials.

Unfortunately, documentation materials vary among programs. Quite often, for instance, course syllabi omit salient details about how

---

[8]This would *not* include "core" courses or courses required of all students in the particular college in which the undergraduate social work program is located. Courses in minor areas, which can vary from one student to another, would also be excluded.

a course is conducted, or they may not be updated to reflect changes in content, or they may be intentionally vague to cover differences in presentation from one section to another. In any event, the accuracy of any analysis of these materials is affected by this lack of uniformity. When this method was being pilot tested, the shortcomings of such irregularities became obvious. To deal with them, the Topic Outline and Budget (TOB) was developed to replace the course syllabus as the basic descriptive instrument. The TOB is completed by the instructor of every required course, including those with multiple sections, to reflect the way in which the course was most recently taught.

The first two pages of a completed TOB for an introductory course appear in Figure C.2.[9] The pilot tests indicated that it typically can be completed by a course instructor in approximately one hour. As can be seen, the document contains several categories of descriptive information. Under the first column, headed "Topic Outline," the instructor lists the major topics covered by the course in the order in which they are presented. Enough details about each topic should be included so that the nature of the material can be readily understood. In the next column, labeled "Time," the instructor indicates the amount of time that is devoted to each topic. The instructor is told to use the most appropriate unit of time, which can range from less than one session to a period of several weeks. This specificity permits the analysts to evaluate the relative emphasis placed on each topic. In the next column, labeled "In-class Instructional Activities," the instructor describes the method(s) of instruction used for each topic. As can be seen in the example, many topics can be taught using several instructional methods. Analysts may use the material under "Out-of-class Assignments" in two ways: they can fill in any gaps that may be found in the topic outline, and they may infer additional instructional activities. (For example, the site visit to a local agency added valuable pedagogical information.) In the last column, "Method of Evaluation,"the instructor describes the methods by which mastery of the subject matter is measured and assessed. (If no evaluation is indicated, the analysts are trained to probe carefully to ensure that no omissions have inadvertently been made.)

During the pilot study of this material, it was found that the information contained in this form greatly enhanced the ability of the cur-

---

[9]To avoid proprietary interests, no actual textbooks or journal articles are cited in the example. The contents of the course, however, are based on an actual MSW course analyzed during the demonstration of the validation procedures in a large social work program.

riculum analysts to arrive at the same rating values for a given course. As stated earlier, however, the TOB does not stand alone. It is supplemented by course syllabi, handouts, copies of tests and examinations, and, in the case of discrepancies or lack of information, by interviews with instructors.

The Level of Preparation Scale

It cannot be emphasized too often that the primary purpose of the validation of a professional school curriculum is to answer the question: "How well does the curriculum prepare students to carry out practice activities of one kind or another?" The operationalized answer to this question is provided by the use of the Level of Preparation Scale (LPS) presented in Figure C.3. The LPS assumes that those desiring to establish the practice relatedness or practice sensitivity of the curriculum will already have developed a practice or job depiction to which the courses will be related (see Figure C.1). In this case, the 18 task clusters that emerged from the national job analyses will be used as the depiction of practice.

Assumptions of the LPS. The LPS reflects the long-held view among a number of learning theorists (Airasian, 1979; Bloom, 1976; Gagné, 1977; Gordon & Gordon, 1982) that learning can be conceptualized in terms of a hierarchy of discrete processes. Although the terminology varies among these researchers, all talk about learning in terms of "being aware of," "understanding the uses of," and "being able to do." Consequently, the LPS has been partitioned into a sequence of three subscales: Presentation, Application, and Utilization. These scales constitute ordinal levels of instruction—any one of the three can reflect the highest level of learning attained but each must be present, in sequence, before the next level can begin. At each level, evaluation is assumed to reinforce the learning process.

Presentation. This level of instruction involves setting forth, portraying, or otherwise bringing content to the awareness of the learner. It represents the first stage of the learning process; its intent is to produce knowledge. Presentation can be accomplished via depiction (oral or visual), definition, discussion, or illustration. Methods of presentation include but are not limited to: assigned written materials (texts, handouts, articles); lectures and discussions (including guest speakers); live performances and demonstrations; audiovisuals (film, filmstrip, videotape, audiotape, CDs); and field visits, trips, or site observations.

Figure C.2. Curriculum Analysis
Topic Outline and Budget

Page 1 of 3
Date: September, 1994

Course #: A-Introductory
Credit Hours: 3

Section#: 1
#Sessions/Week: 3
Instructor: Goodperson

School: Anyschool
Term/Year: Fall 1993

Topic Outline	Time Allocation	In-Class Instructional Activities	Out-of-Class Assignments	Method of Evaluation
I. Concepts of Social Work (as a profession and occupation) A. Various Definitions B. Goals/Domains/Sanction C. The Knowledge, Values and Skill Base required 1. the nature of competence	(3 hrs.) ½ hr. 1 hr. 1½ hrs.	Lecture/Discussion Film: "Social Work" (A, B) Videotape: "The Unmarried Mother" (20 mins.) (B, C.1)	Primary Text: Mimms, Timms, Simms Chapter I—"The Profession of Social Work"	1st of 3 exams given: multiple choice questions. Approximately 30 questions dealing with A, B, C.1

II. History of Social Work as a Profession
 A. Concept of a profession
   1. essential characteristics
 B. Characteristics of Social Work's organizations; its professional association
 C. History of Social Work
   1. early organizations
   2. theoretical positions
   3. major controversies
   4. present structure
	(3 hrs.)
	 ¾ hr.
	 ¾ hr.
	 1½hrs.
		Lecture Discussion (A, B, C.1, 2, 3, 4)
		 Small Group Exercise: Panel discussion about professions/occupations (A.1, C.4)
		 Videotape: "Portrait of a Youth Agency Director" (30 mins.) (A.1, C.2, 3)
			Primary Text
			 Chapter 2—"The Emergence of Social Work as a Profession" (A.1, C.1, 2, 3, 4)
				1st Exam:
				 20 multiple choice questions dealing with A.1, C.1, 2, 3, 4

continued . . .

Figure C.2. Curriculum Analysis
Topic Outline and Budget (con't)

Topic Outline	Time Allocation	In-Class Instructional Activities	Out-of-Class Assignments	Method of Evaluation
III. The Social Work Career Ladder	(1 hr.)	Lecture/Discussion: (A.1, 2, B, C.1, 2, D)	Primary Text: Mimms, Timms & Simms	Short Paper Assigned: Topic: "Making a Living as a Social Worker" (no more than 10 pages) (A.1, 2, C.1, 2)
A. Types of Jobs	¼ hr.		Chapter 3—"Social Work as an Occupation"	Project: Write 10 job descriptions (A.1, 2, C.1)
1. Direct Services				
2. Indirect Services	¼ hr.			
B. Current Labor Force Data	¼ hr.			
C. Nature of Job Classification				
1. Job Descriptions				
2. Merit Systems				
D. Licensing and Certification	¼ hr.			
IV. Social Work and Social Welfare	(2 hrs.)	Lecture/Discussion (A.1) 3 Videotapes: "Nature of Social Welfare" (15 mins.) (A.1, C.1, 2, 3)	Primary Text: Chapter 4—"Social Work and Social Welfare" (B.1, 2; C.1)	1st Exam: 30 questions (multiple choice) dealing with A.1, B.1, 2
A. Concept of Social Welfare	½ hr.		Assigned Article: "The Nature of Social Security and the Safety Net" (C.2, 3)	Short paper dealing with "Who's Entitled to Welfare" (no more than 10 pages) (C.1, 2, 3)
1. Areas of Coverage				
B. History of Social Welfare	½ hr.	"Social Action in the Sixties" (20 mins.) (C.1, 2)		
1. Origins in Europe				
2. Early U.S. Activities				
C. Basic Components	1 hr.			
1. Social Action				
2. Social Services				
3. Entitlements				

(Use Continuation Sheets as Needed)

Figure C.3. **Level of Preparation Scale**

Concept: Extent to which a given course or field experience prepares a student for the performance of a cluster of tasks.

Level Description **Scale Value**

Evalulated?

Presentation:
None—No evidence that any content
related to the cluster is presented. _____ No _____ 0

Some—Up to 10% of time/effort in
the course is devoted to content
contained in the cluster and 1–2 _____ No _____ 1
methods of instruction are used to
present it. _____ Yes _____ 2

Moderate—10–20% of time/effort in
the course is devoted to content
contained in the cluster *or* 3 or _____ No _____ 3
more methods of instruction are
used to present it. _____ Yes _____ 4

Extensive—More than 20% of time/
effort in the course is devoted to
content contained in the cluster _____ No _____ 5
and 3 or more methods of
instruction are used to present it. _____ Yes _____ 6

Application:
None—No evidence that any
experiences in making applications
are provided in the course or
field experience.* _____ No _____ 0

Some—One experience in applying
content contained in the cluster _____ No _____ 1
is provided in the course or
field experience. _____ Yes _____ 2

Moderate—Two to 3 experiences in
applying content contained in the _____ No _____ 3
cluster are provided in the course or
field experience. _____ Yes _____ 4

Extensive—More than 3 experiences
in applying content contained in the _____ No _____ 5
cluster are provided in the course or
field experience. _____ Yes _____ 6

Utilization:
None—No evidence that actual use
of the content contained in the cluster
takes place in the course or
field experience.** _____ No _____ 0

continued . . .

Figure C.3. Level of Preparation Rating Scale (con't)

Level Description	Evaluated?		Scale Value
Some—One experience in using content contained in the cluster is provided in the course or field experience.		No	1
		Yes	2
Moderate—Two to 3 experiences in using content contained in the cluster are provided in the course or field experience.		No	3
		Yes	4
Extensive—More than 3 experiences in using content contained in the cluster are provided in the course or field experience.		No	5
		Yes	6

* In using the Application portion of the scale, look for evidence of application *techniques* (for example, role plays, practice problems) among the course materials. Link the number of these that relate to the contents of any given task cluster. Some of these may apply to more than one cluster. Consequently, a given application could be counted more than once. If no evidence is found in the written materials, probe carefully with the instructor(s) to make sure it has not been inadvertently left out.

** In using the Utilization portion of the scale, look for evidence that the activities contained in the task cluster are carried out under actual conditions of work. Try to identify the number of times, for a given cluster, this takes place. An assignment in a work setting can relate to more than one task cluster. Thus, a given utilization could be counted more than once. If no evidence is found in written materials, especially in field-related courses, probe carefully with the instructor(s) to make sure it has not been inadvertently left out.

Application. This second level of instruction involves the provision of experiences within the course that link or connect content to its uses, either actual or potential. Its intent is to produce understanding. Application techniques include but are not limited to: case analyses; policy analyses; model or "mock" activities (e.g., preparation of dummy proposals, draft legislation or policies, use of practice problems); critiques; and role-playing or other interpersonal simulations. Because one application can cover more than one cluster, a single application can be counted more than once.

Utilization. This highest level of instruction involves carrying out, under actual conditions of work, activities contained in the relevant job or practice area. Its intent is to produce proficiency. At this level of instruction, the hypothetical becomes real—students are exposed to real problems involving real clients and, although the activity is structured, there are real risks (e.g., legal, physical) involved. Methods of utilization typically include, but are not limited to, field placement and volunteer assignments.

Evaluation. Procedures associated with the assessment of performance are an integral part of the LPS. At each of the three instructional levels, if there is evidence that practice-related knowledge or behaviors are evaluated and that this serves as the basis for course grades, the LPS ratings are raised. This reflects the premise that evaluation serves to reinforce the learning process. Methods of evaluation include, but are not limited to, achievement tests; term papers; individual or group projects or proposals; and performance ratings based on observation (e.g., during simulations, field placement).

Describing Field Instruction

Field instruction can be more difficult to describe than classroom instruction. First, the field practicum is usually less standardized in that students tend to have more individualized experiences. Second, descriptions of field experiences typically begin by describing what the students do and then, by inference, work back to an understanding of what they have learned in terms of what is required. Most programs have an evaluation form of some kind to evaluate the students' field experiences. Therefore, instead of using the TOB form to generate descriptions of field instruction, the authors suggest starting with existing evaluation forms to help instructors describe or reconstruct learning objectives for the field.

As with classroom instruction, the best sources of information about what goes on in field placements are those responsible for the teaching and supervision—the field instructors. To be selected to participate in the curriculum analysis, the field instructors should represent a typical field placement in a type of setting, and carry out *direct* field instruction with students in that setting. The instructors should be grouped according to the generic type of placement they represent. In undergraduate programs, they are separated into those teaching in the first and, if applicable, those teaching in the second field placements taken by students. In graduate programs, they would be separated into those in foundation placements and those in various specialized placements.

The field instructors meet in groups (between five and ten in number) with the analysts to generate descriptions of what goes on in their field settings and to help the analysts estimate the level of preparation students receive for each of the task clusters.[10] In the group meetings,

---

[10] A number of meetings will usually need to be held to complete this aspect of the analysis. The meeting should be chaired by someone familiar with the placements, perhaps the director of field education for the program. The number of instructors in any meeting may vary, but should be set to give everyone an opportunity to participate. A meeting typically lasts about two hours.

the starting point is the 18 task clusters. Tasks and activities in the first cluster are described and defined. Using existing field education evaluation forms as a guideline, the instructors are then asked to explain the extent to which the placement type typically provides students with opportunities to carry out that particular cluster of activities. If opportunities are present, the instructors are asked to establish how often the cluster of activity is performed, how the students are prepared to do it, and whether or not their performance is evaluated. For each of the 18 task clusters, the meeting chair leads the instructors through the three scales—Utilization, Application, and Presentation—asking them for evidence of the level of student preparation. The instructors comment systematically on all 18 clusters, helping the analyst generate LPS scores for a group of related field placements. Despite the differences in approach for analyzing classroom instruction and field instruction, the outcomes are essentially the same—a base of information on which ratings for level of student preparation can be made.

Calculating Level of Preparation Scores

Course composite score. In using the LPS for rating preparation in either the classroom or the field, the analyst should proceed systematically, basing each rating on the relationship between the *content* in the course materials and the *content* of the activities contained in a given task cluster. In all instances, the analyst should choose the *highest* level of preparation defensible by the supporting materials.

It should be obvious that the LPS ratings cannot be made until the analyst is thoroughly familiar with the activities contained in each of the 18 task clusters (described in Chapter 1). In rating courses and field practica, the analyst reviews the various materials describing the curriculum component to be validated (e.g., syllabus, TOB, field evaluations, tests, handouts) and determines the level of *Presentation* in that course with respect to the content contained in the first task cluster (Interpersonal Helping). Having done this, a determination is then made as to whether or not knowledge in that content area is formally evaluated as part of the course. The final rating for the presentation component (0 through 6) thus reflects both the level of presentation and the presence or absence of evaluation. Next, the analyst assesses the level of *Application* in the course relevant to the content contained in the first task cluster. A determination is then made about evaluation and a final rating (0 through 6) for the application component is assigned. Finally, using the descriptive materials for the course, the analyst decides on the extent to which the course permits the student to actually carry out the activities associated with the first task cluster and the extent to which these experiences are evaluated. In this manner, the final rating for *Utilization* (0 through 6) is made. In rating materials associated with field placements, the analyst must be present in the meeting with the field instructors. As stated earlier, each rating for each task cluster should be made as the instructors systematically reconstruct the information base on which their assertions of preparation are made.

The Level of Preparation Scale rating for any curriculum component (course or field placement) is calculated by adding together the scores of the three ratings for presentation, application, and utilization. Thus, a course's rating for the first cluster (Interpersonal Helping) could range from 0 (no preparation at all) to 18 (highest level of preparation).[11] Because composite preparation ratings are made for each task cluster, every course will have 18 LPS scores covering the array of practice clusters. It would be expected that practice and HBSE courses would have relatively high LPS scores for the direct service clusters (1 through 8) while policy, research, and specialty courses in supervision, planning, and management would have higher scores in the indirect service clusters (10 through 18).

Curriculum composite score. As described above, each course in the curriculum is assigned 18 LPS scores, one for each task cluster. Determining the composite LPS for the entire curriculum is simply a matter of calculating a weighted sum of the ratings, one cluster at a time, of the individual courses, based on the course's credit hours. Table C.1 shows the LPS ratings for 4 of the 18 clusters for 7 courses (A through G) in a hypothetical curriculum. In the example above, the composite LPS score for the first cluster (Interpersonal Helping) would be $4(8) + 3(9) + 3(6) + 2(3) + 2(3) + 4(3) + 9(9) = 182$.[12] Using this procedure, an LPS score is calculated for every cluster identified in the job analysis. This total (composite) curriculum score reflects the extent to which the required courses in the curriculum prepare students for these practice activities.

---

[11] A variety of logs, work sheets, forms, and procedures have been developed to assist both the job and curriculum analysts in completing their tasks. In the interest of conserving space, these have not been included in this appendix but can be obtained from the authors.
[12] Note that the upper limit of the composite Level of Preparation Scale score is indeterminate because it depends on the number of courses analyzed.

Table C.1. Composite Curriculum Scores (Partial)

Course Number	A	B	C	D	E	F	G
Credit Hours	4	3	3	2	2	4	9
Cluster 1: Interpersonal Helping	8	9	6	3	3	3	9
Cluster 2: Group Work	15	15	3	3	3	3	18
Cluster 3: Individual/Family Treatment	12	11	4	3	3	5	18
.	.	.	.	.	.	.	.
.	.	.	.	.	.	.	.
.	.	.	.	.	.	.	.
Cluster 11: Staff Supervision	4	3	12	11	14	9	5

Synthesizing Job and Curriculum Data

One would assume that if a curriculum prepared its graduates for certain kinds of practice activities or jobs, positive correlations would exist between the importance placed on employment activities in certain practice areas—as evidenced by frequency ratings of practitioners—and the composite LPS scores for relevant courses. This relationship is called "validity" and, in this methodology, it can be determined both visually and statistically. Even the rather limited information contained in Table C.1 can convey useful information. For example, the LPS scores for clusters 1, 2, and 3 suggest that courses A, B, and G prepare students rather well for direct service activities. Similarly, the LPS scores for cluster 11 suggest that courses C, D, E, and F provide a high level of preparation for supervision, an indirect service activity. The inspection process can be greatly enhanced by converting the data to profiles. Figure C.4 shows the profile of a second-year Clinical/Social Treatment Track in an MSW program, analyzed as part of a pilot study of this validation methodology. As the figure clearly shows, the profile reflects a decided emphasis on direct services content, that is, the first eight clusters at the top of the chart. If this profile is compared to Figure 2.5 and Figure 3.4, which depict the profiles of the BSW and MSW direct service workers, one can easily see the practice relevance of the curriculum course work. By the same token, if one compares Figure C.3 to the profile of cluster scores for MSW managers and administrators in Figure 3.7, one finds much less practice relevance.

As mentioned earlier, it is also possible to describe the relationship between job content and curriculum content in statistical terms. As Figure C.1 indicates, the methodology permits analysts to describe both job activities and the curriculum content in terms of the 18 task clusters. The job depiction indicates how frequently each of the task clusters is performed in the normal course of carrying out the job. The

---

Figure C.4. LPS Scores for a Clinical Concentration

Task Clusters

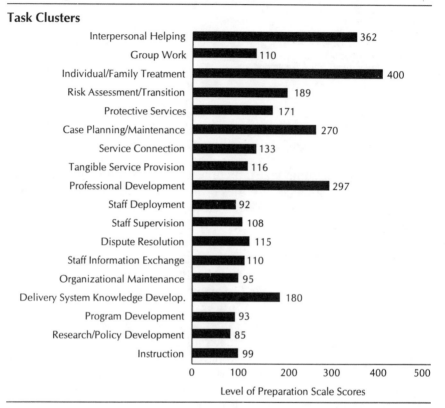

Level of Preparation Scale Scores

---

curriculum is depicted in terms of how well it prepares graduates to perform that job. Thus, the validation methodology yields a pair of scores for each of the 18 task clusters. To determine the strength of the association between the two measures, a correlation, or validity, coefficient can be computed.[13]

In a pilot study conducted to test this methodology, required classroom and field practicum courses in an MSW program were analyzed. In the MSW curriculum, these courses were organized into three components: the foundation year (7 courses), a clinical track (8 courses), and an administrative track (6 courses). Using the methods described above, analysts calculated composite LP scores for each curriculum

---

[13]Because the Level of Preparation Scale scores are at the ordinal level of measurement, a Spearman's Rho (ρ) is the preferred statistic to use. Its value ranges from +1.0 to -1.0. Within the context of the validation model, the desired outcome would be a correlation as close to +1.0 as possible.

Table C.2. Validity Coefficients For Jobs and Curriculum Components

	First Year	Second Year	
		Clinical Track	Administrative Track
Direct Services Jobs (all sites)	.70	.74	-.73
Supervisory Jobs (all sites)	-.71	-.74	.86
Administrative Jobs (all sites)	-.64	-.69	.85

component. During the same pilot study, job analyses were conducted in two agencies: a comprehensive state human services organization and a network of private-sector mental health service providers. In all, JAQ task data were collected from 225 workers in 16 different jobs. The jobs consisted of direct services (9 jobs), supervision (3 jobs), and administration (4 jobs). The job and curriculum analysis results were correlated; a portion of the data is summarized in Table C.2.[14] As can be seen, there is a consistently high positive correlation between the practitioners' ratings of cluster frequency in the direct services jobs and the curriculum analysts' LPS scores for the foundation- and second-year clinical track courses.[15] Similarly, there is a high positive correlation between the indirect service jobs (supervisors and administrators) and the administrative track offered in the second year. Of equal importance are the strong negative correlations between the task ratings in the direct service jobs and the LPS scores in the administrative track. This strong inverse relationship is also true of the indirect service jobs and the courses in the foundation year and the clinical track.

It should be pointed out here that this pattern of relatively independent curriculum components dovetails quite nicely with the findings presented in Chapter 3 about practice. Those data left little doubt that the direct service, supervisory, and administrative jobs held by MSW level practitioners were inherently different from one another. If social work education is practice sensitive, the academic preparation for these graduate practitioners should involve course content that emphasizes very different types of preparation. The program analyzed in the pilot study was typical of many in that students moved from a common foundation year into one of a number of specialized tracks in their

---

[14]Readers wishing a more detailed description of these findings should consult the report of the pilot study (Teare, 1987, 1988).

[15]One should be cautious in interpreting the statistical significance of these correlations. To be of any real practical significance, ρ should be at least $\pm.60$.

second year of training. Also, like many other programs, the majority of students moved into the direct services track. However, almost half (48%) of the MSW practitioners in the national study sample were not direct service workers. This anomaly serves to underscore the point already made in Chapter 3, that an important challenge for social work education will be to provide MSW students with the skills many of them will eventually need to move into supervisory, management, and other system-centered jobs.

Conclusion

The presentation of the curriculum validation methodology in this appendix has been tailored to fit the focus of the book and has thus been abbreviated and simplified. It has dealt entirely with the curriculum analysis. It should be pointed out, however, that the job analysis is of paramount importance since it is those data that provide the frame of reference for the assumption of validity. To repeat what has been said earlier, it is the educational process that purports to prepare graduates for the world of practice, and not the converse. Because of its importance, a complete set of procedures for collecting job data was formulated during the development of this methodology. Although not included here, a detailed description of these procedures can be found in Teare, Higgs, Gauthier, and Feild (1984b). In addition, many of the forms and work sheets that should be used by both job and curriculum analysts (questionnaires, interview guides, rating instructions, analysts' logs, and a variety of summary worksheets) may also be found in the original technical reports describing the two methods (Teare et al., 1984b) or obtained from the authors.

Although this appendix has dealt with procedures that are quantitative in nature, it is important to note that the climate in which these procedures are used will often be highly charged with emotions. This is because participants realize that decisions will be based on the findings—decisions that will often affect the recruitment and selection of program graduates by agencies in the labor market area served by the school. Thus, a validation study is really a policy-oriented investigation and should be identified as such from the outset. It is imperative that investigators clearly communicate what the validation study is and is not, especially when interpreting results to educators, university administrators, and agency officials. Several considerations should be made in carrying out and interpreting a curriculum validation study.

First, because the frame of reference of the curriculum analysis is largely determined by the outcome of the job analysis, the validation may be perceived as an instrument for reorienting the educational process in certain directions. Some might define this mandate narrowly. One must be sensitive to this issue. Care should be taken to convey to educators and agency people alike that a professional curriculum is assumed to be broader than the content of one or more specific jobs.

Second, it should be repeatedly emphasized that this model is designed to reflect *content*, not *quality*. Neither student performance nor curriculum effectiveness is being evaluated. The integrity and academic soundness of the curriculum are not at issue. In this respect, the curriculum analysis is markedly different from an accreditation review.

Third, how does one interpret a validity coefficient that results from a study such as this? What does the presence or absence of a "match" really mean? A correlation coefficient should not be interpreted in a rigidly mechanistic fashion. It is a useful index and, when high in value, indicates that a relationship truly exists between job and curriculum content. But a low correlation does not always indicate a lack of validity. Lack of variability in either or both of the measures being correlated limits the value the coefficient can attain. If a particular curriculum prepared graduates at a uniformly high level in all task clusters, the curriculum analysis would yield a "flat" profile. That is to say, there would be no variation in the Level of Preparation Scale scores. These scores, when correlated with the frequency ratings of the task clusters in the job analysis, would result in a correlation coefficient of zero or very close to it. Thus, a curriculum that results in good preparation for a job could have a low validity coefficient. This type of artifact needs to be understood and taken into account when interpreting results. Obviously, visual inspection of the scores would reveal the problem and cause one to interpret the results with caution.

It should also be stressed that validity is a property *specific* to the jobs and the curricula on which the data are gathered. The national study practice data were used in this study because they were the most comprehensive practice data available at this time. However, a curriculum might be quite relevant to one or more jobs in a local area, but show a poor fit to these national data. The converse could also be true. Thus, the absence of a match (a low correlation) simply means that a *given* curriculum does not contain content relevant to a *specific* job. Similarly, a high correlation between a curriculum and a job should not be viewed as evidence that the curriculum is relevant to or prepares students for all jobs. That same curriculum may show little or no relationship to another job. Because policy decisions may be made on the basis of the findings, it is important that decision makers understand the nature of the methodology and the degree to which generalizations are possible.

Despite these cautions, a curriculum validation methodology can be a very useful tool (Sheafor, Teare, Hancock, & Gauthier, 1985). Taken alone, the curriculum analysis component can permit educators to take an objective look at the degree to which program objectives are operationalized in the classroom and the field. It can facilitate an examination of concentrations and areas of specialization, as well as the balance between these components of the curriculum. In short, it can result in considerable insight into "the water in which we swim." Taken as a whole, the validation process provides an excellent opportunity for schools and agencies to collaborate with one another and to gain useful information on the correlation between academe and job practices. Used properly, this information can work to the benefit of all concerned, especially the clients served by the profession.

Benefits and Considerations for Initiating a Curriculum Analysis

Invited Commentary
by
Barbara W. Shank and Angeline Barretta–Herman
University of St. Thomas and the College of St. Catherine

A fundamental dilemma social work educators face in designing or revising social work curricula is the need to impart skills and knowledge required for current practice, while helping students develop their capacity to handle the practice demands of tomorrow. Clearly, then, social work education must be more than training in response to particular practice needs. Graduates must be prepared to assume leadership roles in an evolving social work profession, to respond to change and, when appropriate, help to bring it about. The information Teare and Sheafor have provided in this volume, especially in this appendix, can be of considerable value in helping social work educators deal with this dilemma. In the narrative portion of the book, particularly in chapters 2 through 4, the authors have produced a clear and detailed depiction of contemporary social work practice at both the BSW and MSW levels. This information is invaluable because we must have clarity about "what is" before we can plan for "what will be."

Teare and Sheafor assert that the information base described in this book can be used in various ways. In this appendix they illustrate one use by outlining a methodology for conducting a curriculum validation study that allows social work educators to determine the practice sensitivity of their curricula. The level of preparation provided by a given curriculum or specialty track can be compared to data from the BSW or MSW national study, or to data obtained from the analysis of the social work positions into which program graduates would be hired. In the latter instance, a program would be "validating" the extent to which its social work credential prepares graduates for jobs in a given labor market area.

We have both used this curriculum analysis approach to describe and analyze curriculum content, looking at the correspondence between BSW practice and the curricula of 8 BSW programs (Shank, 1993), and analyzing the "fit" between social work jobs in a particular area and the BSW curriculum of a school serving that area (Sheafor et al., 1985). In both instances, the curriculum analysis methodology proved to be a useful tool for assessing the relevance, or practice sensitivity, of the curricula.

Benefits of the Curriculum Analysis Methodology

An Empirical Frame of Reference

Curricula evolve over time and are subject to a variety of influences, including faculty preferences, perceived expertise, popularity, cost, or politics. After a while, the organizing principles underlying the curriculum might be hard to infer. Although periodic accreditation reviews temper these disparate influences, they still exist. Performing a curriculum analysis can give faculty the option to base curriculum changes on hard data and move beyond conjecture, assumptions, and personal preference.

A Regional As Well As a National Perspective

CSWE's Curriculum Policy Statement articulates common evaluative standards to which all programs must respond if they wish to be accredited (CSWE, 1994). This material provides only general guidelines for the programs, though, because it is based on an abstract composite of practice as seen from the perspective of policy makers. However, BSW and MSW programs typically prepare practitioners for regional markets that may be quite specific about the tasks that new social workers should be prepared to perform. The technique described here allows a program to vary its focus from national to regional level using the same basic methodology. If the national study data on BSW and MSW practice are used as the standard, curriculum planners can evaluate their programs against a national practice composite described at several levels of abstraction. If task data are collected about jobs in the labor market served by the program, the curriculum planners can evaluate their programs against these local employment expectations. In addition, data contained in chapters 2 and 3 about regional differences in client demography, needs, and problems can help programs fine-tune their emphases.

Specificity about Preparation

In many localities, employers and educators are not clear about the nature of the practice preparation they expect recent graduates to possess. Agency administrators often expect the university to prepare graduates to assume agency responsibilities with minimal agency-based orientation, supervision, or in-service training. This practice framework and curriculum analysis approach allows representatives from the school and the agencies to talk clearly about the tasks that beginning BSW and MSW practitioners should be able to perform. It also permits more focused discussions about future performance expectations or about content that is lacking in either the jobs or the curriculum. With this knowledge, employers and educators can redesign curricula and/or jobs to produce a better match. In addition, with more detailed knowledge about gaps and shortcomings in preparation, each has the information to design in-service or continuing education programs to focus on skills and knowledge not possessed by workers.[16]

A Blend of Options

Using a framework developed independently from any particular curriculum allows educational planners to more objectively balance the program's focus—for example, present/future, narrow/broad, skill/knowledge. Although the job analysis and the curriculum analysis can provide useful information, the data are descriptive, not prescriptive. In other words, curriculum planners still have the option to respond in a variety of ways. For example, if job analysis data show that workers are not engaged in certain types of tasks, curriculum planners may decide to de-emphasize that content in the curriculum. However, they could also assume that workers aren't performing these activities because they don't know how to, and, consequently, elect to *add* curriculum material in those areas.

Clear information about both curriculum and job content can also help a program coordinate with other educational offerings in a given area. For example, the faculty at one school with which we worked recognized that many professional development workshops, seminars, and courses on direct practice were readily available from various organizations in their community. What was not available from the agencies was education focusing on social justice, social change, various indirect practice activities such as policy analysis and planning, and the competencies required to bring about organizational change. Using the curriculum analysis methodology as a guideline, they introduced this content into their own curriculum.

---

[16]It should be pointed out that the curriculum analysis methodology will work with *proposed* as well as *actual* curriculum materials associated with any type of education or training effort.

Considerations When Initiating a Curriculum Analysis

Curriculum evaluation using the approach proposed by Teare and Sheafor should not be entered into lightly. Although some of the considerations examined below have been touched on by the authors in Appendix C, our experiences in working with the methodology suggest that they cannot be emphasized too often.

Faculty and Administration Must Understand and Commit to the Process

Before beginning the process of curriculum analysis, a full discussion of the range of possible outcomes should take place among the school's faculty. All must understand the possibility that considerable curriculum change may result. Our experience suggests that these discussions should include members of the administration (e.g., deans and department chairs) as well as representatives from agencies and the practice community. Because is it so labor intensive, a curriculum analysis should be undertaken only when all parties recognize the high level of commitment in time and resources that is required.

It is also essential that faculty, practitioners, and school administrators understand that this type of analysis is designed solely to relate curriculum content to practice tasks. As such, it is a tool for curriculum development and/or revision, and *not* an evaluation of educational quality. Misunderstandings about this can cause anxiety among faculty, who may feel their instruction is being evaluated when their course syllabi are analyzed and converted into a Topic Outline and Budget. Faculty reactions and suggestions should be solicited throughout the process; this will reduce anxiety, improve candor, and increase the accuracy of the information obtained.

An Infrastructure Should Be In Place

Our experience in using the methodology highlighted the importance of having a structure in place to carry out the curriculum analysis. A competent individual should be designated as the curriculum analysis manager. It is important that this individual have credibility with the faculty in addition to having academic rank, teaching experience, and curriculum expertise. Whoever takes overall responsibility for managing the analysis serves as a facilitator, coach, motivator, and consultant. Expertise, credibility, compassion, and good humor were found to be indispensable in facilitating the process without getting bogged down in details.[17]

The Topic Outline and Budget Should Be Prepared Carefully

Perhaps the most important element in producing an accurate set of descriptive materials is the careful preparation of the Topic Outline and Budget (TOB). Its contents are derived from a course syllabus, handouts, examinations, and interviews with faculty members responsible for the course. If the materials on which it is based are too abstract or incomplete, analysts are often tempted to make inferences about course content. Thorough training of faculty in how to complete the TOB is absolutely essential. We found that training faculty in a group was highly desirable because it was efficient and ensured a consistent understanding and interpretation of the requirements for completing this task.

Despite the work, faculty found that the process had a number of unexpected benefits. Preparing TOBs for their own courses helped faculty members clarify course objectives, analyze their teaching methods, and review their assessment strategies. When shared, the TOBs became valuable tools for tracking content through the curriculum and informing faculty of content taught in other courses. In multi-section courses, inconsistencies among sections were quickly spotted. In one school in which we worked, the process revealed that faculty had (unknowingly) placed excessive reliance on certain teaching techniques and evaluation procedures, and that content assumed to be included in specific courses was actually lacking. This latter situation was particularly evident in courses in which different faculty had modified content over time and where new content had forced curtailment or elimination of particular material. (Ah, our old friend, disjointed incrementalism!) Once these omissions were spotted, faculty addressed the gaps and made the necessary corrections.

Analyzing Field Practicum Materials Is Especially Challenging

Difficulties associated with the preparation of TOBs for field practicum courses deserve special mention. Because field placements

---

[17]If a job analysis is carried out, there should also be a job analysis manager who is familiar with that methodology and has responsibility for collecting that data within the agencies and coordinating with the curriculum analysis manager on the campus. A recommended organizational structure for the entire process has been described in the original NASW technical reports. Further details can be obtained from Teare and Sheafor.

vary considerably and practicum courses do not typically have syllabi as such, a wide assortments of materials must be used to develop the TOBs. These include field manuals, field evaluation forms, and learning contracts required by the various agencies. We found it essential to interview faculty responsible for field instruction as well as agency-based field supervisors representing the full range of student placements. Only these individuals can supply information on typical student experiences and how they relate to course objectives and clusters of practice activity.

Curriculum Analysts Should Be Carefully Selected and Trained

Individuals who are selected to serve as curriculum analysts should be chosen carefully. Ideally, they should not be members of the school's faculty, but this cannot always be done. If they are faculty, they should be as free of conflict of interest (relative to the outcomes of the study) as is possible. A mix of analysts with curriculum experience at the appropriate degree level and practitioners with extensive experience greatly enhances the process. The group should be able to work as a team.

We both found that it was important to begin the training of the curriculum analysts by having them all carry out a pilot analysis of three or four courses. This was helpful in determining if they were consistently applying the rating scales and in detecting any biases in their analyses. We also found that preparing a manual with descriptions of the task clusters, the Level of Preparation Scales, and examples of course materials greatly increased the reliability of the analysts' ratings.

Community Practitioners Must Be Involved

Involving agency-based field supervisors and community practitioners is essential to the integrity of the curriculum analysis process. Although faculty may be initially reluctant to subject the curriculum to the scrutiny of outsiders, these individuals are subject matter experts and their knowledge of practice realities can result in important insights in the interpretation of data. We found that the involvement of practitioners had multiple long-term benefits: the faculty gained new respect for the practitioners, and the practitioners gained a healthy respect for the rigors of curriculum development. Long after the analysis was over, the practitioners continued to provide crucial support for subsequent changes the faculty made in the curriculum.

Final Comments

In the schools in which we worked, we found that information generated by means of an empirically-based methodology, with clear guidelines and procedures, had more credibility in the eyes of both faculty and practitioners than data collected in less systematic ways. It produced a common language by which both parties could communicate, a more thorough understanding of the curricula, and a more rational process for making decisions about the educational process. Because all parties were clearer about performance goals and objectives, the result was an increase in "practice-sensitive" curricula.

References

Peter W. Airasian, *Formative Evaluation Instruments: The Construction and Validation of Tests to Evaluate Learning Over Short Time Periods*. Unpublished doctoral dissertation, University of Chicago, 1979.

American Psychological Association, *Standards for Educational and Psychological Testing*. Washington, DC: Author, 1985.

Anne Anastasi, *Psychological Testing*, 4th ed. New York: MacMillan, 1976.

Benjamin S. Bloom, *Human Characteristics and School Learning*. New York: McGraw-Hill, 1976.

Council on Social Work Education, *Handbook of Accreditation Standards and Procedures*, 4th ed. Alexandria, VA: Author, 1994.

Lee J. Cronbach, "Test Validation," in Robert L. Thorndyke (ed.), *Educational Measurement*, 2nd ed. Washington, DC: American Council on Education, 1971.

Robert M. Gagné, *The Conditions For Learning*. New York: Holt, Rinehart & Winston, 1977.

Robert Gatewood and Hubert S. Feild, *Human Resource Selection*, 3rd ed. Fort Worth, TX: Dryden Press, 1994.

William E. Gordon and Margaret S. Gordon, "The Role of Frames of Reference in Field Instruction," in Bradford W. Sheafor and Lowell E. Jenkins (eds.), *Quality Field Instruction in Social Work*. New York: Longman, 1982.

Walter W. Hudson, *The Clinical Measurement Package: A Field Manual*. Chicago: Dorsey Press, 1982.

Jum C. Nunnally and Ira H. Bernstein, *Psychometric Theory*, 3rd ed. New York: McGraw-Hill, 1994.

Todd N. Lennon, ed., *Statistics on Social Work Education in the United States: 1992*. Alexandria, VA: Council on Social Work Education, 1993, pp. 44-45.

Barbara W. Shank, *An Exploration of the Relationship Between the Generalist Practice Framework and Job Tasks Performed by Baccalaureate Social Workers*. Unpublished Dissertation, University of Minnesota, 1993.

Bradford W. Sheafor, Robert J. Teare, Mervyn J. Hancock, and Thomas P. Gauthier, "Curriculum Development through Content Analysis: A New Zealand Experience," *Journal of Social Work Education*, 21 (Fall 1985): pp. 113-124.

Robert J. Teare, *Validating Social Work Credentials for Human Service Jobs*. Silver Spring, MD: National Association of Social Workers, 1987.

Robert J. Teare, "Establishing the Validity of Educational Credentials as Job Requirements," in *Proceedings of the 28th National Workshop on Welfare Research and Statistics*. Baltimore: National Association for Welfare Research and Statistics, July 1988, pp. 137-143.

Robert J. Teare, Catherine Higgs, Thomas P. Gauthier, and Hubert S. Feild, *Classification Validation Processes for Human Services Positions: Overview, Vol. 1*. Silver Spring, MD: National Association of Social Workers, 1984a.

Robert J. Teare, Catherine Higgs, Thomas P. Gauthier, and Hubert S. Feild, *Classification Validation Processes for Human Services Positions: Job Analysis Procedures and Instruments, Vol. 2*. Silver Spring, MD: National Association of Social Workers, 1984b.

Robert J. Teare, Bradford W. Sheafor, and Thomas P. Gauthier, *Classification Validation Processes for Human Services Positions: Curriculum Analysis Procedures and Instruments, Vol. 3*. Silver Spring, MD: National Association of Social Workers, 1984.

U.S. Bureau of Labor Statistics, *Occupational Outlook Quarterly*. Washington, DC: U.S. Department of Labor, 1992, p. 33.